Theresa Schaller • Ruth Würzle
Mobile Schools

Theresa Schaller
Ruth Würzle

Mobile Schools

Pastoralism, Ladders of Learning, Teacher Education

Verlag Barbara Budrich
Opladen • Berlin • Toronto 2021

All rights reserved. No part of this publication may be reproduced, stored in or introduced into a retrieval system, or transmitted, in any form, or by any means (electronic, mechanical, photocopying, recording or otherwise) without the prior written permission of Barbara Budrich Publishers. Any person who does any unauthorized act in relation to this publication may be liable to criminal prosecution and civil claims for damages.

You must not circulate this book in any other binding or cover and you must impose this same condition on any acquirer.

A CIP catalogue record for this book is available from
Die Deutsche Bibliothek (The German Library)

© 2021 by Verlag Barbara Budrich GmbH, Opladen, Berlin & Toronto
www.barbara-budrich.net

 ISBN 978-3-8474-2512-0
 eISBN 978-3-8474-1656-2
 DOI 10.3224/84742512

Das Werk einschließlich aller seiner Teile ist urheberrechtlich geschützt. Jede Verwertung außerhalb der engen Grenzen des Urheberrechtsgesetzes ist ohne Zustimmung des Verlages unzulässig und strafbar. Das gilt insbesondere für Vervielfältigungen, Übersetzungen, Mikroverfilmungen und die Einspeicherung und Verarbeitung in elektronischen Systemen.

Die Deutsche Bibliothek – CIP-Einheitsaufnahme
Ein Titeldatensatz für die Publikation ist bei Der Deutschen Bibliothek erhältlich.

Verlag Barbara Budrich
Stauffenbergstr. 7. D-51379 Leverkusen Opladen, Germany

86 Delma Drive. Toronto, ON M8W 4P6 Canada
www.barbara-budrich.net

Jacket illustration by the authors
Picture credits: Theresa Schaller and Ruth Würzle
Technical editing by Anja Borkam, Jena, Germany – kontakt@lektorat-borkam.de
Printed in Europe on acid-free paper by docupoint GmbH, Barleben

Table of Contents

Preface – Why Do We Ask Questions? 9

Introduction 11

Part I Daasanach Pastoralists and Education Provision 13

1. How Do Daasanach Pastoralists Live? 14
   - 1.1 Homeland Area 15
   - 1.2 Livelihood 18
   - 1.3 Social Organisation 21
   - 1.4 Celebrations 29
   - 1.5 Indigenous Knowledge 32

2. Why Is Education Provision for Daasanach Pastoralists Difficult? 36
   - 2.1 Kenyan Primary Education System 37
   - 2.2 Ambiguity about Schooling and Education 39
   - 2.3 Standardised Curriculum 40
   - 2.4 Language Barrier 41
   - 2.5 Fixed Schools for Mobile Communities 42
   - 2.6 Lack of Infrastructure 44
   - 2.7 Alienation from Traditional Cultural Identity 45
   - 2.8 Lessons Learned 47
   - Personal Notes of the Authors 47

3. What Are International Approaches to Mobile Education? 50
   - 3.1 Tent Schools in Iran 50
   - 3.2 Radio Education in Mongolia 51
   - 3.3 Quranic Schools in Somalia and Kenya 51
   - 3.4 Mobile Schools in Kenya 52
   - 3.5 Lessons Learned 54

4. What Are the Wishes of Daasanach Pastoralists with Regard to Education? .. 58
   - 4.1 Which Form of School Service Is Desired? 58

4.2 What Should Be Learned at School?..61
4.3 Who May Attend School?..62
4.4 What Are the Future Perspectives for Pupils?..63
4.5 Who Should Teach?..65
4.6 Lessons Learned...67
Personal Notes of the Authors...68

Part II International Cooperation..69

5. What Is the Pedagogical Perspective on Development?......................................70
5.1 Development Education..70
5.2 Education Should Foster Maturity..71
5.3 Culture Dependency of Development...72
5.4 Montessori's Development Pedagogy...74
5.5 Lessons Learned...75
Personal Notes of the Authors...76

6. What Is the Pedagogical Perspective on Development?......................................78
6.1 Changing Concepts and Definitions..78
6.2 International Cooperation of INES..79
6.3 Participation and Partnership Approach..81
Personal Notes of the Authors...83

7. What Is the Plan of the INES Project?...86
7.1 Central Issue...86
7.2 Forces and Actors...87
7.3 Project Vision and Mission...88
7.4 Partner Landscape...90
7.5 Desired Outcome and Progress Markers...91
7.6 Strategy Map and Tasks..92
Personal Notes of the Authors...93

Part III Learning System and Teacher Education..95

8. What Is the System Ladders of Learning About?..96

    8.1 Ladders of Learning Come from India 97

    8.2 Mobile School Concept with the System Ladders of Learning 99

    8.3 (De)Construction of Learning Contents 99

    8.4 Support System for Learning and Teaching 104

    8.5 Daily School Schedule 110

    8.6 Prepared Learning Environment 112

    8.7 Monitoring Tools 118

    Personal Notes of the Authors 119

9. How Do the Learners Start Schooling? 122

    9.1 Relatedness-oriented Background 122

    9.2 Linear Structure of the Ladder of Learning 125

    9.3 Each Milestone Introduces a Different Domain 127

    9.4 Joyful Learning Activities 130

    Personal Notes of the Authors 132

10. How Do the Learners Acquire Literacy? 136

    10.1 Literacy in the Mother Tongue 136

    10.2 Pastoralist Lifestyle in the Design 138

    10.3 Guidelines for the Learners 140

    10.4 Learning Activities 144

    10.5 Development Process 146

    10.6 Differences and Similarities of the First Two Ladders of Learning 147

    Personal Notes of the Authors 149

11. How Does INES Develop Ladders of Learning? 152

    11.1 Analysis of the Mathematics Curriculum and Textbooks 153

    11.2 Mathematical Test with Daasanach Children 154

    11.3 Mathematical Field Researches in the Catchment Area 157

    11.4 Development Process of the Mathematics Ladder of Learning 158

    Personal Notes of the Authors 165

12. How Does INES Empower Mobile Teachers? 168

12.1 Community Participation 169

12.2 Becoming a Mobile Teacher 170

12.3 Preparation Module 173

12.4 Module 1 - Basics 175

12.5 Module 2 - Introduction Ladder of Learning 180

12.6 Module 3 - Start of the Mobile School 182

12.7 Further Modules – Additional Subject Ladders of Learning 185

Conclusion 187

Afterword – What Do We See Now? 189

Appendix – Photographs and Graphics 191

Works Cited 223

Preface – Why Do We Ask Questions?

Why do more than 60 million children and youths do not attend school (UN 2019)? The answer is clear. They are exposed to armed conflicts, climatic and environmental challenges, precarious economic conditions, and child labour. Why are there still no sustainable educational solutions for these children and youths on the move? The answer is more complex. When education providers want to treat and organise everything and everyone equally, they are not oriented towards the basic needs and necessities of people in seemingly invincible life situations. When we take a close look at the cultural and social needs within the individual life situations of children and youths, we come across unexpected resources these special life situations entail for a sustainable future.

We like to ask questions. We enjoy asking Daasanach pastoralists out in the remote and dry savannah of Northern Kenya about their families, livestock, their culture, their living conditions, their dreams, and visions. At the same time, we continuously question the approaches of the Illeret Nomadic Education System (INES) and our role and work in it. Likewise, people like to question us. They want to know whether we act in accordance with the Daasanachs' wishes regarding education. They question how Daasanach women, men, and children envision their future and whether the planned mobile schools will support them in their vision. They ask why a non-governmental organisation like the Benedictine Fathers in Illeret has taken over a service, which is actually a governmental task. The primary question behind all the question remains: who has the right, the responsibility, the capacity, and the will to provide basic education to one of the most marginalized children in the world?

We do not claim to have found the answers to all these questions. Most of the solutions, which we present here, were developed in a long process of trial and error and sure enough, there are other innovative approaches to the education provision of mobile pastoralist. Nonetheless, after several requests from Daasanach pastoralists for an alternative educational system INES was started in 2014 by Father Florian OSB, who has been active as a Benedictine missionary in Kenya since 1984. The vision evolved in long talks with the Daasanach themselves. Daasanach pastoralist children live and shift with their mobile families, support the pastoralist production team, and participate in educational activities in so-called mobile schools with ladders of learning. The long term vision is that Daasanach men and women, who are mobile pastoralists themselves, visit the mobile teacher education programme of INES, gradually building up their school offer of various subject ladders of learning and thus support individualized learning in multi-age and multi-level learning groups.

We have had the incredible privilege to be part of the INES project implementation team from the beginning. We are grateful for the diverse group of partners, supporters, and colleagues, with whom we develop questions and seek answers.

In the course of our work within the INES project, as well as in the process of writing this book, we greatly benefitted from the action research done in India and Germany but most importantly from the intense dialogues with our Kenyan partners, German colleagues, and the RIVER team in India. At this point, we would like to particularly thank Father Florian OSB, the founder of the INES project, who invited us into the project as expatriate co-workers and consultants. We thank Edwin K. Changamu, the devoted pedagogical manager of INES and the small project implementation team of INES. Our thanks also go to Dr. Thomas Müller, associate professor from the University of Würzburg, who supported us in the process of writing this book as well as Sara Schuster for her language support.

Dear reader, we hope that this book will challenge you to remain open to questions and innovations regarding education provision and we hope you will enjoy reading about some of our most precious moments in Northern Kenya.

Introduction

Education provision for mobile pastoralists remains a difficult and emotive issue. Because the children of mobile pastoralist are involved in the economic production from an early age to contribute to their livelihood and because the pastoralist families have to stay on the move to find suitable grasslands and water points, there is hardly any time for the children to regularly attend fixed schools in settlements. With the infrastructure in Northern Kenya and the current school system, Daasanach pastoralist are therefore faced with a difficult choice: The first possibility is they give up their livelihood as mobile pastoralists, settle in a town and send their children to fixed schools. This is only possible if the parents generate an alternative income. The second possibility is to send their children to distant boarding schools where the children eventually lose touch with pastoralism and the sustainable lifestyle of millions of people eventually dies out. The third, and most common, choice is not providing their children access to formal education altogether.

For this reason, this book not only deals with the necessity but also the development of a mobile school system for Daasanach pastoralists in Northern Kenya. The publication gives a practical insight into the INES project of the Benedictine Fathers (Illeret Nomadic Education System), which offers Daasanach pastoralists in Northern Kenya access to alternative basic education through mobile schools, taking into account their livelihood of mobile livestock production. In order to implement this extensive pilot project, an innovative mobile school system with its own local learning material development and a teacher education centre for Daasanach pastoralists is being developed.

As you move through the three parts of this book, you will notice different writing styles and approaches to the title questions. On the one hand, this shift derives from the specialist fields of cultural, psychological and pedagogical studies. On the other hand, we want to provide a practical example of school development cooperation supported by technical literature. At the end of some chapters, we attached personal notes in which we want to share some of our thoughts and the most precious experiences we were able to make.

We would like to invite our readers to start by understanding the living conditions of the mobile Daasanach pastoralists in Northern Kenya (chapter 1) and why education provision for pastoralist groups is difficult (chapter 2). In chapter 3, we present selected international approaches to pastoralist education and outline which lessons the INES project learned from these school development projects. In chapter 4, we summarize the perspectives and dreams of Daasanach women, men and children regarding learning, teaching and schooling, which, we believe, to be fundamental in partnership-oriented development cooperation. If you may, this first part of the book provides the (problem) analysis of this international cooperation project.

In the second part of the book, we want to give an insight into our understanding of development and conceptual plans of the INES project of the Benedictine Fathers Illeret. We shortly approach the term development from a psychological and pedagogical point of view (chapter 5) and challenge the concept, idea and principles of international (development) cooperation (chapter 6). Chapter 7 provides an overview of the INES project, with forces, actors, partners, vision, mission and strategies.

The third part of this book gives a practical insight into the different working fields of INES – mainly learning material development and teacher education – with cross-references to technical literature and related projects. In chapter 8, we provide the pedagogical concept of the mobile school system with its ladders of learning, its Indian origin of the MultiGradeMulitLevel-Methodology and the Kenyan adaption. Chapter 9 focuses on the importance of the cultural context for the development of learning materials. This is exemplified with the Introduction ladder of learning of INES. Chapter 10 describes how learners move independently in the complex arrangement of the Daasanach ladder of learning. In chapter 11, the focus lies on Mathematics and our readers learn how whole subject ladders of learning with its learning materials for several grades are developed, based on the Kenyan curriculum and with regard to the cultural characteristics of the local Daasanach. How the modularized teacher education system works practically with mobile pastoralists is presented in chapter 12. Finally, we invite the readers to close with a brief description of the excellent pedagogical work we believe to see with Daasanach pastoralists, who offer girls and boys in their mobile stock camps access to alternative basic education.

Part I Daasanach Pastoralists and Education Provision

Daasanach like to keep their traditions.
Paul Gosh Kwanjang', Daasanach elder and linguistist

1. How Do Daasanach Pastoralists Live?

The Daasanach belong to one of the smallest and most marginalized language communities in Kenya (Tosco 2001).[1] Until the late 1970s, the Daasanach were unknown from an ethnographic point of view, as well as, linguistically. Only a handful of anthropological and linguistic studies were published in the 1980s and 2000s. The partial information on the Daasanach life, language and social organisation provided in the following chapters are mainly based on personal experiences of the authors and their interviews with local Daasanach in Northern Kenya. Cross references to other authors and scientists who studied the Daasanach people in Ethiopia reveal further interesting facts about the language, social life and economy.[2]

Fig. 1.1: Joshua Esho with his wife in traditional dress with two of their daughters at the *'dimi* celebration (Source: Ruth Würzle).

---

1 In literature, different spellings can be found for Daasanach, e.g. Dhaasanach, Dassanetch or Dasenech.
2 There are a handful of papers and monographs by Claudia Carr (1977), Uri Almagor (1972, 1978), Mauro Tosco (2001) and Peggy Elfmann (2005) who studied the Daasanach mainly in Ethiopia.

1.1 Homeland Area

Numbers. Mobile pastoralists (nomadic herders) make up several tens of millions of people, mainly in Africa, the Middle East, South, South-West and Central Asia. Official figures for Africa vary but a conservative estimate by the International Institute for Environment and Development is approximately 50 million mobile pastoralists in the drylands across the continent (Car-Hill & Peart 2005). The arid and semi-arid lands of Northern Kenya cover more than half of the country and is home to 2.5 million pastoralists with eight different language groups. As with many mobile pastoralists, the Daasanach are a cross-border language group. Most of the Daasanach live in southwest Ethiopia (38,000 in 2010). In Kenya, they make up one of the smallest pastoralist language groups with an estimated 9,000 (2010) pastoralists in the remote region of Marsabit County at the northeastern shore of Lake Turkana and the area around Illeret (Lewis 2009).[3]

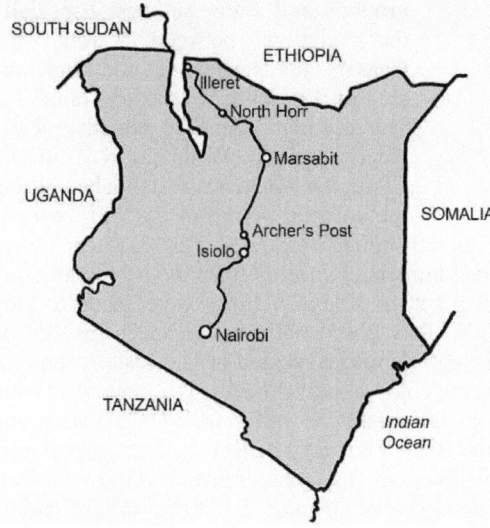

Fig. 1.2: Journey from Nairobi to Illeret (Source: own illustration).

Remoteness. Arid Kenya, with its deserts, savannahs and grasslands, covers 80% of Kenya's land mass and has historically been at the periphery of national development. In these arid lands, the mobile pastoralists find their economic livelihood. The total homeland area of the Daasanach pastoralists is comprised of 2,300 square kilometres and stretches mainly along the West and East banks of the Omo River, the largest river in south-western Ethiopia. Only in the course of the last century with prolonged droughts, the Daasanach had to shift southwards to the north-eastern shores of Lake Turkana in Kenya. It is a four days journey with a car or lorry from Kenya's capital, Nairobi, following the country's tarmac highway towards the North. In Marsabit, the newly constructed tarmac road ends and turns into a dirt road which leads northwestern, along the Chalbe desert to North Horr. After North Horr you hardly see any vehicles and once you have crossed the stony and dry homeland area you reach the Gabra pastoralists. Leaving behind Buluk, a desolate police outpost, a bumpy desert road leads through the Sibiloi National Park and then finally reaches Illeret, 18 kilometres from the Ethiopian-Kenyan border.

---

3   The last national census in Kenya was carried out and published in 1994. The data showed a net population increase of 1,5% per year. Even the Kenyan government uses data from Lewis M.P. (2009). In August 2019 a national census was conducted and to date, there are no official numbers.

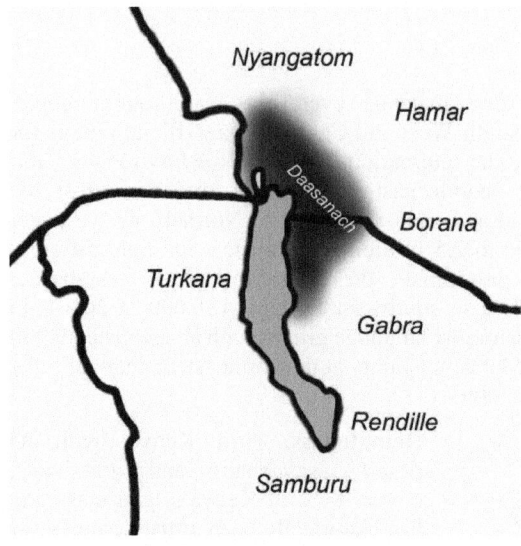

Fig. 1.3: The Daasanach homeland and the neighbouring groups (Source: own illustration).

Neighbouring Groups. The Daasanach territory in Kenya borders the homeland of the Gabra, Borana, Rendille and Samburu, as well as, the Turkana. In Ethiopia, they are neighbours to the Hamar, Borana and Nyangatom. Most of the time the Daasanach have good relationships with their pastoralist neighbours and also maintain trade relations of grain, tobacco, ironwork, clay pots, coffee, textiles, spears, knives, bracelets, toilet soaps and riffles. Time and again, however, tension and conflicts arise over attractive pasture grounds and water sources. Especially the relation between Gabra and Daasanach is tense since the homeland area of the Gabra is very dry, rainfall is scarce and borders are not historically clearly marked. When the Kenyan and Ethiopian border was established during the colonial period of the 20th century, Gabra and Borana were officially recognised as transboundary groups. The Daasanach were defined as Ethiopians although their traditional homeland spreads from the Ethiopian Omo delta to the north-eastern shore of Lake Turkana in Kenya. Efforts were made to stop Daasanach from inhabiting Kenyan territory (Galaty 2005) but the Daasanach insisted on their historical rights to grazing near the lake and therefore resided on the eastern shore of Lake Turkana. In order to secure the frontier, the colonial power decided to move the Gabra and Borana away from the Kenyan and Ethiopian border zone. Later, in 1948, a small group of Daasanach was officially "tolerated" in the British territory of Kenya. The cross-border feeling of togetherness between Kenyan and Ethiopian Daasanach remains very high and is demonstrated, for example, in their collaboration of carrying out raids. The rewards of raiding are cattle, girls and prestige. Almagor (1978) argues that hostilities and raiding are usually reciprocal between the neighbouring groups with no substantial gain. As long as, certain conventions and rules are not violated, the movement of cattle and small stock back and forth is acceptable. Traditionally raiding happens on a small scale and occurs spontaneously among peers in their twenties.

The long and strife-ridden history between Gabra and Daasanach can be perceived differently because of the acquisition of firearms during the last decades. Registered rifles, as well as, illegally obtained rifles are officially permitted for use by the home guards to secure property and land. This easily leads to unfortunate recurring fatal escalations (Galaty 2005).

Water. Lake Turkana is the second largest lake in Kenya and the largest permanent desert lake in the world. It has no outlet and receives more than 90% of its waters from the Omo River, which rises seasonally and irregularly in Ethiopia (Carr 2017). The distribution of rainfall along the 200 kilometre long and 40 kilometre wide east side of the lake is unreliable and its occurrence is irregular.

During the rainy season, numerous natural river beds flood within minutes allowing no crossover for some days. When the water level sinks again the Daasanach girls and women dig out wells along the bank sides and first find groundwater after 2 to 3 metres of sand. The groundwater is traditionally filled into hollow calabashes however, today plastic jerricans and buckets are used and are carried on their heads to the none permanent homes. Lake Turkana is the most saline lake in East Africa and the second most saline lake in Africa and as salinity is already at a critical level for various fauna, the lake is only borderline potable for humans and livestock. However, a study found that herd animals regularly refuse the saline water even though it is technically borderline potable and the villagers' health problems can also be attributed to a high salinity of living at the shore of Lake Turkana (Carr 2017). As long as the grass provides enough feed for the livestock and there is sufficient water in the puddles and wells of the riverbeds the Daasanach families settle in these spots. Since the Daasanach pastoralists live off their livestock, household mobility is a constant requirement to keep the animals safe.

Fig. 1.4: Eastern shore of Lake Turkana with view on Northern Island (Source: Ruth Würzle).

Lake Turkana's volume has significantly decreased over the past 30 years because of higher temperatures, changing weather patterns and the construction of huge dams for hydroelectric power production in Ethiopia. Hydrologists predict that the downstream impact of the dams, which were inaugurated in 2016, will reduce the flow to Lake Turkana up to 70%. The inevitable impact this will have on the Daasanach pastoralists is unclear, however, it will transform the natural habitats to the more than 50 species of fish which have been identified in Lake Turkana so far and kill ecosystems (Carr 2017).[4]

---

4   In 2018, Lake Turkana was added to the list of endangered World Heritage Sites. The World Heritage

1.2 Livelihood

The Daasanach see themselves as pastoralists, even though their homeland area along the river Omo in Ethiopia also allows agriculture. Mobile pastoralism is a lifestyle based upon animal husbandry which mainly feeds on natural vegetation. In turn, the pastoralists live off the animal products. As most mobile pastoralists, the Daasanach inhabit remote areas because their livestock and production strategies are adjusted to the grasslands and generally harsh ecological conditions which are not suitable for agriculture as an example. Contrary to common misconceptions, mobile pastoralism is not an archaic form of husbandry and pastoral techniques are not antiquated. On the contrary, pastoralism is highly sustainable due to high productivity (Dyer 2016).

I especially like when the weather is good and there is food for the animals. I get food from my animals.
Joshua Esho, elder

Grazing areas vary seasonally according to the rainfall which determines the dry and wet seasons. In each season the herds are shifted to make the best use of the different kinds of grass. Herding involves both daily treks from the more permanent settlement (*manyatta*) and extended periods out to the temporary stock camp (*forich*).[5] A family's stock of goats, sheep, cattle, donkeys and camels is not grazed together. Cattle graze before small stock to protect the pasture and in the dry season goats are given priority and therefore sheep are often separated from the goats. There is no clear pattern of shifting, scouts and herders move rather freely and whoever identifies a specific pasture first grazes it, as long as, there is sufficient water in puddles and wells for drinking. The seasonal movements save the land from overgrazing and deterioration (Carr 1977; Almagor 1978). As long as the livestock is provided with water and grass, the Daasanach pastoralists are able to survive the harsh environmental conditions of Northern Kenya.[6] Strong population growth in recent years has increased the number of small flocks in the region fivefold and overgrazing of the already highly stressed ecosystem has become a problem. Hunger is the result due to loss of livestock and larger families. Since slaughtering animals in large numbers is only justifiable during ceremonial feasts or when food is short, animal husbandry is considered as a mode of subsistence and animals are usually not for sale (Milimo 2004; Elfmann 2005). The close relationship between the Daasanach and their livestock is not only shown in the fact that they live with them side by side but also in their language. There are, for example, more than 30 different names for oxen like *long'ollekóu* (lit. ox with a white head and black body), *loso'guel* (lit. ox with long slim horns) or *ng'elluka* (lit. ox with one horn bent upwards and one downwards) (Tosco 2001).

Committee expressed concern about the disruptive effect of Ethiopia's Gibe III dam on Lake Turkana and the changes affecting the hydrology and the ecosystem (https://whc.unesco.org/en/news/1842/).

5 Almagor (1978) and Carr (1977; 2017) describe in detail the social and ecological conditions, which determine the process of livestock and family shifting, as well as, ecology and economy of the Daasanach.

6 Milimo (2005) describes the mobility of the whole production family as a prerequisite requirement of pastoralists due to the surrounding ecological conditions. She illustrates the organisational skills which are necessary to plan the migration tours in the course of a year, which are all too often affected by numerous uncertain events in Northern Kenya such as floods, droughts, ceremonies, political events and hostilities with neighbouring groups. However, according to the World Initiative for Sustainable Pastoralism, one of the main misconceptions about pastoralism is that mobility is unnecessary, chaotic and disruptive (Dyer 2016).

Fig. 1.5: A Daasanach boy tending goats and sheep (Source: Ruth Würzle).

Moreover, Daasanach do not count their livestock, they simply know them. Counting is considered evidence of incapability and numbering downgrades the animals in their sight.[7] The degree of mobility and sedentarisation varies between groups and individual families. There are 'pure' mobile pastoralists, where all members are on the move, semi-permanent pastoralists, who are settled and perhaps only young men travel with their livestock for several months, to agro-pastoralists, who engage in crop production and animal husbandry depending on the season.

Nutrition. The local diet is mainly based on *bie kulláá* (lit. hot water) prepared by the woman of the house upon an open fire in the round hut. Three stones on the left side of the entrance hold the cooking pot. In the morning and the evening, women and girls milk the livestock and then coffee-hulls or tea leaves are boiled in water together with milk and sugar. Some of the milk is reserved for toddlers and the production of yogurt. The nutritious milk is poured into a calabash together with water and the branch of a certain tree to produce different dairy products. The calabash is shaken and beaten and then allowed to rest for 24 hours before consumption. The yogurt has a smoky taste because the calabashes are cleansed and purified

---

[7] The anthropologist Melville Herskovits (1895-1963) introduced the term "cattle complex" in his PhD thesis "The Cattle Complex in East Africa". With this term, he describes the system of values made up of cattle ownership which governs and directs everyday life in large parts of East Africa. Thereby Herskovits does not refer to sole cattle-keeping in itself. "Cattle complex" according to Herskovits is the fact that cattle more than anything is the focal point in the people's lives. Cattle are the provider of food, however, should only be slaughtered to mark special occasions such as birth and funeral – the great transitional events of life. Moreover, "most enduring social relationships were mediated through the loan, gift or exchange of cattle." (Barnard & Spencer 1996: 91).

with smoke. Traditionally, no food is eaten throughout the day. Toddlers, girls and women who stay near the settlements consume some milk or leftovers from breakfast. The boys and men, who spend the day out grazing the animals only carry some water. If available, the women cook *rubba* (sorghum) either as whole grains or ground as porridge and occasionally add meat. In Kenya, sorghum, as well as, sugar, tea leaves, maize and beans can only be purchased in the shops in Illeret and Silicho. This traditional diet of sorghum is grown and sold by the Ethiopian Daasanach along the river Omo. When food runs out in the stock camps or there is not enough milk for all family members, some boiled, roasted or dried meat is added to the meals. All in all, slaughtering remains a special event, reserved for traditional celebrations. Occasionally, the Daasanach also drink blood from a healthy bull but this happens rather seldomly since the number of cows is rather low. During special occasions, the bull is held by at least three men while the neck of the bull is stabbed with a kind of arrow (*bilte*). The blood is collected in a container, mostly a calabash, and served to men, women and children likewise.

Pastoralism is important because we get all we need from the animals.
Lokolom Long'ada, mother

Agriculture. Pastoral production is the main source of subsistence in Northern Kenya, since the soil, heat, lack of rain, deep groundwater and alkaline water of Lake Turkana prohibit agricultural farming. Reed grass is one of the few plants which grows in alkaline water. Only the Ethiopian Daasanach living near the Omo River can do some subsistence farming. When the Omo rises once a year and inundates the riverbanks and surrounding flats, sorghum crop, maize, beans and calabash can be grown. Depending on the rains there can also be a second and third harvest (Almagor 1978). Empty calabashes are cut in two halves, lavishly decorated with dried shells and colourful beads and used as drinking bowls (*'daate*) for the *bie kulláá*.

Fishery. Even though the Daasanach in Kenya live on the eastern shore of Lake Turkana, which contains many different kinds of fish, such as Nile perch (*lates niloticus*) and different types of mudfish; Daasanach pastoralists traditionally dislike fishing and the sale of fish. Fishing is considered poor people's work. To date, there are many restrictions on social relations with fishermen. Traditionally, fish is only eaten occasionally during dry seasons as a supplement or when a family has lost their livestock and has no other means to survive.

Today, however, it can be observed that more and more businessmen, mainly Kenyan Somalis and Ethiopians, settle along the shore employing young locals as fishermen and then hire ice lorries to carry and sell fresh fish to central Kenya and dried fish, as far as, Uganda. Since the western part of Lake Turkana is heavily overfished and long sections of the lake are now under the protection of the Sibiloi National Park, fishing along the shores between the Omo delta and Illeret seems to be a lucrative business at present. In earlier days, a subgroup of the Daasanach (Elmolo) would also hunt crocodiles which mainly live around the Central Island, but today, deliberate hunting of crocodiles is strictly prohibited.

Fig. 1.6: A Daasanach man with traditional hair drinking *bie kulláá* from a *'daate* (Source: Ruth Würzle).

1.3 Social Organisation

Traditional African life is based on the idea of communalism which can be seen in the collective activity and mutual help that extends from the family, over the extended family and the brotherhood derived from it, to the community at large. In a communalist group, the loyalty primarily lies within the community above any other loyalty, as, for example, loyalty to a country (Farrant 1980).[8]

---

8   The political theory of communalism has its roots in the ethnic and cultural diversity of Africa. Communalism inspires cooperation between individuals within a certain group rather than competition. Features of communalism are also seen in how a certain community claims united actions in major challenges and how in a crisis collective resources are arranged to help those members in trouble. On the other hand, communalism can also lead to clashes between different communities if each group denies the fact that they have more commonalities with other communities than they have differences. This can result in groups becoming hostile to one another, which has given communalism negative connotations (Farrant 1980).

Various aspects of communalism can be seen in the way Daasanach society is organised in segments, clans, moieties, generation sets, bond friendships and families which all carry meaning, restrict certain relationships and distribute rights, chores and ritual duties.[9]

Clans. The most general groups are the clans. Daasanach belong to one of the eight tribal sections, which are each seen as coterminous with a territorial section (Tosco 2001). The clans are described as having certain duties and rights which are of importance in Daasanach life and include everyday rituals and special activities. The eight clans are hierarchically structured. Members of the first clan, *Tuurnyerim*, are the first to get circumcised during a circumcision ceremony and the first to slaughter bulls and goats during a traditional *'dimi* ceremony. Then the remaining seven clans mentioned above follow in turn. The clan system follows a patrilineal inheritance structure: Children belong to the clan of their fathers' and inherit their tasks, duties and talents. When the spouse is from another clan, the wife officially changes to the husband's clan, however, without adopting the gifts of the new clan.

Lydia, for example, belongs to the *Galbur* clan, since her father inherited this tribal section. After she married a man from the *Fargááro* clan, she now officially belongs to this clan of rainmakers and snake healers but does not share the skills with her husband. It is perceived, that Lydia still has the ability to stop crocodiles from hurting livestock and people, the skill of *Galbur* members. Their children will follow the lineage of the father and be part of the *Fargááro* clan with all their rights, duties and skills.

Clan Name	Attribution
Tuurnyerim	Clan of rainmakers and snakes; *Tuurnyerim* are perceived to bring rain, to heal snake bites and to converse with god.
Fargááro	Clan of rainmakers and snakes; *Fargááro* share the same duties and rights with the *Tuurnyerim*. They can pray for rain if no *Tuurnyerim* is nearby.
Tuurat	Clan of fire; *Turaat* are perceived to be able to heal burnings.
Galbur	Clan of crocodiles; *Galbur* are said to prevent crocodiles from hurting livestock and people. *Galbur* are perceived to protect livestock from crocodiles especially during river crossings.
Ílli	Clan of scorpions and spiders; *Ílli* are said to have the power to heal scorpion bites.
Edhe	Clan of wind catchers; *Edhe* are perceived to stop strong winds and they are said to treat eye sickness.
Múrle	Clan of insect controllers; *Múrle* are perceived as being able to stop flies and other insect.
Tieme	Clan of pancreas; *Tieme* are said to have the power to heal a swollen pancreas by blessing the affected person.

Fig. 1.7: Overview of the eight clans (Source: own illustration).

---

9   According to Claudia Carr, Daasanach society is structured into eight tribal segments (*en*): *Inkabela, Inkoria, Naritch, Eleli, Koro, Oro, Randel, Rieli*. Each *en* functions as an autonomous fighting unit during warfare and has its own traditional tales of origin and is subdivided again into clans, moieties and generation sets. There are no marriage boundaries between these eight tribal segments. Out of the eight segments, *Inkabela* is the largest and most dominant one which serves as a reference structure to the others. *Inkabela* are said to be the oldest *en* with other tribal segments originating later (Carr 1977). In the Kenyan Daasanach homeland around Illeret, all informants referred to the *Inkabela* segment when speaking about the social structure of the Daasanach. Therefore, the information on clans, moieties and generation sets stated in this book are based on the *Inkabela* segment.

Moieties. Daasanach are divided into moieties – *baadiyet* (lit. outside people) and *geerge* (lit. stomach people). Everyone belongs to the *dolo* (moiety) of the grandfather on the father's side. Generations alternate in the father-child relationship. Moieties are not externally recognizable. This division cuts across territory, tribal clan and the age system grouping (Almagor, 1978). Marriage in the moieties is regulated in that members of *baadiyet* are not allowed to marry a person from the moiety of *geerge* and vice versa. In the moiety each tribal section celebrates the *'dimi* ceremony separately and depending upon your moiety you execute specific ceremonial functions. The moieties association with fertility – *baadiyet* is derived from the male and the *geerge* of the female and is stressed in the ceremony.

Generation Sets. The central defining principle of Daasanach social organisation is called generation set. Every man belongs to a *hari* (generation set) and to one of the two existing age groups (Almagor 1978). The generation set is determined at birth and a man always joins the alternate set to that of his father. The age differences within a generation set may be forty years or more since the entry into one set depends on when its alternate one starts bearing children. Women's generation sets are much less important than the men's because group affiliation is more entangled in domestic cares. The transition from girl to wife to mother and old woman occurs on an individual basis (Elfmann 2005). Marriage is, without exceptions, only possible within the same generation set. The membership of unmarried girls to a *hari* is shown by the colour-coding of their hair accessories. Men and married women do not show their belonging to a *hari* openly. The generation set *nabus* is shown by red-green colour-coding while *kobier* is depicted by red and yellow beads.

A concrete example illustrates this complex system of generation sets: Samuel is as a member of the red-green generation set *nabus* and thus can only choose a partner from the same set. To find a husband for their daughter, a special celebration called *'gúol* is organised by the family where the appropriate *hari* (generation set) is invited. Additionally, the moieties have to be taken into account. Gosh, being a *kobier* and a *baadiyet*, was only allowed to choose a wife from the same generation set and moiety.

Bond Friendship. Finally, bond partnerships play an important role in Daasanach social organisation. From the standpoint of increasing their array of social and economic relations, they are mainly of importance for men (Carr 1977).

Among men, there are five bond partnerships with each bond characteristic of a particular stage in life: *bond partnerships of lips* are established between teenage boys; the *bond partnership of gifts* is established between men from twenty to forty years of age; the *bond partnership of smearing* is established between a boy reaching physical maturity with a man from his *hari* which is an unbreakable bond. During circumcision, the *bond partnership of holding* is created. The *holder* supports during circumcision and afterwards gives him a *kára* (stool, headrest), beads, necklaces, a *'daate* (drinking calabash) and a skirt. The strongest bond of all according to Almagor is the *bond partnership of name-giving* which is created when a newborn child is named after someone at the name-giving ceremony. Between women, there is only one bond (*friendship of holding*) which is established when a girl gets circumcised and is held by another female who has already undergone the procedure. Because the female bond usually elapses after a while it is considered rather weak and is not referred to as a bond.

Fig. 1.8: Generation-set *nabus* (green pearls) and *kobier* (yellow pearls) (Source: Philipp Laurer).

Family Structure. Many Daasanach live polygamous which means men may have several wives. The amount of wives displays the wealth of a man since he can feed and care for a larger family. A second wife is also coverage in case one of the wives is absent or passes on. If the mother is absent, the other wife naturally takes care of the children. This is demonstrated within the extended family who live closely together and where there are no differences made between the biological children and those of the other wives. The children are brought up and nurtured by all the present females. If a community member catches a child doing something wrong, it is this person who deals with this misbehaviour. All children of a man are siblings, no matter if they have different mothers. No difference is made between siblings and half siblings. Nonetheless, each wife has her own domain, house and fireplace within a settlement, if all marriage partners are living in the same area. In this case, toddlers and young children go to their biological mother for food and to sleep. Boys only sleep in the huts with their mothers during the first few years. At the age of eight, the age mates become more important and boys group together to sleep outside with the animals and men. It is more common however for their wives to live in different places providing the men with several homes and possibilities to graze their stock. Nowadays, many men have a wife in town (Illeret or Silicho) and one in the mobile settlements of the stock camps.

Daasanach marriage includes the lifelong overwriting of livestock to the bridal family. The amount of livestock and when the payment is due is agreed upon between the two families at the wedding ceremony. Marriage is seen as a contract between two families whereby livestock is traded in for a woman's fertility (Elfmann 2005). If the husband no longer transfers livestock to the wife's family this is interpreted as not being capable to provide for the family and the in-laws are entitled to take the wife and children back. The *'gúol* ceremony, in contrast to weddings, where men are looking for a wife is a big ceremonial event.

Gender Roles and Tasks. In the east of Africa among mobile pastoralists, the major differences in the roles and tasks of men and women are deeply rooted in a male rule. This is evident in the basis of family, clan and tribal organisational structures, as mentioned earlier (Buke 2012). The general rule is that tasks performed by men are controlled by men and those performed by women are controlled by women. Men control grazing and watering of animals, wage earning and trading activities. Women control young animals, donkeys, milk and milk products, water and fuel for domestic use, as well as, grain grinding, meal preparation, house cleaning and clothes washing.

Depending on age, sex and season, every community member has clear tasks and chores to fulfil as illustrated in the following case of Joshua Esho and Lokolom Long'ada.[10]

Fig. 1.9: A Daasanach man tending his goats (Source: Ruth Würzle).

> Joshua Loki Esho is 29 years old. He and his wife have five children between the age of 1 and 14 years. Esho has a couple of cows, camels and donkeys, as well as, numerous goats and sheep. During the dry season, first thing in the morning he has his breakfast which consists of a cup of sugared tea, which is prepared and served by his wife. Then he checks on the animals which were locked up in the *boma* (thorn hedge where livestock is kept)

---

10 In 2017 interview guidelines were developed by Höldrich and the German INES research team (that time: Lichtinger, Schaller & Würzle). In Illeret, Schaller carried out interviews with a relevant cross section of Daasanach and asked about their everyday lives and their expectations of education, schooling and teaching. For results see chapter *4. What Are the Wishes of Daasanach Pastoralists with Regard to Education?*.

during the night. Meanwhile, usually the oldest son (or in the case of Esho's family his daughter) gets up, eats breakfast and is now ready to meet the father to discuss where the small animals should be tended throughout the course of the day. During the dry season, the livestock leaves the *boma* at around 8 o'clock in the morning and the children tending the small animals (sheep and goats) often have to walk several kilometres to find appropriate pasture. During the rainy season, however, the livestock leaves the *boma* as early as 5 o'clock in the morning to graze nearby so that by approximately 9 o'clock the goats, sheep and cattle return to the *forich* to feed their kids and calves and to get milked subsequently. While his children take the livestock for grazing, Esho follows his duties as a scout. Together with the other elders of his community, he searches for good pasture grounds and where the *forich* community will migrate to. This requires not only organisational skills since the herds often have to be split due to the special needs of the livestock, ecological conditions and also the long-distances that need to be walked. Upon his return to the larger *forich* and his report to the community, the decision will be made where the animals will be taken the following day by the elders. In a single household *forich* the family man decides alone. During the dry season warriors (mainly young men who are not yet elders) patrol closely to the *forich*, keep a lookout for enemies (warriors from neighbouring tribes) and protect their livestock, families and settlements, if necessary, by force of arms.

Boys take part in animal husbandry from an early age. His area of responsibility constantly broadens once he has proven capable of tending the livestock (first young kids, who are kept near the *forich*, then sheep and goats and finally cattle).

Fig. 1.10: Daasanach woman together with her grandchild (Source: Ruth Würzle).

> Lokolom Long'ada is one of her husband's two wives and has several children. Women mainly stay in the settlements if they are not out for shopping or visiting. Lokolom describes the beginning of her daily routine with the preparation of breakfast for her husband (if he is with her), her children and herself before she goes to the animals to oversee the feeding of the kids and calves and finally milks them for the family's food. Later in the morning, she fetches water from a well, which often she must dig herself.
> In this case, the water source belongs to her and she oversees who may or may not draw water. During the day, Lokolom Long'ada takes care of the house (including assembly and dismantling of the round hut), packing, unpacking, carving, cleaning wooden utensils, washing clothes and if available grinding sorghum. Breastfeeding and taking care of young children is not seen as a task, as such, they are rather carried out simultaneously. In the evening she collects firewood, milks the animals a second time and prepares dinner.

The duties of girls also increase with age: at the age of six, they learn to collect firewood and how to fetch water from the wells. They practice balancing the carriers on their heads and begin with small containers, which eventually hold up to 20 litres. At the age of 10, girls are taught how to milk goats, sheep, cows and camels. If the family has boys, herding is less necessary, instead, they support their mothers with duties such as smoking milk containers to cleanse and purify or milking the animals. Later on, in preparation for their future household, girls also learn how to produce commodities, for example, carved milk containers from a tree, woven load-bearing scaffolds for the donkeys, so-called *noonos*. Sometimes girls also stay with the household of an older sister or close relative if they are needed to care for children or the elderly.

Fig. 1.11: A Daasanach girl milking a goat (Source: Philipp Laurer).

Structure of Settlements. Usually, a *forich* is constructed in a round structure. The size of these stock camps depends on the number of community members which move around together. Along the border areas of the traditional territory of the Daasanach, the *fora* tend to be larger comprising up to 100 people in order to defend themselves against their neighbours, if necessary. The average or a *forich*, however, comprises around 30 people. When a *forich* is rather larger and comprises several huts they are arranged in a circle. The small houses in these temporary camps are thatched with grass, skin hides, sacks or black tarps. The *forich* is surrounded by a *boma* (circular thorn hedges) to protect the livestock from wild animals and raiding enemies during the night. Within each *fora* there is a fixed meeting place, called *nááb*.

In big settlements this gathering place is in the centre of the *fora*, in smaller communities which may only include one elder, the *nááb* is in front of the elder's house. This assembly place is used for daily gatherings of the community to discuss topics concerning migration and grazing grounds. When an elder is not in the *forich* he is immediately informed at the *nááb* about everything that has happened during his absence.

Fig. 1.12: A small *forich* with a few round huts, covered with black tarps (Source: Ruth Würzle).

During the rainy season (*irr gudua*, lit. big rain) the communities of a *forich* speak of the time of plenty and shift several times per months. The herders take their stock to the remote pasture grounds where the grass is plenty but far off from permanent water sources. As long as there is enough water for the people, as well as, the herds the pastoralists settle here.

When the water supply runs dry, they migrate to the next pasture ground. During the dry season, Daasanach speak of the time of want, the pastoralists settle near river beads with permanent water supply. During this time the Daasanach live in more permanently and larger built huts with more equipment. Due to the eventually diminishing pasture, the livestock produces less milk and if the drought season prolongs these *manyatta*, more permanent dwellings, can remain up to three years in one spot.

Fig. 1.13: A hut with an iron sheet roof in a *manyatta* (Source: Ruth Würzle).

1.4 Celebrations

Many different ceremonies are part of the unique Daasanach culture. The most important ceremonial functions are *'gúol*, where fathers are on the lookout for an appropriate husband for their daughter, *bilte*, the circumcision ceremony, *suoryó*, purification prayers and *'dimi*, where men receive the status of an elder.

'Gúol – Finding a Wife. This ceremony is organised within one of the two generation sets either *nabus* (red-green colour-coding) or *kobier* (red-yellow colour-coding). Since marriage is only possible within the same generation set, *'gúol* ceremonies are celebrated separately by each of the two groups. During *'gúol* the girl wears her father's big white ostrich feather to indicate that the celebration is held on her behalf. Ostrich feathers are a status symbol only worn on special occasions. The black and white feathers are considered to be more special than grey ones. The male guests of *'gúol* wear small white ostrich feathers in their lavishly decorated hair, which is dyed with red, white and brown clay. During the ceremonial dancing and singing, the female guests snatch the young men's feathers to indicate their interest. During the *'gúol* ceremony both sexes observe each other, however, in the end, it is the father who chooses the wife for his son. After *'gúol* the lad asks his father to visit the family of the girl and to propose. If both families agree the wedding is arranged. Between this engagement agreement and the actual wedding, some years may pass.

Fig. 1.14: Daasanach men celebaring *'gúol* (Source: Philipp Laurer).

***Bilte* – Circumcision.** The *bilte* ceremony is the circumcision of both, boys and girls, whereby the ceremony for the boys is more important to the Daasanach. Males, as well as, females establish a close bond partnership to the *holder*, a supporter who has already undergone the procedure. Girls are usually circumcised between the age of 12 to 13 and are then considered mature enough to be married and to bear children. However, the firstborn daughter of a man cannot be circumcised before her father has held the *'dimi* ceremony on her behalf (Elfmann 2005).

In 2011, the Kenyan government enacted a law making female genital mutilation illegal. According to the Kenya demographic health survey of 2014, the prevalence mainly among pastoralists' communities has dropped from 38% in 1998 to 21% in 2014, but there is still a large number of unreported cases (Kenya National Bureau of Statistics 2015). Traditionally seen circumcision remains an important part of becoming of age.

***Suoryó* – Purification.** The purification ceremony takes place when the community members perceive that they have offended their ancestors. For example, by not offering sufficient tobacco or milk during a *'dimi* ceremony. Especially during prolonged droughts or phases of severe fighting with enemies (neighbouring language communities) the *suoryó* ceremony is held to ask the ancestors for forgiveness or blessings, peace, rain or healing of illnesses.

***'Dimi* – Becoming an Elder.** The most important celebration among the Daasanach is the *'dimi* celebration.

Any Daasanach man who has not graduated from 'dimi is not a real Daasanach and he will not attend elders' meetings.
Paul Gosh Kwanjang', elder

Fig. 1.15: A Daasanach man celebrating *'dimi* in Nang'oleiy in 2016 (Source: Ruth Würzle).

The *'dimi* celebration can only be held by a man whose firstborn daughter has not yet had her first menstrual bleeding. *'Dimi* is very demanding, costly and thus often very lengthy. The preparation can take years and may first start, as early as, the birth of the firstborn daughter. Only with a 'dimi celebration can a Daasanach man become an elder. While the firstborn daughter is the reason for the celebration, it is her father, who is the main character. A *'dimi* ceremony can be held for a single man, but often several families unite and celebrate 'dimi together. It is not unusual to find hundreds of Daasanach gathering together in a huge camp for several weeks or even months during the dry season to have *'dimi* together.

The ceremony normally spans three months climaxing with the slaughtering of a bull at the end of the celebration. Each family celebrating *'dimi* slaughters one bull no matter how many families have merged for a *'dimi*. The evening before, every candidate slaughters a goat and a sheep. Traditionally, the goat, sheep and the bull are slayn with a stone between the eyes. Unlike the normal practices of slaughtering (killing animals without numbing), during *'dimi* no blood is supposed to be spilled while slaughtering. During a large *'dimi*, the ceremonies of slaughtering may stretch over several days, because each clan has their appointed time. First, the candidates from the first four clans (*Tuurnyerim, Fargááro, Tuurat, Galbur*) conduct the slaughtering ceremony. Then, a few days later, the men from the remaining clans (*Ílli, Edhe, Múrle, Tieme*) follow. The clan hierarchy is shown by the structural arrangement of the round huts, all the round huts of the first four clans are arranged in the inner circle, while the members of the other four clans set up their huts in the outer circle.

The *'dimi* ceremony demands a strict dress code. The man celebrating *'dimi* wears a leopard skin as a cloak tied around his neck demonstrating bravery shown in his ability to kill a leopard. Nowadays, however, these skins are either bought or borrowed. Along with traditional leather skirts, the wife of the elder-to-be wears a colobus monkey skin coat tied around her shoulders. The loincloth for the man is traditionally made of the skin of a sheep. During the months of preparation, the man celebrating *'dimi* wears a big white ostrich feather in his lavishly decorated hair.

At the climax of the celebration, this single white feather is replaced with an intricate headdress of black ostrich feathers. This crown of black feathers is only worn for *'dimi* to show the outstanding position of an elder. The forearms are fully covered with tight bracelets of copper and other metals. Furthermore, he and his immediate family's bare skin is covered with yellow powder. In addition to his normal shepherd's crook, the man carries a three metre long stick (*naaso*), which he not allowed to lay down for the entire ceremony. Before and parallel to the slaughtering, there are a series of ritual dancing, singing, prayers, discussions, speeches and other performances which are all directed by the senior elders reigning from a specially established *nááb* (meeting place) in the centre of the 'dimi camp.

1.5 Indigenous Knowledge

The Daasanach are one of the more than 30 pastoral communities in Kenya whose lives are based on animal husbandry. Two-third of Kenya's landmass is arid, unsuitable for planting, but through their mobile lifestyle, the pastoralists and their livestock use the pasture grounds and water points in the high valleys, savannahs and steppes. This requires a great deal of technical knowledge about livestock management, animal husbandry, ethno-veterinary and animal production. This indigenous knowledge is transmitted orally and the skills are acquired by apprenticeship (Dinucci & Fre 2003).

From an early age, Daasanach children are taught by their parents, grandparents, elders and older members in the age group of the child.

Oral Tradition. When asked what the mobile pastoralists do in their spare time they say *making stories*. Orally transmitted proverbs, genealogies and narratives in form of storytelling or singing are recurring events in the daily lives of pastoralists. Since taking care of animals, fetching water or collecting firewood is done mainly along the *nááb* (meeting place in a settlement), *él* (well or water puddle), *bíl* (round hut) and *ðáb* (non-permanent settlement) are popular spots where news is exchanged and stories are told, preferably with a cup of freshly brewed tea with sugar and milk.[11]

Indigenous Technical Knowledge. From an early age, Daasanach children learn that the better they feed their animals, the more valuable and healthier the food they receive from them because the right forage plants not only increase the amount, but also the quality of the milk and products derived from it, such as butter, cream cheese and yogurt.

---

11 For more information on orally transmitted face-to-face education in traditional East African communities see chapter *2.1 Kenyan Primary Education System*.

I take good care of the livestock because I get the daily bread from the livestock.
Jakob Lon'gada, elder

Over the generations, the Daasanach carefully select and breed their animal races to be resilient, tenacious and adapted to the harsh climate. Hereby the pastoralist children learn to seek four basic characteristics in their livestock: milk productivity (the animal should be a high milk producer), size and coat colour; loyalty to their owners and hostile towards strangers and walking endurance (the ability to walk long distances). Pastoralist children come to understand that good management of the livestock and the production team is a crucial factor in productivity and livelihood. Seasonal migration, searching for water and grazing, moving to a healthier environment and protecting livestock from raiders are essential requirements for good animal husbandry.

My father told and showed me how to get animals and how to take care of them.
Nyingole Felix Anini, young man

Children learn from their parents which grass types contain the most nutrients and which plants heal. It is also necessary for the Daasanach to have basic knowledge about all major stock diseases as this influences the daily decision concerning grazing locations that should be utilized and how to recognise and isolate diseased animals (Carr 1977). The fact that the Daasanach pastoralists possess a rich, mostly unwritten, veterinary vocabulary shows their indigenous knowledge. This covers a wide range of diseases, causes and miscellaneous ailments affecting a wide range of multi-species and single species livestock.[12] *Gál gil ógká* (lit. people who know how to use their hands; gifted women) pass their indigenous knowledge on human medicine to one of their female children whom they consider to also be gifted. Their knowledge covers identification of various diseases and which plants can prevent, alleviate or cure illnesses. The mother shares her versatile knowledge with her daughter so that she will become the next *gál gil ógká*.

Written Language. *Af 'Daasanach*, (lit. mouth of the Daasanach) is an East Cushitic language of the Omo-Tana branch (Sasse 1975) and thus shares lexical and morphological language material with Arbore, Elmolo, Bayso, Rendille and Somali.[13] Until the 1970s, the Daasanach were unknown from an ethnographic point of view and linguistically, as late as, 1990s.[14] Jim and Susan Ness of Bible Translation and Literacy (E.A.) and Wycliffe Bible Translators have devised a practical orthography for the Daasanach and published three primers mainly for adult literacy courses, which explains why there are quite a number of Daasanach who have never been to school, yet know how to read and write in Daasanach.[15]

---

12 Dinucci & Fre (2003) studied the indigenous knowledge of pastoralists in Eritrea and showed that their veterinary vocabulary is extremely rich includes internal parasites (worms, ect.), ecto-parasites (ticks and fleas), contagious diseases, ailments caused by accidents, diseases caused by malnutrition and exhaustion, environmental ailments and so on. Also the Daasanach' language shows a complex vernacular terminology for the listed areas, the stock animals and the major stock diseases (Carr 1977).

13 The genetic affiliation of the Omo-Tana branch genealogically derives from Afroasiatic, Cushitic, East Cushitic languages. The Omo-Tana are divided into three branches, Western (Daasanach, Arbore and Elmolo), Central/Northern (Bayso) and Eastern (Rendille and Somali). The membership of the Daasanach within the Omo-Tana is well established since there is notable morphological correspondence to Somali and shared lexical material between Daasanach, Arbore and Elmolo (Tosco 2001)

14 Uri Almagor published a major anthropological description of Daasanach life and social organisation in 1978.

15 Jim and Susan Ness published a trial edition of the Gospel of Mark in Daasanach in the orthography in 1997 using Latin script. Komoi & Kwanyang' have published a transition primer for Bible Translation and Literacy (E.A.) under the title *Af 'Daasanach Veeritle Kí Onot* (lit. Let's learn to write Daasanach). Jim & Susan Ness

The Daasanach language operates with 26 consonantal phonemes and five vowels, which may be short or long, plus two diphthongs which are shown in figure 1.16.

orthography	IPA	orthography	IPA	orthography	IPA	orthography	IPA
/'/ (word – finally only)	ʔ	/dh /	ð	/'j/	ʃ	/s/	s
		/e/	ɛ	/k/	k	/sh/	ʃ
/a/	a	/ee)	ɛ:	/l/	l	/t/	t
/aa/	a:	/f/	f	/m/	m	/u/	ʊ
/b/	b	/g/	g	/n/	n	/uu/	u:
/'b/	ɓ	/'g/	ɠ	/ng'/	ŋ	/v/	v
/ch/	c	/h/	h	/ny/	ɲ	/w/	w
/d/	d	/i/	ɪ	/o/	ɔ	/y/	j
/'d/	ɗ	/ii/	i:	/oo/	ɔ:	/ie/	iɛ
/d/ (between vowels)	d	/j/	ɟ	/r/	r	/uo/	uɔ

Fig. 1.16: Orthography of the Daasanach language compiled by BTL/Wycliffe (Source: own illustration).

---

have also prepared A Preliminary Language Learning Lesson Series for The 'Daasanach Language (Lokono & Kwanyang' 2013a, 2013b). These primers were used in literacy courses for adults. In 2014 Bible Translation and Literacy (E.A.) published the complete New Testament and an illustrated children's Bible.

A school building is not good. Maybe tomorrow the grass is good somewhere else and we have to migrate.

Joshua Esho, first Daasanach mobile school teacher

2. Why Is Education Provision for Daasanach Pastoralists Difficult?

Education provision for mobile pastoralists is a highly complex, controversial and emotive issue (Krätli 2000).[16] Much of the lifestyle of mobile pastoralists and the formal education programmes appear incompatible. Many attempts have been made to establish education services to meet the learning needs of children from mobile pastoralists' communities but they have, overall, failed (Carr-Hill & Peart 2005). With the *World Declaration on Education for All* (*WDEFA*) from 1990 and the *Millennium Development Goals* (*MDG*) to provide access to basic education to all children by 2015, it is frightening that millions of children worldwide still do not have adequate access to schooling. Children of mobile pastoralists are among the most disadvantaged worldwide (Little, Hoppers & Garder 1994; Dyer 2006). After the deadline of 2015, the *Global Agenda* (2030) with its 17 *Sustainable Development Goals* (*SDG*) replaced the *Millennium Development Goals*. While the *MDG* focused primarily on poverty reduction in the most affected countries, the *SDG* focus on broad sustainable development around the world, taking into account economic, social and environmental dimensions.[17]

Despite the great efforts of the Kenyan government to provide full primary education at no cost, 80% of children in the arid regions of Northern Kenya, where most of the mobile pastoralists' communities reside, still lack basic education (Kibera, Gakunga & Imonje 2013). According to David Siele, former director of education from the Ministry of State for Development of Northern Kenya and Other Arid Lands (MDNKOAL), educational participation and achievement are much lower in pastoral areas of Kenya than the national average, as in many countries in Africa. The remote location of the Daasanach pastoralists and their mobile lifestyle pose great challenges for the conventional Kenyan school system with its fixed school buildings.[18] According to the *World Initiative for Sustainable Pastoralism*, one of the ten most widespread misconceptions about pastoralism is that they should settle to benefit from services like schooling (Dyer 2016).

---

16 Saverio Krätli has worked as an international consultant focussing on pastoralism, engaging with the whole spectrum of pastoral development agencies, from grassroots pastoral associations and local NGOs to governmental and international organisations and research institutes. In 2000, he published a worldwide review of the literature on education provision to nomadic pastoralists. In 2009, Krätli and Dyer published a book which describes the conceptual difficulty of pastoral education and gives insights to international innovative approaches (Mobile Pastoralism & Education: Strategic Options). In 2010, the Kenyan Ministry of State for Development of Northern Kenya and Other Arid Lands held a workshop in Nakuru, Kenya on Nomadic Education, where Dyer and Krätli were key consultants on policy guidelines and strategies for improving education among nomadic communities in Kenya.

17 The *Sustainable Development Goals* (*SDG*) are much more ambitious than the *MDG*. For example, *SDG* 4 states to ensure inclusive and equitable quality education and to promote life-long learning opportunities for all. *SDG* 4 states to build and upgrade education facilities that are child, disability and gender sensitive and to provide safe, non-violent, inclusive and effective learning environments for all. By 2020, the number of scholarships for developing countries, in particular, *Least Developed Countries* (*LDC*), *Small Island Developing States* (*SIDS*) and African countries should be expanded. Moreover, the supply of qualified teachers should be increased, including through international cooperation for teacher training in *developing countries*, especially in *LDC* and *SIDS* by 2030 (BMZ 2015).

18 The incompatibility between mobile lifestyle and sedentary schooling is not only an issue for education providers of pastoralists. 52% of the 68.5 million refugees (UN General Assembly, *Universal Declaration of Human Rights*) who are on the move or live in camps are younger than 18 years and there are still no educational offers which fit pupils on the move.

The following chapter sets out to analyse the conceptual difficulty between education users and the current education providers concerning the Daasanach pastoralists. The colonial history of Kenya explains the design of the formal primary school system and why there is still an ambiguity between the concepts of schooling and learning. This excurse into Kenyan history helps to address the conceptual difficulty between education users and providers from two perspectives: the constraints of the conventional school system and the conditions of mobile pastoralism itself.

2.1 Kenyan Primary Education System

Pre-Colonial Education in Kenya. Strictly speaking, there was no national country Kenya until the 20th century. First borders were not set until the Berlin Conference, also known as the Congo Conference (1884 – 1885) which was organised by Otto von Bismarck. This conference regulated European colonization and trade in Africa during the New Imperialism period. The African continent was divided to avoid the Europeans warring amongst themselves over territory. Strictly speaking, the pre-colonial country of Kenya is the area and region which later was determined as being Kenya.[19]

Like many African countries, Kenya is characterized by a triple heritage: traditional African, Arabic and Western European. This is also reflected in the way education has been introduced into the country (Närman 1995). Education was not a social service brought into Kenya by the colonial European power, there is a rather long history of oral face-to-face education. For thousands of years, education has been a community responsibility and also the *teachers* were part of the community: Fathers taught the young generation farming, fishery, craft and pastoral production, while mothers imparted knowledge about domestic tasks and arts. Elders and priests traditionally passed on the oral religious traditions of the group and were therefore closely related to the community and the environment (Anderson 1970). No formal organisation was needed but, despite its apparent informality, traditional face-to-face education had its clear goals: Education is for every child and exists to strengthen the community. This traditional idea of inclusive education has no drop-outs because it is not based on selection (Farrant 1980).

Although Christianity has a long history in Africa, it is Islam that holds the distinction for having established the oldest surviving system of formal education. Pioneer Muslim traders arrived on the Swahili Coast of East Africa around the 8th century as part of their annual trade migration around the Indian Ocean.[20] In East Africa, mosques hold the oldest surviving system of Islamic formal education, since they are not only established for the community's worshipping but also as a place for literacy, numeracy and social organisation (Eisemon 1988).

---

19 In 1870, only 10% of Africa was under European control. By 1914, it had increased to 90% of the continent. When borders were set, some areas were divided and the local communities were officially recognised as transboundary groups. The Daasanach were defined as Ethiopians at first but later on tolerated in the British territory of Kenya. For more information see chapter *1.1 Homeland Area*.

20 Many of these first pioneer Muslim traders set up trading posts along the seaboard, intermarrying with Africans and creating the culture that later became known as Swahili. The language Kiswahili is structurally a Bantu language with heavy borrowings from Arabic.

Colonial Education in Kenya. Christian formal education in Kenya started at the beginning of the 19th century with the arrival of the first missionaries.[21] In the beginning, missionary schools in Kenya tended to be concentrated around major mission stations along the coast and the lakes (Cowan 1970).[22] The educational development expanded at the beginning of the 20th century, as the more central parts, the highlands of Kenya, were also cultivated by British farmers and came under the influence of Christian missions. In that time, the colonial government did not actively participate in education but contributed to the work of the missions by granting land for the establishment of mission stations (Meck 1971). Formal education was almost exclusively in the hands of missions (Cowan 1970). In 1911, the colonial government created an Education Department to oversee the activities of missionary societies. This establishment was the first step towards a direct government involvement in Kenyan education. The Education Department promoted the development of education through financial help for mission schools and the successive foundation of governmental schools (Eisemon 1988). Following, the British school system, three school types were installed: elementary education, primary and secondary education.[23] The colonists were particularly interested in the possibility for training better skilled labour forces, as well as, installing the European interpretation of law and order among the native populations. All in all, during the colonial period, education was an exclusive right offered only to a minority of children (Närman 1995).

Post-Colonial Education in Kenya. In 1963, after gaining independence, a 7-4-2-3 system, modelled after the British education system, was established with about 6,000 primary schools (Närman 1995). This system was designed to provide seven years of primary education, four years of lower secondary education, two years of upper secondary education and three years of university studies. Education was promoted actively since the country was in immediate need for skilled workers to hold positions previously held by the British. In 1985, the system changed into an 8-4-4 system, similar to the U.S. education system. This was designed to provide eight years of primary, four years of secondary and four years of university education. Emphasis was placed on Mathematics, English and vocational subjects. Vocational education was aimed at preparing students who would not continue with secondary education (Närman 1995). In 2002, the curriculum was reviewed and the number of subjects was reduced to English, Kiswahili, Mother Tongue, Physical Education, Creative Arts, Mathematics, Science, Christian Religious Education, Hindu Religious Education and Islamic Religious Education. However, the 8-4-4-system has been widely criticised for being heavily loaded in terms of content and for being too exam-oriented, putting undue pressure on pupils and students.

In line with the attainment of universal primary education and *Education for All*, Kenya's government made education a constitutional right in 2003 (Articles 43 and 53 of the Constitution of Kenya). As a consequence, fees in primary schools were abolished, further

---

21 In 1920, the East African Protectorate became crown colony of Kenya and thus was administrated by a British governor. From 1920-1963 the colony and protectorate of Kenya was a part of the British Empire in Africa.

22 The first Christian missionary school was established in coastal Rabai in 1846 by two Germans Krapf and Rebman (Närman 1995). However, the Germany expansion took mainly place in the neighbouring country Tanzania.

23 Until 1940, elementary education, comprising the first five years of school life, was almost exclusively in the hands of missions. In 1940, the Education Department began to open its own schools (Meck 1971). At the same time, first independent schools started, which were entirely financed by voluntary contributions from the population and managed by local committees selected by the community (Cowan 1970). Early secondary education for African pupils was exclusively provided by Christian missions (Meck 1971).

day and boarding schools were built, school feeding programmes initiated and secondary schools introduced bursary funds for bright but poor learners. As a result, nearly three million more children were enrolled in a primary school in 2012 than in 2003 and the number of schools grew by 7,000 during that period (Clark 2015).

In 2017, a curriculum reform took place and Kenya's new 2-6-6-3 education curriculum framework was tested in 470 selected primary and pre-primary schools countrywide. According to education cabinet secretary Amina Mohammed, the full implementation was scheduled for January 2020. The new system involves two years of pre-primary education for children aged between 4 and 5 years before proceeding to primary school for six years. Primary schools have lower and upper tiers with each covering three grades. From primary school, learners move on to junior secondary school for three years and then another three years of senior secondary school depending on their competencies and natural talents. In senior secondary school level, students are divided amongst three tracks (Creative Arts and Sports; Social Science; STEM (=Science, Technology, Engineering and Mathematics)). Finally, students can proceed to three years of university or other tertiary education.

In regard to quantity, Kenyan education after independence can be described as a success story. However, the *Education for All Global Monitoring Report* by UNESCO of 2012 also states that over a million Kenyan children are not in school, especially girls: One in two girls in rural areas is not in school. According to the report, Kenya is ranked as the 9th country in the world with the highest number of school drop-outs. Despite the efforts to promote pastoral education by the government and educational stakeholders, over 80% of children of school-going age in nomadic pastoralists' areas still do not have access to free primary education.[24] School enrolment remains low, there are high drop-outs and imbalanced teacher-pupil ratios (Kibera, Gakunga & Imonje 2013). The conventional school system does not fit to the Daasanach pastoralist way of life for reasons which are addressed below.

2.2 Ambiguity about Schooling and Education

There is a frequent ambiguity about what is meant by schooling and education. In Kenya, there is a tendency to use the term education when what is really meant is schooling. Education and schooling are used as if these terms were interchangeable when they are not. Education refers to an act or process of acquiring knowledge, whereas schooling more narrowly defines the process of teaching or being taught in a school. Education, therefore, includes what is learned at home by face-to-face education or by apprenticeship. Mobile pastoralism, for example, is a form of apprenticeship, *learning on the job*, which in this case is only possible within the family. Daasanach pastoralist children grow up learning pastoral production and life from their parents, their grandparents, the elders, the community and their age group.

My grandfather taught me how to look after animals and how to live in a family. He taught me the family rules.
Paul Lokono, young man

---

[24] In 2010, a policy framework for nomadic education was launched and a National Commission on Nomadic Education in Kenya (NACONEK) was established.

Even though child labour is merely described in negative terms in the mainstream literature, mobile pastoralist children and their parents often perceive children's work commitment as a process of crucial educational value, which is not available in the conventional education system:

> Children's work is perceived as a process of socialisation, progressively initiating children into work and transmitting skills that will enable them to support themselves and their parents and contribute to the community. [...] The most important thing one can do for a child is to teach him or her to work. Death can overcome the parents at any time; that's why it is essential to train children young to the work of the parents. (Molteno, Ogadhoh, Cain & Crumpton 2000: 92).

The narrowing of the broader notion of education to mean schooling explains why governmental boards and other educational stakeholders often assume it is sufficient to construct school buildings and to employ teachers to provide education for the Daasanach pastoralists. If they, in turn, do not use this form of education provision, it is often explained as *nomadic ignorance*.

Interestingly enough, the Universal Declaration of Human Rights defines elementary education to be compulsory but makes no mention of schools or schooling. Rather, parents are granted the prior right to choose the kind of education that shall be given to their children. The *World Declaration on Education for All* also reinforces article 26 of the UN General Assembly, proposing a holistic, broadly conceived vision of education and stressing the need to broaden the means and scope of basic education (UN General Assembly, art. 26). While formal schooling is seen as the main delivery system of universal primary education, the *WDEFA* explicitly states that "supplementary alternative programmes can help meet the basic learning needs of children with limited or no access to formal schooling, provided that they share the same standards of learning applied to schools, and are adequately supported" (World Declaration Education for All 1990: 6).

2.3 Standardised Curriculum

If a curriculum is what Lawton describes as a selection from the culture of society and if culture is a way of life of a group of people, including its body of accumulated knowledge and understanding, then it is questionable whose culture is selected for curricula content in Kenya (Lawton 1975; Thaman 1993). Cultural pluralism makes the definition of indigenous Kenyan culture very fluid and elusive. However, it is important to acknowledge that the Daasanach, like any other indigenous people, have what Dei portrays as "underlining commonalities and affinities in their thought systems" (Dei 1994: 6). These were historically repressed through colonial education and with the current national curriculum still are (Shizah 2005). Of course, it can be argued that for every child around the globe there are parts of the assigned school curriculum which are irrelevant or even controversial to traditional knowledge. However, for indigenous children, Western concepts of knowledge and science are perceived as especially irrelevant and promote the marginalization of non-Western knowledge systems (Shizha 2005). As with all curricula in post-colonial Africa, the Kenyan curriculum was constructed mainly by the British colonial power and shaped by white, middle-class mainstream school knowledge. As mentioned above, the first schools were established by British Christian missionaries in the highlands of Southern and Central

Kenya where the majority of pupils came and still come from households of farmers and labourers. To date, the Kenyan school textbooks emphasise communities and lifestyles in towns and green highlands with sedentary agriculturalists, livestock farmers and labourers. Textbook protagonists live in permanently built houses, drive bicycles, buses or cars, enjoy a certain diet, go to stone-built schools, play specific games and prefer a *Western* style of clothing. Also, the (targeted) omission of pastoral images and cultural knowledge in Kenyan text- and workbooks not only degrades pastoral lifestyles but also supports the widespread tenor that mobile pastoralism is environmentally destructive, economically irrational, culturally backwards and an archaic form whose time has passed (Dyer 2016).

2.4 Language Barrier

The language barrier is a tremendous problem in the Kenyan education system. Most children, especially in rural areas, are raised in their mother tongue associated with their ethnic group. In school, however, English is the classroom language taught from class one and Kiswahili is the national language.[25] This trilingual system causes several challenges.

Firstly, when literacy acquisition is taught in a foreign language, children cannot build on their own mental concepts. Just as with language acquisition, children become best acquainted with letters and sounds when they can try these out. When for instance letters are introduced with unfamiliar initial sound pictures such as *apples* and *bananas* for the graphemes *a* and *b*, Daasanach children need to put much more effort developing a mental concept and memorising than children with English as their mother tongue. It is not only unlikely that these pastoralist children ever come across apples and bananas, but also the articulation of the graphemes *a* and *b* is different in English and Daasanach.[26]

Learning motivation becomes a problem when literacy acquisition takes place in a foreign language because the children do not become aware of the fact that writing and language are mutually translatable. They do not experience the communicative function of reading and writing and the social relevance of these skills (Brügelmann & Brinkmann 1994). Even though the Kenyan curriculum urges teachers to use the pupils' vernacular, it is very unlikely that the government teachers in rural and marginalized communities, such as the Daasanach, speak the local language.

Secondly, all educational resources and textbooks (except for the subject Kiswahili) are written only in English, which demands challenging and time-consuming code switching for both teachers and learners.

To date, schoolbooks do not include texts in vernacular languages and technical terms are mainly in English, which demands pupils to learn definitions and explanations in Science or Mathematics by heart, often without a conceptual understanding of the term. Moreover, the fact that many English concepts are not transportable into a traditional vernacular, such as Daasanach, poses learning motivational difficulties.

---

25 There are over 42 such language groups with different indigenous languages and dialects in Kenya (http://worldpopulationreview.com/countries/kenya-population/).

26 The INES development team has published an initial sound chart based on the Daaasanach language. The grapheme *a* is symbolized by *aadho* (lit. sun) and the grapheme *b* is represented by *bóte* (lit. melon, pumpkin). For more information see chapter *10. How Do the Learners Acquire Literacy?*.

This leads to the third great challenge: In Kenya, the national examinations of all subjects are in English. This means pupils are not only tested in the subject matter but also in their English skills. Since the performance in the exams solely decides whether a child moves on to the next grade and exams are written in English, only those can proceed who bring along language skills and are good at learning by heart. There is no clear alternative for pupils with language problems.

2.5 Fixed Schools for Mobile Communities

In 2014, the Benedictine Fathers of Illeret carried out a field study with the parents of 884 Daasanach children in 13 semi-permanent settlements to assess how many children were enrolled in one of the two government primary schools in Illeret and Silicho or one of the four non-formal nursery schools in El-Bochoch, Illolo, Nang'oleiy and Aiy'beete. The results showed that only 22% of the children, who temporarily happened to live in one of the semi-permanent settlements during the field study, were enrolled in one of the two primary schools or non-formal nursery schools. 78% of the children did not go to school but the reasons why they were not enrolled were not further analysed then.

On the one hand, there are frequent voices who argue that the mobile pastoralists of the Daasanach cling to pastoral production with its typical features of mobility and children's work commitment and therefore shun schooling altogether. On the other hand, there are pastoralist parents who want their children to be educated, yet stress the failure of the current education system in terms of relevance, the location of schools and delivery methods.

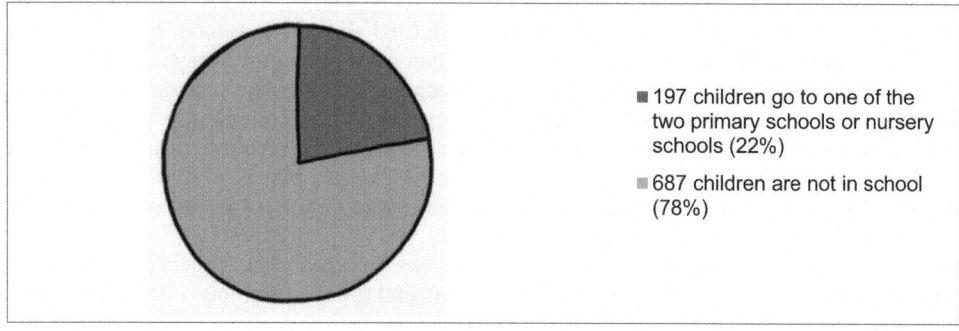

Fig. 2.1: Enrolment of Daasanach pastoralist children in 13 semi-permanent settlements (Source: own illustration).

Schröder (2012) points out that permanent sedentarisation is one of the fundamental preconditions for a school system to administrate pupils. So, for those pupils whose lives are marked by permanent mobility, it is central that the educational providers have to search for new administration forms. Mobility is the key to the production strategy of mobile pastoralists but it poses a serious challenge to a system heavily reliant on school-based education in permanent settlements (Milimo 2004).

Standardised curriculum delivery services are usually designed for the majority of the population. Across the globe, the majority of people lives in sedentary communities even though 80% of Kenya's landmass is homeland to mobile communities. Thus, the widespread notion of schooling in permanent settlements is through classroom education. Due to the limitations imposed by the conventional sedentary school-based system in Kenya, only few Daasanach families send their children to school, as mentioned at the beginning of this chapter. Krätli and Dyer (2009) present typical consequences for pastoralists whose direct business is animal production in dryland conditions, who want their children to be educated but are using a conventional school-based education service:

A first consequence could be that the household – the production team – has to be split in a way that is functional to school attendance but not to the running of a family enterprise. Children's commitment to work has long been and still is very closely related to the livelihood of the whole community. Since nomadic pastoralism is a form of *learning on the job*, which is tailor-made to their needs and not available anywhere else, children's involvement and responsibilities within the household's economy from an early age. This, however, competes with the requirements of school calendars and timetables of formal schools. Daasanach boys take turns herding small livestock such as goats and sheep during the day and the traditional chores for girls are fetching water and collecting firewood during the morning hours and taking care of siblings during the day.[27]

The Kenyan school year is divided into three terms, beginning in January and ending at the end of October with national exams. Each term has around 14 weeks with a two-week break in April and in August and a two-month break in November and December. Primary school timetables request the children to attend school from 8 am to 4 pm with tea and lunch breaks in between. This causes incompatibility between education providers and mobile pastoralists. The parents have to decide who is sent to school and who stays at home to help with animal husbandry and with household chores.

The parents decide whom to take to school. Maybe two children go to school and two assist at home.
Joshua Esho, elder

Those kept within the pastoral system tend to be firstborn children (to perform rituals and take over the father's tasks) and those with the greatest affinity for looking after animals. If a Daasanach family man has large herds he can afford several wives – one wife living in a permanent settlement to accommodate the schoolchildren and other mobile wives with the children assisting at home. In order to send a child to school, the pastoral household must renounce the labour power of this individual child with all the economic consequences that this involves.

A common feature, therefore, is that children are enrolled for a short period, while the family is staying near a school and then drop out again. A second possible consequence of sending children to a conventional school is having to modify herd management and livestock mobility patterns in ways that impact their productivity and ultimately the reliability of the production system as a whole.

Right now, I am not looking for animals because of school.
Helekua Nyabatang', boy

The families who want to send all their children to a conventional school regularly have to settle near Illeret or Silicho, which automatically means having to employ herders, who shift

---

27 For more information on gender roles and tasks see also chapter *1.3 Social Organisation*.

between the pasture grounds, or to downsize the herd drastically to have sufficient fodder near the settlement. Both cases imply a serious financial risk for the whole family especially if the family has no other means of income.

2.6 Lack of Infrastructure

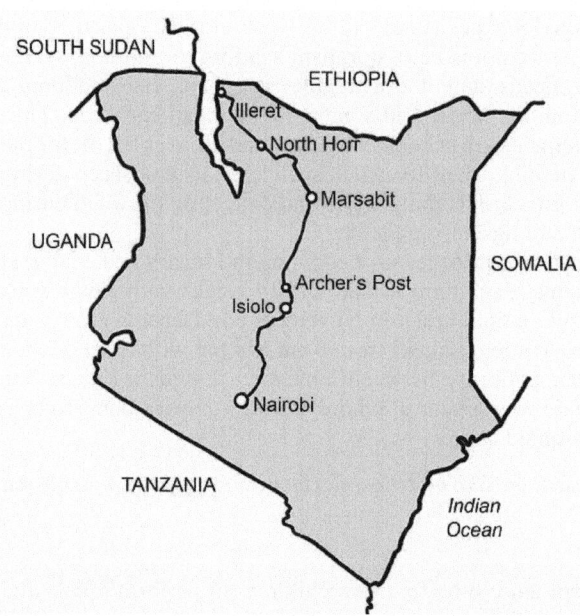

Fig. 2.2: Four-days-travel from Nairobi to Illeret (Source: own illustration).

Generally, it is argued that the harsh environmental conditions in Northern Kenya, as well as, the scattered population and economic poverty of the Daasanach, besides funding problems, malnutrition, lack of infrastructure and insecurity in Marsabit County, are the main reasons that impede the efforts of education development. For sure, the harsh conditions in Northern Kenya negatively affect education provision of conventional school designs. Often being an advantage for pastoral production, scattered populations in rural areas cause a problem for realising economies of scale in school-based education. Building and maintaining schools in isolated, harsh and remote rural areas is costly (Krätli & Dyer 2009) especially when there is hardly or no tax income and barely any infrastructure as in the case of the Daasanach in Northern Kenya. Illeret, the largest permanent settlement of the Daasanach in Kenya, is located 18 kilometres south of the Ethiopian border and at 250 kilometres distance from North Horr, where the nearest secondary school is located. Illeret itself has a primary school, a small health centre and a police station. Some small shops have developed in the course of the last years since humanitarian agencies have brought money into circulation. To reach Illeret via car from Kenya's capital Nairobi, it takes a three to four days journey passing Isiolo, Marsabit and North Horr. From North Horr, Illeret can only be reached with great difficulty after a six to eight hours journey, since the roads are in a bad condition or partially non-existent.

As with school funding, staffing and training of teachers is difficult in harsh and remote rural areas. Well-trained teachers refuse to live in highly remote areas, often go somewhere else or leave at the first opportunity because the teachers often do not come from a pastoral background (Krätli & Dyer 2009). Their cultural identity, language and living standards differ highly from those of pastoralist children. For these reasons, staffing is difficult and teacher training costly. The relatively small amount of schools in remote areas further increases the probability of imbalanced pupil-teacher ratio, which, in return, impedes the low standard of education: The few schools are overcrowded. The rigid school routine in conventional schools is interrupted when teachers are not present – a common phenomenon in Northern Kenya. Since Kenyan government teachers usually come from non-pastoralist backgrounds and economically, as well as, ecologically more stable areas of the country than their pastoral pupils, they do not live off pastoralist's diet and fear to move to areas of severe drought and low food-security. Thus, after holidays it sometimes takes an unreasonably long time until teachers find their way back into the remote areas, such as Illeret, where they have been sent for teaching.

The Kenyan government entitles only registered schools with trained teachers to the school feeding programme and the distribution of meals is bound to the presence of a head teacher. Evidence shows that schools are usually successful in increasing school attendance when food is supplied but success vanishes as soon as the meal provision is interrupted. Daasanach children who attend one of the two primary schools in Illeret or Silicho or the nurseries in Nang'oleiy, Aiybeete or Illolo are reliant on school meals because they are not out in the fields herding the flocks or near the home where they receive water, milk and food. So, when ecological conditions and animal needs force the parents to leave the area near the nursery or primary schools, children usually abandon the school in order to survive with what the family's livestock provides them with. The school routine is thus continuously interrupted due to the absence of pupils and the school boards deplore the high rates of pupil drop-outs or even complete abundance of school buildings.

The sparsely populated area of Northern Kenya inevitably also leads to security problems. As with many pastoralist groups, the Daasanach have a tense relationship with their neighbours – the Gabra. To reach Marsabit, the county's main town, Daasanach have to cross hostile Gabra terrain. Territorial conflicts and cattle raiding maintains a tense and largely unresolved relationship between the Daasanach and the Gabra. Travelling is considered a risk and the border zone remains a conflict-prone region. Having to walk long distances to attend a school in Gabra homeland presents serious risks especially for girls who also have to fear sexual harassment. Since the police station in Illeret and Darate are mal-equipped and far off, officers are often not able to follow-up incidences among the scattered population and the rivalling communities. Therefore, Daasanach children are hardly sent to schools in North Horr.

2.7 Alienation from Traditional Cultural Identity

The expansion of boarding schools in mobile pastoralist areas is a popular means of enhancing school enrolment and attendance. Evidence shows, however, that boarding schools in pastoralist areas mainly enrol students from non-pastoralist backgrounds (Krätli 2000; Kibera, Wangu, Gakunga & Imonje 2013). There are also research findings that boarding schools in several countries in Africa constitute rather unfriendly learning and living environment for boarding students from a pastoralist background. A Maasai-Kenyan scholar explaining the failure of the Kenyan education policy with day and boarding schools underlines "the practical irrelevance of an imported Western model of schooling and its basic incompatibility with prevailing social and cultural values and practices" (Carr-Hill & Peart

2005: 107). The prevailing school culture is often anti-pastoralist despite the pastoral surrounding. Poor educational attainment and behavioural problems in boarding schools are said to arrive from the overall poor living standards, cultural and linguistic barriers to other students and teachers, who are rarely from pastoral backgrounds and the seldom visits home (Krätli 2000). Pastoralist parents dislike the idea of giving custody of their sons and daughters to people they do not know, to whom they are not related, whose moral integrity they cannot be sure of and who live far off. Parents are particularly reluctant to sending girls away from the familiar contexts where they can be protected and controlled. In many pastoral communities, girls are considered to be bearers of the family honour, the traditional values and the cultural continuity. Parents therefore ardently protect their daughters against any risk of pregnancy and therefore find it often impossible to send their daughters to a day or boarding school, if that involves distant travel or loss of sight of the girls for long hours (Krätli 2000).

I don't like early pregnancy with girls. That is why Daasanach don't want girls to go to school.
Artukatch Nylim, elder

Girls also drop out more often than boys or are never sent to school for reasons of cultural alienation.[28] In part, the low education participation of girls is because females are particularly associated with cultural continuity. As with many pastoralist communities, Daasanach girls move to a different household with marriage and paying (often very high fees) for their higher education is not considered a good investment, as the girl will leave her family and will not be in charge of her parents' retirement. Often school experience is seen as providing the opposite of education:

"Children not only fail to learn how to secure a livelihood but lose what they were taught in early life and absorb alien and negative values and lifestyles. At school they are 'softened', humiliated, trained into dependency, laziness, irresponsibility, lack of discipline and self-esteem" (Krätli 2000: 28).

A study on education provision for pastoralists carried out by UNICEF Somalia points out that pastoralists in Somalia view both schools and schooling as "alien things that do not contribute to the pastoral way of life" and they believe that "such facilities will alienate their children from them and the society at large" (Jama, quoted in Krätli, 2000: 28).

Also, the economic benefits of schooling are not easily evident for the nomadic pastoralists. As stated above, formally educated Daasanach children hardly have any possibilities to work as labourers without having to leave the community altogether. To make matters worse, when children do not succeed through schooling they often become equally hard to employ in the livestock economy because they are not fully equipped with the necessary skills (Krätli & Dyer 2009). Most Daasanach boys with secondary education do not find work in Northern Kenya and also do not return to traditional pastoral production for reasons of lack of skills and motivation. Formal education is therefore often seen as training children into dependency or leaving the community. In regard to the lack of economic prosperity for formally educated children, with the view to the increasingly high costs of schooling and the context of general pastoral impoverishment, it becomes clear that many Daasanach pastoralists do not see any economic benefits of formal education.

---

28 The pastoral office of Marsabit diocese published a booklet on abuses of girls by cultural practices in pastoralist areas of Kenya in 2012. These include not to inherit property, unconsented and early marriage and female genital mutilation which are also reasons why girls are rather kept at home.

On the contrary, even within a responsive approach, school education is seen as something ultimately meant to equip children to leave their pastoral community and their homeland area for good. So, the decision to keep a child out of school is usually taken with the best interest of the whole household in mind (including the individual child), even if formal education as such is desired. Even though some Daasanach feel that formal schooling weakens the power and authority of traditional systems and there are objections that formal education does not value their culture and traditional way of life. They are not hostile to education altogether. On the contrary, many recognise the potential of formal education and state that it will better their lives.

2.8 Lessons Learned

The conceptual difficulty of pastoral education has shown that education users and providers have to recognise that traditional approaches to force children in or out of school cannot be the solution. Daasanach children have a right to receive formal education but to assure a livelihood through pastoralism they have to stay within the production team. Only through the compatibility of schooling and pastoral production can children assume their right to education and support with the livelihood of the whole community. This way, their working power is not deducted and also the indigenous technical knowledge about livestock management is carried on. According to pastoralist experts like Krätli and Dyer, there is no other group that spares the environment as much as mobile pastoralists. In times of recurring and severe droughts in the arid and semi-arid lands, they easily change their grazing routes and thus better cope with lack of rain than sedentary farmers – whereby farming is feasible in many arid areas anyway. Their animals provide approximately 50,000 people of the Daasanach with meat, milk, horn, skin and coat and the mobile pastoralists maintain an ecological balance in their homeland area. They use camels and donkeys as migratory and load animals and the trade with goats, sheep and cows provides the herders with cash to purchase foodstuffs, garments, mobile phones, rain shelters etc.

For this reason, education provision for pastoralists implies for education providers to review schooling and curriculum contents, as well as, to develop flexible learning systems which allow children to remain in their pastoral household while also dedicating themselves to learning. At the same time, education users have to organise the daily work commitment of pastoralist children and even shifting habits of the whole household in a way that allows boys and girls to find time for learning.

Personal Notes of the Authors

We feel that many Kenyans think that the common and easier way to increase educational participation among mobile pastoralists is to take the children out of their families and to accommodate and educate them in boarding schools. In Illeret, we repeatedly observe this method of (foreign) benefactors who finance the boarding school education of one or more Daasanach children. Their motives might be noble: helping deprived children to a better future. However, the biographies of these sponsored children show that they will either never return to their homeland area or will face challenges of being integrated into their traditional society. The mobile lifestyle and animal husbandry has become alien and unattractive to them. These supposed *development attempts* are based on the idea that mobile pastoralism is anachronistic and not promising.

At this point, we ask the reader to allow us to doubt this view and to critically question the method of taking children out of their communities. We believe it is a fatal misjudgement to describe the mobile form of animal husbandry as anachronistic or hindering for the development of Kenya (and other countries). We observe how Daasanach pastoralists live a highly flexible and sustainable life even without relief aids. We hope that mobile schools will fulfil the wish of the Daasanach pastoralists that families can stay together and children receive a traditional and formal education.

The national education system is not designed for mobile pastoralists.

Father Florian OSB, founder of INES

3. What Are International Approaches to Mobile Education?

There are limited examples of so-called alternative basic education for mobile pastoralists, which have performed some degree of success. The Quranic schools in Somalia, for example, are implemented into the existing cultural environment and thus respond flexibly to changes in society. The tent schools in Iran succeeded because they supported the existing pastoral ideology whereas the radio schools in Mongolia were matched with pastoral development policies in decreasing labour intensity and freeing children from the household's labour demand. More recently in East Africa, cooperations were started between the national governments, UNICEF and the local pastoralist communities. Several attempts have been made to train young men and women from pastoralist communities in Sudan, Uganda, Ethiopia, Somaliland and Kenya to offer lessons in their pastoralist communities with mobile or tent schools, whereby the degree of school mobility varies.[29]

These initiatives mainly have a non-permanent structure as school area (shade of a tree; tents or huts, which can be assembled or dismantled) and a local school graduate who receives basic teacher training (or not) offers traditional teacher-centred learning with a poor endowment of learning materials. A closer look at the early approaches in Mongolia, Iran, Somalia and Kenya, which are analysed and portrayed in the following chapter, as well as, the situational framework conditions in Kenya give valuable impulses for a mobile school system for the Daasanach pastoralists.

3.1 Tent Schools in Iran

A local young man with a law degree introduced tent schools in Iran together with the financial support of the United States. Krätli and Dyer (2009) see the programme as a radical change to previous attempts of the Persian government to permanently settle pastoralist communities since it was genuinely committed to developing mobile education. Along with hundreds of schools, which were built in the settlements, 600 tent schools were introduced to provide education for mobile households. With these, the equipment was kept at the minimum with one blackboard, one case of equipment for science and nature studies and the teacher's and pupil's books.

The standard national curriculum was adopted but corporal punishment and regimentation – a frequent occurrence – were abolished. Teaching was in Persian, a foreign language for many pupils, nonetheless children could read and write within a few months and appeared exceptionally outspoken and willing to participate in lessons in comparison to their city cousins. Well qualified city teachers were a failure in the beginning, so a training centre for unskilled local teachers was opened in 1957. At its peak, the programme reached 10% of the school-age children.

Today, the state authorities provide boarding schools for the pastoralist communities in Iran. According to Dyer (2016), there is mutual engagement and negotiation over acceptable terms of including mobile pastoralists into formal education. However, there is resistance to

---

29 There are attempts of pastoral education with mobile schools by local NGOs in partnership with UNICEF or Kindernothilfe. Example reports are delivered on the respective websites e.g. www.unicef.org and www.kindernothilfe.de.

education inclusion as an overarching term, because much depends on the context and assessment of the pastoralist groups, their future viability and their livelihood.

3.2 Radio Education in Mongolia

Radio education in Mongolia was introduced in 1996 with the aid of UNESCO and DANIDA, a Danish aid agency, with the aim to provide non-formal education to women of the six Gobi provinces, who have a mobile lifestyle. The education programme was designed to fit the current situation and lifestyle of the women, using as much of the existing resources as possible. With the project, the government was trying to support nomadic people to adjust to the country's transition into a market economy and democratic government. According to the descriptions of Krätli (2001), the learning materials of the programme were based on reading materials and radio broadcasts. All participating learners were women. They received a three-day crash course in one of the district centres, where they were provided with booklets, papers, pens, batteries and a radio and they met their future visiting teachers. Each teacher was made responsible for 15 learners, visiting the women twice a month. The teachers were educated local vets, doctors and teachers, often with a nomadic background themselves, who worked part-time on a voluntary basis. The subjects covered health education, income generation and literacy. To be of practical use for the women, subject booklets and radio broadcasts focused on felt making, family planning, making camel saddles and traditional garments, preparing milk and meat products, working with leather, growing vegetables, converting animal dung into fuel, civics and small business skills. Even though the programme targeted women, often whole families got involved and the levels of participation and responses were high.

After interviews with the nomadic families, which provincial and district officials, as well as, community leaders, carried out as early as 1992, the needs of the nomadic people were analysed and a pilot project was run from January to May 1995. In the main phase of 1996, in total more than 600 teachers were trained, three local radio studios were re-equipped, twenty-three subject booklets were produced and more than 15,000 women aged between 15 and 45 from 62 districts were enrolled (Krätli 2001).

Since Mongolia's transition to a market economy in the 1990s, there has been a reduction in state-provided services, investment and governance, which also undermines the nationwide school and boarding school network. Collectives of animal herders were disbanded by governmental subsidies, which in turn increased the demand for children to contribute their labour in the family's household leaving the challenge with which Mongolia is now grappling (Dyer 2016).

3.3 Quranic Schools in Somalia and Kenya

Quranic schools have existed for a long time. In remote and mainly Islamic regions such as in Somalia and North-East Kenya (e.g. Wajir county), they sometimes even outnumber formal schools. These Quranic schools are single teacher schools in which the lessons are centred on reading, reciting and memorizing the Quran. Besides Arabic language acquisition, the lessons are aimed at elevating the moral and spiritual character of the pupils. Although pupils are taught literacy skills, they are often not able to read and write in their mother tongue because Somali is written in Latin script. Teaching and learning materials are reduced to a copy of the Quran, wooden barks and charcoal. Since Islamic teaching is considered a religious duty for learned persons, the pupils pay no formal fees to a teacher. Spiritual leaders, who are also administering Islamic law in cases of marriage, divorce, inheritance, conflict and dispute, mainly offer to teach on a voluntarily. They are also often involved in the community as healers, diviners and prayer leaders.

Quranic schools offer the advantage of multiple entry points and flexibility of attendance since pupils (both children and adults) are instructed side by side on an individual basis and with individualized assignments. There are no formal examinations or qualification and even though there may be underachievers or slow learners, there is no concept of failure. Discipline is strict and direct, which is a teaching and learning approach similar to the apprenticeship patterns in herd management the pupils are familiar with. Overall, these schools usually allow a high degree of community ownership and appear to be culturally non-intrusive since lessons are taught in the early mornings and evenings, outside the times reserved for pastoral duties. They are not employment oriented and thus present little risk of pupil alienation from the households.

There are approaches today of combining religious education, provided within the community, and secular inputs, offered by external providers. The governmental organisation Education for Marginalized Communities in Kenya runs mobile schools for 5-14-year-old Somali pastoralists in Wajir county in which acquisition of basic literacy and numeracy skills are combined with Muslim religious traditions of the conventional Quranic schools. According to Dyer (2015), each of these *dugsi* (lit. school) comprises basic learning equipment, two camels and a secular teacher who is selected by the community and trained by sponsored local partners.

Somali children learn the Quran for two years, typically attending the *dugsi* for six to seven hours each day, while also taking care of younger siblings and herding livestock. The secular curriculum wraps around these commitments, offering basic literacy and numeracy for two hours in the morning and evening. In March 2012 three mobile schools enrolled some 80 children and 14 transitioned to a nearby boarding school to complete the primary level (Dyer 2015).

3.4 Mobile Schools in Kenya

Kenya's commitment to the *Millennium Development Goals* and the *World Declaration on Education for All* is perhaps the best in Africa (Krätli & Dyer 2009). The Kenyan Ministry of Education has taken several steps towards meeting the distinctive needs of the country's estimated four million pastoralists, a substantial number of whom are nomadic. In 2008, the Ministry of State for Development of Northern Kenya and Other Arid Lands (MDNKOAL) was established. A Policy Framework for Nomadic Education was launched in July 2010, which, among others, committed the government to establish a National Commission on

Nomadic Education in Kenya (NACONEK).[30] In addition to the expansion of boarding schools, several education providers, including the Ministry of Education, have experimented with alternative models of service delivery in pastoralist areas such as mobile schools and shepherd schools.

These alternative strategies are obliged, according to the MDNKOAL, to use the national curriculum to ensure equivalence with the rest of Kenya. However, the adaptation of material to the specific conditions of pastoral livelihood systems may take place at the stage of design. In the case of the production of radio learning modules, teachers should be supported with a specific handbook for each district. Further, the framework by MDNKOAL from March 2010 (Getting the Hardest to Reach: A Strategy to Provide Education to Nomadic Communities in Kenya through Distance Learning), specifically asks alternative basic education systems to install evaluation and examination systems which would enable children to move back and forward between the so-called distance learning programmes and the conventional formal education system.

MDNKOAL asked the charity SOS Sahel International UK to help ensure that a draft policy for nomadic education meets the expectations of mobile pastoralists and accommodates their production strategies. In 2009, the *Education for Nomads* team attached to the International Institute for Environment and Development (IIED) elicited the views of girls, boys, men and women of four of Kenya's pastoralist groups – Gabra, Boran, Somali and Turkana – using the scenario planning method. According to one of the Turkana facilitators, the government of Kenya is asking how education and livestock herding can be combined. It was stated that the government of Kenya wants the pastoralists to succeed in both and wants them to be part in planning and implementing alternative education systems (Birch, Cavanna, Abkula & Hujale 2010).

The conclusions from these consultations were presented at a high-level meeting attended by senior officers from both the Ministry of Education and the MDNKOAL. The publication by Izzy Birch, Sue Cavanna, Dauod Abkula and Diyad Hujale from 2010 (Towards Education for Nomads: Community Perspectives in Kenya) shows that these four pastoralist groups in Kenya – Turkana, Gabra, Somali and Boran – generated a common critique of the education system, highlighting how it separates children from their culture and way of life. If the families wish to educate their children they must, therefore, make hard choices. The parents described the criteria they use to decide which children are sent to school and which are kept within the pastoral system. All four pastoralist groups were aware that alternative models of education already existed on a small scale. There was a universal desire for children to learn within the pastoral system and a curriculum that reinforces it. In the second round of consultations in 2010, the same pastoralists groups were briefed about the inter-ministerial meeting and since then there have been developments in these areas independent of the programme.

In 2010, about ninety mobile schools existed in six arid districts (Wajir, Garissa, Moyale, Ijara, Turkana and Samburu), including around fifty funded by the World Bank Arid Land Resources Management Project (MDNKOAL 2010). According to the study, children who were still too young even to herd small stock like goats and sheep attended the school during the day. Other children, tending the small stock during the day, had the opportunity to attend school at night. It was planned that pupils would be enrolled in a conventional boarding

---

30 Krätli and Dyer published a preparatory study in 2009 (Mobile Pastoralists and Education: Strategic Options). From 2009 to 2010, Krätli was the scientific advisor to the project *Education for Nomads* with the MDNKOAL and had a key role in the design of the strategy and the technical manual (MDNKOAL 2010).

school after three years of learning in the mobile schools. In addition to children, adults often also visited the mobile schools. The teachers came from a pastoralist background and were therefore attached to a nomadic family or group of families.

In their case study on mobile schools in Turkana and Marsabit area, Kibera, Gakunga and Imonje (2013) investigated factors such as teacher training, teaching and learning facilities, household's economic status and child labour influencing provision of education for pastoralist children specifically in four mobile primary schools in Marsabit North, Kenya.

There are no references to sources of further information on classroom management, learning content and to what extend the teachers received a teacher training. However, the interviewed teachers highlighted the importance of in-service and pre-service training especially for teaching young learners in mobile primary schools (Kibera, Gakunga & Imonje 2013).[31]

Generally, the MDNKOAL (2010) highlights the advantage of mobile schools because children can continue their household work without having to leave their production team. Moreover, there are no hidden costs for learners and their families. MDNKOAL concedes, however, that mobile schools are expensive because of the small number of pupils and the difficulty to staff, manage and monitor the schools. Further, the government of Kenya recognises that unqualified teachers have to face multi-grade teaching requirements and have little support from teaching and learning materials. Moreover, according to the official government papers, classroom models of teaching based on the continuity of attendance are difficult for pastoral households as they scatter at any time, forcing children to move in and out of the system with negative consequences. In practice, therefore, most mobile schools tend to fill formal school service gaps in semi-permanent settlements but do not reach all mobile households (MDNKOAL 2010).

3.5 Lessons Learned

The consultation of the four presented approaches to the education of mobile pastoralists demonstrated possible models of education service that are in harmony with the nomadic way of life. They showed the following common features shown in figure 3.1, which seem to complement or promise success. Additionally, the example of the radio schools in Mongolia showed that education users considered the learning materials which covered relevant topics for pastoralists such as health education and income generation as a major benefit. The Quranic schools in Somalia and Kenya offer the advantage of multiple entry points and flexibility of attendance. Further, the children in the Quranic school pay no fees.

Ezeomah (1997) gives a list of lessons learned about nomadic education specifically in East Africa:

– Recognition of nomadic culture is necessary for programmes to be successful and more research is needed.
– Nomads dislike Western delivery systems but not education as such.
– Education should be taken to nomads on the move by various means.
– Education offers need to be developed to suit the nomadic lifestyle in order to succeed.

---

31 A case study from 2013 from Kibera, Gakunga & Imonje counts 15 mobile schools in Turkana Central district, 22 in Turkana West, 12 in Turkana North, 6 in Loima and 4 in Marsabit North district.

- Nomads should be involved in planning, implementing and evaluating their education programmes.
- Development of suitable skills and knowledge will improve individual nomads, their societies and their nations.
- Nomadic education is an international responsibility, as nomads spread across national borders.

Feature	Iran	Mongolia	Somalia	Kenya
interlace with existing government institutions for education and development	x	x	x	x
planning and implementation with the local community	x	x	x	x
supported financially by the world community and local governments	x	x	x	x
compatibility of work commitment and learning	x	x	x	x
not aimed at sedentarization	x	x	x	x
take place in informal settings and the school environment allows parents to maintain a close surveillance over the physical and moral security of their children	x	x	x	x
special teacher training centres are installed	x	x	x	
teachers are locals with nomadic background and basic education			x	x
national curriculum is adopted but teaching and learning methods and materials are adjusted to specific needs and requirements	x	x		
schools use existing resources as much as possible	x	x	x	
subjects cover literacy and numeracy	x	x	x	x
equipment is kept at the minimum	x	x	x	

Fig. 3.1: Common features of successful alternative basic education programmes for nomadic pastoralists (Source: own illustration).

According to Carr-Hill and Peart (2005), successful non-formal education programmes are based on two-way processes. They are highly flexible in structure and content and they maintain flexibility over time to be able to respond to changing needs.

Further, the literature review prepared by UNESCO and the International Institute for Educational Planning summarizes that *alternative*, non-formal approaches to pastoral education have proved more successful, cheaper to implement and complement pastoralism as a livelihood, rather than provide an exit from it. Carr-Hill and Peart (2005) concede, however, that as long as non-formal education is not recognised at the same level as formal schooling, both, in administrative terms and people's perceptions, its success will only be measured in terms of capacity: to convey out-of-school children into otherwise unsuccessful, unresponsive formal education systems. Mobile schools, in particular, remain subject of complex logistics because assuring availability of a viable group of pupils is difficult. The combination of reasons such as migration routes, seasonal herding, community organisation, deteriorating security and drought, that bring groups of pastoralist children together are transient and unpredictable (Dyer 2016).

Schröder (2012) generally concedes that through inappropriate linking of educational offers and existing life situations worldwide school systems often do not diminish disadvantage but contribute to increasing it. This is achieved in particular by the fact that schools, in their general character and the supposed insight that they must treat all and everything equally in administrative and methodological-didactic terms, are not oriented towards the basic needs and necessities of children and their families.

Education is the key for our life.

Felicitas Muer, first female Daasanach INES teacher trainee

4. What Are the Wishes of Daasanach Pastoralists with Regard to Education?

To make pastoral education programmes a success, Ezeomah (1997) suggests for mobile pastoralists to be involved in planning, implementing and evaluating these programmes. Therefore, the INES team has made several attempts to find out what the Daasanach wish concerning education and schooling.

In 2014, the Benedictine Fathers, Illeret surveyed Daasanach parents of 884 children in 13 semi-permanent settlements to survey the number of children enrolled in one of the two government primary schools in Illeret and Silicho or one of the non-formal nursery schools in El-Bochoch, Illolo, Nang'oleiy and Aiy'beete. This was undertaken to show the need for schooling. The parents were also asked whether they were willing to send their children to a mobile school which would migrate with the communities. Additionally, the German INES project team (Höldrich, Lichtinger, Schaller and Würzle) carried out 26 interviews with Daasanach girls, boys, men and women in 2017 to inquire about the experience, relevance and expectations of education, schooling and teaching.[32] The participatory method aimed to include various views and perspectives and marshal the interviewees' own arguments and evidence to advocate for the future of their educational system with or without mobile schools.[33] During the interviews, all interview partners expressed a common wish for education – for themselves, their children and community members.

Education will change our life.
Joshua Esho, elder

4.1 Which Form of School Service Is Desired?

To start with, the Daasanach were very clear to distinguish between the terms schooling and education. Even though many interviewees stated they had not been to school, all of them experienced education through their parents, grandparents, elders, the community and their age group. Traditional education was explained to happen through oral communication and apprenticeship, a form of *learning by doing* and copying.

---

32 The interviews were conducted by means of a translator. At some points, the interview partners also animated other community members to join the discussion so that a dialogue with more participants evolved. According to Bagele Chilisa and post-colonial indigenous research, this open discussion form is typical for relatedness-oriented communities and should be considered in the research design.

33 In 2010, a study was carried out by a team of researchers (Birch, Cavanna, Abkula & Hujale) in the course of a broader action research programme to support the Kenyan government in questions on nomadic education. The Kenyan government is striving for alternative forms of schooling for pastoralists, which gives them new perspectives and access to education and, at the same time, does not compromise the pastoralists' way of life. The survey among Boran, Somali, Gabra and Turkana pastoralists in Northern Kenya inquired their ideas on possible forms of nomadic education. Thus, the aim of the discussions and interviews with these four selected groups of pastoralists was to hear the voices and perspectives of end users and to inquire their opinions, needs and ideas. The findings show that the Boran, Somali, Gabra and Turkana support a way of formal schooling which is in harmony with their traditional mobile way of life. However, sceptic voices are raised about the sincerity of the government when it comes to a new approach of education for pastoralists (Birch, Cavanna, Abkula & Hujale 2010).

My father talked to me and sometimes showed me by taking care of animals together.
Nyingole Felix Anini, young man

Interesting parallels were drawn between the conventional classes in a school and the levels of instruction and performance in traditional learning.

I was educated by my father and neighbours. First, I was told to look after the small kids, then goats and sheep and then cows. That is how I learned. It is like a school where you first go to nursery, then class 1 and so on.
Jakob Lon'gada, elder

Fig. 4.1: Theresa Schaller conducting surveys in Illgele (Source: Theresa Schaller).

There was a universal desire for children and other community members to receive an additional formal education. Where opinions differed was on how further education should be delivered. All interview partners talked about a school, yet not all about a school building. Pastoralists explained that the education models should ideally accommodate the changing fortunes and places of the pastoral system and that a static system did not fit.

My dream school will be mobile. It cannot be a construction because we cannot put it on a donkey. It is too heavy.
Lokoringole Hakualata, elder

They stressed the priority that all children who wanted to go to school should have access – no matter where they were moving to or staying at.

School should be next to where there are children.
Bonaya Yierar, young man

One interview partner, a young man, addressed the difference between the two options of mobile schools and schools in permanent settlements. According to him, mobile schools were important for mobile or semi-mobile pastoralists because they would be able to accompany the community on their shifts between pasture grounds. However, when Daasanach settle permanently, fixed school buildings would also be necessary. The two existing governmental school in Silicho and Illeret were stated to not be sufficient. More should be installed. Asking for reasonable locations where the permanent schools should be located, he suggested having the moving patterns analysed with a view of permanent water supply and pasture grounds.

Mobile schools can be everywhere. We need mobile schools because they move with us. In manyattas, the school can be in a permanent building.
Joseph Naliye, young man

Pastoralists were clear about how a mobile school could shift with the communities:

The teacher should be given a donkey to move with them because when we migrate we use donkeys to put luggage on them.
Jakob Long'ada, elder

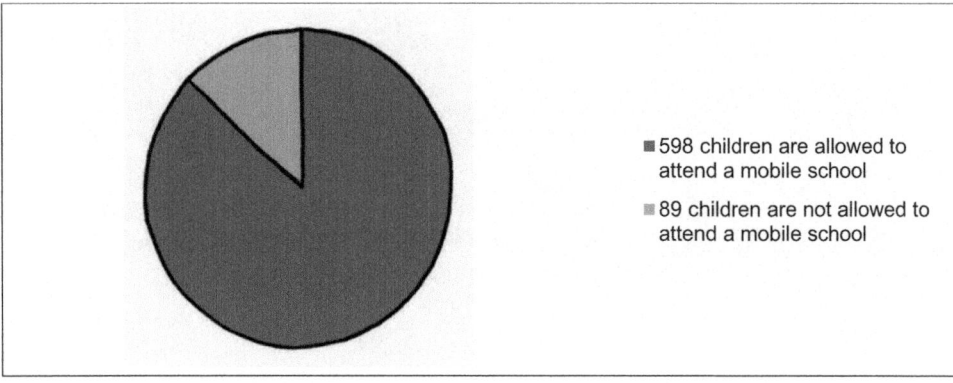

Fig. 4.2: Permission of Daasanach parents for their children to attend a mobile school (Source: own illustration).

During the field research in 2014, the parents were asked if they were ready to send their children to a mobile school, given the school would move with the communities. The diagram shows that the parents of 598 out-of-school children (67%) would send their children to a mobile school. Only the parents of 89 of the out-of-school children (10%) would not allow their children to attend a mobile school. It is unclear which reasons or underlying narratives of education lead to this specific result.

It was seen as ideal that a school offer recognises the children's commitment to specific tasks within the community and allows children to learn at different times. According to the interviewees' proposals, the school should take place in the morning hours after the young animals were watered, the household water was fetched and firewood prepared for the evening. Young boys are usually out during the day to take care of the small livestock. They should receive the chance for schooling in the evenings or in the mornings when a brother has taken over the tending. Girls should learn alongside boys. There was a universal agreement that school should fit together with the duties of the children to ensure the compatibility of formal education and the traditional household chores because the whole community with all its members is seen as one production team.

I have to compare my school with the daily life of the community before I decide when my school takes place. I observe carefully when they get up and take the animals for grazing.
Bonaya Yierar, young man

The interviewees also explained that all education models should ideally accommodate the changing fortunes of the pastoral life. For example, when pasture and water are plentiful during the rainy season, the herders and the livestock leave the stock camp early in the morning at around 5 o'clock but come home early. During the dry season, however, the children tending the livestock do not leave before 9 o'clock in the morning but come back late in the afternoon. These changing calendars should be taken into account when setting the daily school schedule. Each community should be allowed to determine their own schedule.

Before I start my school I call for a community meeting and explain everything to them. They have to make their decisions.
Joshua Esho, elder

The interview partners suggested a school committee that would hold regular meetings and ensure a smooth operation of the school.

I will be part of the school committee. I will discuss with the rest if there are problems and if yes, we will look for a solution.
Jakob Long'ada, elder

4.2 What Should Be Learned at School?

There was a universal desire for new school systems to not only cover lower primary levels but to prepare the pupils for a possible shift to a governmental upper primary school or even to a secondary school. For that reason, parents would like the schools to cover the Kenyan national curriculum to ensure the possibility for further learning and the taking of national exams.

My dream school would be based on the Kenyan curriculum.
Mary Nabul, young woman

The interviewees would like learning to take place in the mother tongue in the early years and criticised about the present system that teachers do not speak the vernacular in school.

The local language should be introduced.
Paul Lokono, young man

Yet, there was no desire for pastoralists to be literate only in their own language. With the progress of schooling, they would like learning to also take place in Kiswahili and English.

They learn ABC up to Z.
Helekua Nyabatang', boy

Even though all would like to have teachers who understand their environment and who would act as role models for their children, only some addressed the wish for the curriculum to include subjects relevant to pastoralism such as animal husbandry or range management.

The teacher will teach how to take care of animals.
Bewa Nyatemura, boy

Nonetheless, education should help families thrive within their environment and reinforce the rich and complex learning that takes place within pastoralist societies.

4.3 Who May Attend School?

There was a common agreement that schooling should be on a voluntary basis. Nobody should be forced to go to school or to send their children there.

School should not be forced upon the family.
Joshua Esho, elder

This notion was explained with the fact that many Daasanach parents have to take children out of school when their livelihood as pastoralists is at risk and they need the children's work commitment. Besides, if the parents were not allowed to choose education freely, they might take their children out of school at the first opportunity and impose other duties on them out of defiance.

Parents decide whom to take to school. For example, two children go to school and two assist at home. I don't know if there is a way of sending all children to school. The parents have to decide.
Joshua Esho, elder

During the interviews, there was a general agreement that the schools should be offered to the youngest children first. Further, they expressed their hope that the learning programmes would also be to the benefit of older children who have already taken over more complex tasks within the community and later even to the whole community as such.

With time, the school offer should also address adults who could, for example, join for evening classes. The interviewees stressed the concern, however, not to mix the classes since children tend to be very shy in the presence of adults and the cultural norms would demand teachers to pay closer attention to adults than to children. This could have negative effects on school.

We cannot mix elders and children because children will see the elders as superior because of their age. The children would then not concentrate very well.
Lokoringole Hakualata, elder

Some interviewees, therefore, mentioned splitting classes for children and adults but with identical learning materials. There should be school times when children are free while their parents and adults are at work and learning times for other community members when the children do not participate.

Elders and parents have to go to an adult education class. To be in school is good for all because you get knowledge.
Yierite Ar'gudo, mother

Nonetheless, even during the children's learning time, parents and adults should be conferred to function as observers of the daily classes and to assess how the teacher did his works.

Parents are also part of the same school. They have to come and assess if the teacher is there and is sober. Parents are not there for learning and are not allowed to interrupt.
Bonaya Yierar, young man

4.4 What Are the Future Perspectives for Pupils?

Most community members shared their hope that formal education would open new chances and opportunities to those going to school but also their families. The whole community would profit from the education of some. From those children who have received education in a school and who have the chance for employment, it is expected that they will support their families and communities financially.

Education will change your life even though you are a pastoralist. For pastoralists, the living standard is only livestock. People who are not pastoralists can get employed and work somewhere. With Daasanach going to school both is possible.
Bonaya Yierar, young man

The worldview of Daasanach was also explained during the interviews. Daasanach believe God created two types of people – those living settled and the others mobile.

I think God separated people differently. He has given Daasanach livestock and called them pastoralists. Those in towns he has given knowledge and fields. Daasanach do not know anything apart from livestock. It is God's nature that Daasanach are pastoralists.
Lokoringole Hakualata, elder

This revealed a profound belief in widely varying economies and differing ways of life. The important link between literacy and taking responsibility for the extended family was expressed repeatedly. The social security system is based on family and community ties, so the social and economic development of the individual would mean the improvement of the whole community. Daasanach pastoralists are looking for additional sources of income in order not to be fully and exclusively dependent on their livestock and unpredictable factors such as severe droughts and heavy rains.

Education is important because you get knowledge and you get employed and you can assist your parents.
Bewa Nyatemura, boy

The intense interest in education among adults, youths and children was clearly evident. The Daasanach interviewees are looking for a form of education that promotes alternative local sources of income. While education is recognised as a possible way out of pastoralism, it should not ultimately lead to the migration of youths to towns like Marsabit or even Nairobi. They desired that education would help families thrive within their environment and reinforce the rich and complex learning that already takes place within pastoralist societies. Some of the interviewed adults recognised that education could open local alternatives to pastoralism, such as small local businesses or other services. Only if the educated remained close to their home, culture and way of life would the development of the individual be to the benefit of the whole community.

After leaving school, the school leavers can look for employment, come back home and start a business. The children can decide which business they want to start. Maybe they can start with maize, beans, then also traditional shoes and necklaces.
Nyakaro, elder

In the long-run, education is also seen as a potential sector for employment.

After leaving school you can be a teacher.
Artukatch Nylim, elder

According to the interview partners, Daasanach pastoralists are convinced that education cannot be addressed in isolation. Many factors, including drought, disease, conflict and the availability of infrastructure and technology will have an impact on learning in pastoralist areas. It is not their aim that education should only bring financial benefit to the community but it should also help to overcome social disadvantages. According to many community members, basic education will not only positively affect the cohabitation of Daasanach but also reduce conflicts with neighbouring groups – Gabra, Turkana, Rendille, Samburu – who possess a higher educational level and are thus more involved in civic activities, for example, membership in the county government.

The offices in Marsabit are all occupied with Gabra. The Daasanach are wondering why Gabra are ahead. Daasanach are behind the rest because they have not taken their children to school.
Bonaya Yierar, young man

The interviewees were aware that many conflicts and disputes between the rivalling neighbouring groups are incited by communication problems. Because each group has its own language, they need an understanding of Kiswahili to have a lingua franca.

Education changes the way of living with people. First, when you see Gabra or Turkana in the fora, you see them with fear. If you go to school you can interact with them. The communities can talk. You realise that Gabra and Turkana are brothers and sisters. You don't have to fear them anymore.
Jeremiah Loki Teete, young man

4.5 Who Should Teach?

All interview partners had similar and definite ideas on who should be the teachers and how they should interact with the pupils. Men and women can be teachers likewise. There were no gender preferences. In larger schools, two or more teachers could be possible even of both sexes. Especially female interviewees, however, expressed the concern that married couples should not teach in the same school because the social position of a wife could negatively influence collegial cooperation and decision-making processes.

The husband is the boss at home and also in school.
Mary Nabul, young woman

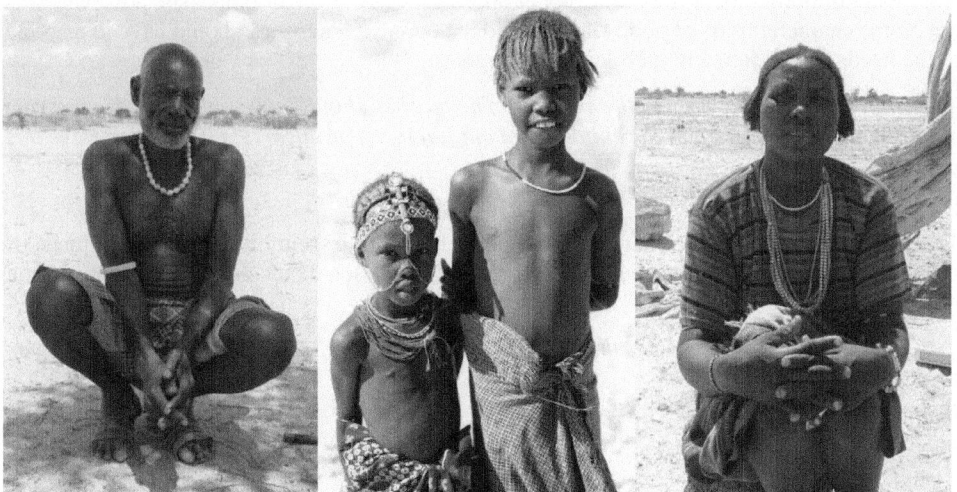

Fig. 4.3: Interviewee Lokoringole Hakualata; two Daasanach girls with traditional hairdress and interviewee Laboro (Source: Theresa Schaller).

The interviewees were particularly clear on the topics of caning, teacher absenteeism and drunkenness, some of the most recurring and much-discussed topics in Kenyan classrooms, especially in very remote areas such as Northern Kenya.

A teacher should not be drunk, harsh, caning and coming late to school.
Jeremiah Loki Teete, young man

It is not good if the teacher canes the children and the stick is very bad.
Nyakaro Habara, elder

I do not like that my teachers cane strongly.
Helekua Nyabatang', boy

A teacher should not be allowed to be very harsh on children because the children are still young and need help. A teacher should not be drunk because then the teacher is very harsh.
Nyakaro Habara, elder

The fear of caning was especially high when the teacher is known to be drinking. Even though the Kenyan board of education has abolished caning from schools, it remains a highly controversial and emotional topic, since many parents still make use of it at home in child rearing. Caning also occurs within the Daasanach social cohabitation when the hari (generation set) disciplines one of its members.[34] So, many interviewees gave their agreement to caning if it was not too harsh and served a purpose.

Caning is not bad but for a good reason.
Nyakaro Habara, elder

According to the interviewees, caning as such is not necessarily seen as the problem. It is considered problematic if alcohol is involved, if physical punishment is not proportional to what was committed or if the extent is not appropriate. A stronger emphasis, however, was put on the character traits of good teachers and the competencies they should have to respond to the needs of children and their learning progress.

A teacher should be friendly to the children. The teacher should have polite words to attract children and should listen to the child to find out if it has a problem and if yes, also solve this problem.
Paul Lokono, young man

Teachers are seen as important role models, helping to reinforce both the values of pastoralism and the benefits of education through their personal behaviour and the interaction with the pupils.

A teacher should properly lead the children and show good practice so that children can copy that.
Joshua Esho, elder

Nevertheless, teachers should not only be role models in the way they behave but also in their appearance.

A teacher has to show a good picture of hygiene and should clean the class area, should not be dirty, brush his teeth and show the children how to wash their face. Also, a teacher should not urinate around the classroom.
Joshua Esho, elder

Public schools in Kenya have a clear dress code for teachers, while all pupils wear uniforms. Daasanach interview partners were generally dissatisfied with the fact that pupils were not allowed to wear traditional hairstyles and jewellery in formal schools. Concerning teachers, the opinions differed on whether the teachers should dress traditionally or not.

A teacher should wear usual clothes, trousers and a shirt.
Helekua Nyabatang', boy

The teachers should dress according to the Daasanach way, not in a modern way because it shows that the teachers have lost the cultural way of the community.
Bonaya Yierar, young man

---

34 For more information on the social organisation of the Daasanach see chapter *1.3 Social Organisation*.

Opinions about the degree of cultural attachment in outward appearances varied for gender. It was generally agreed that male teachers could wear a *shuka* (a blanket or piece of cloth tied around the waist) and sit on a *kára* (a traditional small carved stool for men) while teaching. It was generally agreed that trousers should remain for men.

A female teacher cannot wear trousers. Men yes but not women.
Felicitas Muer, young woman

According to the interview partners, female teachers can wear modern or traditional skirts and jewellery but should wear shirts for schooling. In summary, there was a universal desire that teachers should dress decently but also with clear markers of their cultural background. While the consultation process demonstrated the clear expectations to cultural awareness, it also revealed that teachers could be anyone with moral principles, with a certain amount of intelligence and who has undergone a basic teacher training.

Anyone who likes the task of teaching, not stealing school property and who has undergone some training can be a teacher.
Jeremiah Loki Teete, young man

Someone clever can be a teacher.
Yierite Ar'gudo, mother

It became clear, that pastoralists are well aware that neither the mainstream education system through settled schools nor alternative programmes with laypersons as teachers are working well. Most importantly, the interview partners highlighted the importance of an inner attitude of ownership for the school. Only the teachers could bring about the necessary changes in how learning is organised and managed.

Teachers should own the school because they give the children knowledge if they own the school and treat all children like their own.
Lokoringole Hakualata, elder

Just as learning should take place within the pastoral environment, the teachers should be part of the pastoralist society, too. Only if the teachers have respect for pastoralism and an understanding of their way of life will they act as positive role models for their learners.

The teacher should be from the same community to know their way of life.
Bonaya Yierar, young man

4.6 Lessons Learned

The consultations with the men, women, boys and girls demonstrated a genuine interest in education, if the model of service delivery is in harmony with their nomadic way of life, if the teachers come from their own communities and if the curriculum reinforces pastoralism. There were definite ideas on how education will improve their way of life as pastoralists but also the lives of those community members who seek alternative means of livelihood. There were no genuine ideas of how and where schooling should take place but the interview partners were clear that static school constructions do not fit nomadic pastoralists – only those who have settled down permanently. There were also remarkable perceptions of how learning processes succeed in the Daasanach' traditional form of apprenticeship and the interviewees made specific statements regarding the role and exemplary behaviour of teachers. All in all, the interview partners showed great appreciation for the consultation process which was felt to be credible and appreciative.

Personal Notes of the Authors

"On my way to the first interviews in El-Maasich, I was pretty nervous and not sure whether I would meet people who were ready to talk to me. I had heard that sometimes Daasanach are paid by different non-governmental organisations (NGOs) who want to do research or conduct interviews. I feared that the communities would not talk to me *for free*. I was also uncertain, whether potential interview partners would be present in El-Maasich because a ceremonial *'dimi* celebration was held nearby.

Despite the busy preparations for *'dimi*, I was welcomed warmly and the men, women and children who surrounded me at my arrival were curious why I was there. The fear that no one would want to talk to me without *expense allowance* left right away when Nyakaro – the tallest Daasanach elder I have ever seen – immediately invited me to have a seat with him under a shady tree. I was accompanied by Bonaya Yierar as Daasanach translator. The interview started and the atmosphere relaxed below the tree because my dignified interview partner and I had much to talk about and together with curiously watching children and young warriors there was much to laugh. All of a sudden, it did not feel like an interview anymore but rather like a casual conversation in a good atmosphere. In the interviews, I was talking with very remarkable people: the very shy young woman Maas, the open-minded boy Helekua, the self-confident young woman Felicitas, the thoughtful and farsighted elder Joshua, the elderly man Lokoringole who told stories about colonial times or the courageous young girl Loboch. All of them were not only willing to talk to me but even showed great appreciation that I asked them to share their experiences, thoughts, hopes and expectations.

I will surely never forget the question of Laboro, a mother of many children, who asked me whether I thank my parents repeatedly for sending me to school. She hopes for her children to go to school one day and then to be able to master foreign languages to be able to communicate without a translator. Laboro is sure her children will appreciate the gift of education." (Theresa Schaller, June 2017)

Part II International Cooperation

It takes a whole village to raise a child.

African proverb

5. What Is the Pedagogical Perspective on Development?

Development is a term that is used in many different areas. Usually, changes in a person's characteristics in the course of life are referred to as development but the concept of development cannot be clearly defined. Many different research areas are concerned with human development: developmental psychology, pedagogical psychology, developmental education to name only a few. They each have a different focus, ask different questions and work with other methods. Developmental psychology, for example, raises the questions of whether development is continuous or discontinuous[35], which aspects influence the development and how genetic material and the environment interact with each other.[36]

From a pedagogical perspective, the inescapable question arises as to what contributions education makes to development. Are there developmental processes which should be promoted? If yes, is that possible? Where does the development process lead us? What is the goal of development? Are developmental goals universal?

The authors of this book do not intend to answer these questions, however, it is necessary to specify the term development from a pedagogical point of view since the INES project is providing a learning environment for children in which they should be able to evolve and develop individually and according to their needs. Therefore, the system Ladders of Learning focuses on the pedagogical perspectives of development and refers to it, which is, inter alia, visible in the arrangement and design of the learning materials.

5.1 Development Education

While psychology looks at the scale position children achieve in relation to their age group, educators are predominantly concerned with the learning progress as a whole no matter what scale position a child has in relation to others. Educators ask what reasons have contributed to the increase in performance and whether any barriers impede the child's development. Education providers examine which learning and teaching processes enable improvement of the individual performance of a child or adolescent and how they can provide assistance so that the individual child or adolescent reaches their optimum potential possibilities.

---

35 Humans are constantly evolving and experience an increase in competencies, not just age-related. However, especially in childhood, numerous developmental progress can be observed. This often raises the question of whether children make qualitative *leaps* in their development or whether development is more of a continuous process of small changes. There are several well-known stage theories (e.g., Jean Piaget's theory of cognitive development according to which children go through four stages between birth and adolescence, each characterized by a particular type of cognitive process). All stage theories underlie the idea of a general developmental sequence that children of a certain age show great similarities in certain situations and have clearly identifiable behaviour, depending on their age. Although the stage theories were very influential, opinions have changed over the last 20 years viewing development more as a continuous process characterized by gradual rather than a sudden change.

36 Does the environment in which we grow up or our genes determine our life? Attempts have been made to reduce this question to an either /or proposition, however, this question misses the significant focal point. According to current developmental psychology, there is a consensus that both our genes, as well as, our environment influence the development of human characteristics. It is more reasonable to explore how genetic materials and environment work together than to focus on the question which of the two has more influence.

From a pedagogical point of view, the focus does not lie on testing and the allocation of scale points (e.g., what is the level of reading and writing in comparison to age and schoolmates?). Beyond dispute, this information is important and helpful to assess the individual learning processes or the functionality of the learning system as such, especially in the process of adapting a new learning system and developing innovative learning materials. However, to support and assess the individual learner, it takes more than providing ranking lists. Developmental education examines how education provision can be made more appropriate and effective concerning the whole person and thus asks questions like:

- How does the child's personality develop through schooling?
- Does the educational offer support the development of the individual learner and if yes, why and how?
- Does the child develop self-confidence or anxiety in school?
- Does the schooling environment provide an atmosphere where the child is encouraged to explore, to ask questions and to find solutions to a given problem?

The educational providers of the system Ladders of Learning seek to focus more on the educational than the psychological point of view making the development process of each learner important.

5.2 Education Should Foster Maturity

The educational scientist Heinrich Roth defines maturity as the general objective of education. Outside influences should be replaced by self-determination, as far as possible. Erich Weber defines maturity as the main pedagogical objective as being the ability and readiness of someone to lead a responsible life based on own reasoning, drawn upon understanding and critical judgment and by independent decisions. This also includes a continuous effort of improving the social living conditions, since the individual maturity is dependent on a responsible society (Weber 1974).

Maturity has to be interpreted as competence in a threefold sense: a) as self-competence – the ability to be responsible for your own action; b) professional competence – the ability to act and judge in a particular profession, and be held responsible; c) social competence – the ability to act and judge, and be held responsible, in professional or social areas that are relevant in social, societal or political terms. (Hartig, Klieme & Leutner, 2008: 6)

All three spheres of competency (self-, professional and social competency) are equally important in the maturing process. Thus, there can be no development to self-competency without training professional and social competency at the same time. Since the three are mutually dependent, all three areas are consciously encouraged and served in the system Ladders of Learning. Interviews, personal conversations, as well as, close analysis of the Kenyan curriculum are of importance because in an international team for education provision (such as INES) the question arises whether there are culturally perceived variations of self-, professional and social competency.[37]

---

[37] In the Kenyan Curriculum launched by the Ministry of Education in 2017, every learner should achieve the

In the interviews with the Daasanach, parents were asked what their children should learn in school. The interviewees mainly mentioned aspects of professional competency:

The children should learn ABCD, Swahili, Counting, English and Daasanach.
Jakob Long'ada, elder

The children should learn 123, ABC and Swahili.
Artukatch Nylim, elder

However, the interviewees also highlighted they wanted the teachers to safeguard their cultural heritage in school, which indicates that self- and social competency are also regarded as desirable learning objectives.

In school, the child should also be taught about the Daasanach culture, for example, about the ceremony of 'dimi.
Nyakaro Habara, elder

Although promotion of social competency was not explicitly formulated as a learning goal, almost all respondents emphasised that alongside with teacher based learning processes, children should also interact and learn with their classmates.

The learners should assist each other.
Lokolom Long'ada, elder

This illustrates that the school should create learning situations where children have to cooperate as partners or groups to achieve a task or produce creative work.

To impart the maturity of the three spheres of competency in a tangible way, they have to be broken down into manageable more comprehensible educational sub- and intermediate goals depending on the culture. In independent, individualistic Western cultures, such as Germany, maturity in people is regarded as apparent when they show behavioural patterns such as productivity and critical thinking. Often these are regarded as measurement and characterization of high level performance, while in other cultural contexts mature behaviour may be characterized differently (Willemsen & Gottschalk 2015). The international question of controllable conditions that influence the development towards a mature adult is valid. The general concepts, however, of what a mature personality is and how these people act are different from culture to culture.

5.3 Culture Dependency of Development

Around the globe, there are different efforts to help track and facilitate children's development. Even though all children develop unique personalities, it is not surprising that cultural influence encourages and trains certain cultural behaviour.[38] As stated above,

---

following competencies: Communication and collaboration, critical thinking and problem-solving, imagination and creativity, citizenship, learning to learn, self-efficacy and digital literacy.

38 Culture can be defined as "the set of attitudes, values, beliefs, and behaviours shared by a group of people, communicated from one generation to the next" (Matsumoto 1997: 5). "[…] Researchers typically discuss two cultural phenomena: 1) independent, individualistic, or Western cultures and 2) interdependent, collectivistic, or Eastern and Southern cultures." (Rubin & Menzer 2010: 2). These two cultural models are, however,

different socialisation goals and different views on what a mature person is may exist depending on the prevailing, surrounding culture (Keller 2011). Even if a certain behavioural pattern appears identical across various cultures, this could in fact be interpreted and evaluated differently depending on the predominant customs and beliefs (Rubin & Menzer 2010).[39] The cultural influence reaches so far that it makes an impact on the achievement of different developmental milestones of children.[40]

Child development is a dynamic and interactive process. Children show an extraordinary sensitivity to their environment, they interact with and imitate it. All cultures follow different socialisation goals, embody different parenting ethno theories and emphasise different behavioural practices, which in turn can broadly be classified into relatedness-oriented or autonomy-oriented backgrounds (Keller 2007).[41] Growing up in different cultures children receive different and specific inputs from their environment. These are strongly dependent on the parents' behaviour and parenting strategies, which in turn are influenced by certain culturally adapted beliefs and practices. In her studies, Keller found inter alia that mothers from different cultures use different communication strategies when they interact with their children. These different forms of communication affect, on the one hand, the child's interaction with other people and, on the other hand, has an impact on the child's primary self-perception. Early social experiences form the basis of psychological development and help infants to construct and co-construct the world around them (Keller 2003). Moreover, the cultural context also defines who is entitled to educate children.

While education in autonomy-orientated backgrounds is primarily reserved for the parents and close relatives, in more relatedness-oriented backgrounds and traditional contexts the extended family, neighbours and the surrounding community members educate the children together. Further, an international study on autobiographical memory with children from different countries showed that children from autonomy-oriented cultures tend to describe themselves around their unique traits and characteristics such as, *I am clever* or *I am good at painting*. In contrast, children from interdependent societies with a great focus on relatedness describe themselves more often around their relationship with others and mention their social role, for example, *I am my parents' child* or *I am a good friend*. How children describe themselves depends on their cultural background. When asked to describe themselves, 60% of Kenyans described themselves in terms of their role within groups while 48% of Americans used personal characteristics to describe themselves (Ma & Schoeneman 1997).

---

prototypes and most countries and cultures are a mix of both of them.
39 Socialisation refers above all to the social dimension of human development. In socialisation processes, the human being becomes a socially capable subject https://asset.klett.de/assets/64e4908b/6ddd94c0fe2e74bd35 ddad1ad7cdc09597062682.pdf).
40 Vital milestones of neurological development are skills such as neck control, smiling for the first time, sitting without support, taking the first step, etc. These Milestones have a range of normal variation. However, additional to cultural differences in the timing of certain developmental milestones, there are often culture-specific expectations about when children reach or should reach certain milestones (Osamor, Owumi & Dipeolu 2015). According to that, some behaviours may be encouraged and supported while others, which are not a main culture-specific socialisation goal, may not be promoted or even neglected.
41 For more information read chapter *9.1 Relatedness-Oriented Background*.

5.4 Montessori's Development Pedagogy

Children come into the world with unlimited potential and are eager for self-construction with what they take from their environment (Feez 2010). Montessori is one of the representatives who emphasise that the development of children is organised through the influence of the environment and who express the necessity for educators to develop a culture-sensitive view (Borke & Keller 2014). Maria Montessori works with the anthropological assumption that the child is, from birth, a creature capable of self-activity, spontaneity and born with creative potential and an absorbent mind (Feez 2010). Children are the master builders of themselves.

Scientific observation then has established that education is not what the teacher gives; education is a natural process spontaneously carried out by the human individual, and is acquired not by listening to words but by experiences upon the environment. (Montessori 2007: 3).

The approach of Montessori is to provide children with didactic materials that encourage children to use them independently. Care is taken to design learning materials which capture the children's attention and interest. Montessori builds up her entire pedagogy on the perspective that the goal of every child is a gradual self-development to a mature personality. Hereby, Montessori underlines the child's own activity, as well as, the child's development towards autonomy and independence (Borke & Keller 2014). It is not surprising that Italian-born Montessori highlights autonomy and independence, values, which are typically attributed to autonomy-oriented backgrounds. However, with a closer analysis of her learning activities, there are also many instructions which are attributed to relatedness-oriented contexts. The exercises of practical life, for example, in which children complete real-life activities aim at promoting socially relevant and culturally appropriate activities, skills and performances. Moreover, in the initial demonstration phases of the Montessori pedagogy, the educator uses clearly defined meaningful gestures and precise language while the individual learner observes closely. Thereafter, the child is not only encouraged to imitate the sequence of movements but also to find their own, to move beyond mere copying. This sequence of demonstration, observation and copying is typical for relatedness-oriented contexts (Borke & Keller 2014). Since all human beings have to develop self-, professional and social competency for themselves, parents and educators must understand their roles as helpers. From the child's perspective in Montessori's word: *Help me to do it myself.* It is not advisable for parents and educators to anticipate learning experiences by only demonstrating knowledge or a certain performance without allowing the child to copy and explore.

Children show extraordinary sensitivity to certain learning processes at certain points of time in their development. Montessori refers to these sections of heightened interest as sensitive periods because they signal the opening windows of developmental opportunity (Feez 2010). During these sensitive periods, environmental stimuli are absorbed and correlated. Following this approach, the children's environment should arouse, activate and motivate the hidden creative power of the child. Sensitive parents and qualified educators pay close attention to these specific developmental needs and prepare a positive learning environment and materials.

5.5 Lessons Learned

The pedagogical perspective on development affects and shapes the various fields of work of INES and mobile schools. For education providers, it is essential to be sensitive to the fact that not every child develops in the same way and at the same pace. This attitude is particularly represented in the individual learning paths of the system Ladders of Learning. The focus is not on a child's scale position (position on the ladder of learning) and/or on the pace (individual speed on the ladder of learning) but rather on the fact that the child keeps moving. Moving on the ladder of learning indicates that the learning is in progress although at a different pace which shows that each child needs its own time to explore and understand. This attitude is also encouraged and discussed in the INES teacher education programme.

Besides, the overall goal of helping learners to develop towards maturity remains the focal point in the mobile schools whether in establishing school routines or during the individual learning ladder time. The system Ladders of Learning promotes self-, professional and social competency in a unique way because it values the three as equally important for the maturing process. Self-regulated learning processes are promoted through the fact that learners follow the learning path at their own pace and evaluate themselves. Self-regulated learning in return promotes self-competency. Professional competency is trained with the milestone topics and the activities of the different subject ladders of learning and their learning materials, whereas social competency is, inter alia, promoted through the different social forms of the activities. With the integrated help system of advanced learners and teacher's help, social competency is also trained through role modelling. Moreover, the daily procedure in the mobile INES schools with opening and closing assemblies, as well as, plenary sessions helps to foster social competency. The whole structure and procedure of mobile schools is adjusted to the Daasanach attitudes towards social cohabitation.[42]

The questions of how learners can be supported in their individual learning process is discussed worldwide and in different contexts. Thus, there is a growing interest in Montessori's pedagogy, as well as, other reform education and pedagogical movements which place the child in the centre of their interest. INES uses several concepts and material ideas from Montessori because they promote activity-oriented and self-determined learning and they help children to manage their (life-long) learning and education. Moreover, the Montessori pedagogy puts emphasis on the cultural context of the catchment area of the school and encourages educators to integrate meaningful traditions into the classroom. Especially the initial demonstration phase of the Montessori pedagogy (demonstration, observation, copying) bears a striking resemblance of how Daasanach teach their children in their relatedness-oriented context of pastoralism.

---

42 For more information on the daily routines of the INES mobile schools and the system Ladders of Learning, as well as, the MultiGradeMultiLevel-Methodology and its ladders of learning see chapter *8. What Is the System Ladders of Learning About?*.

Personal Notes of the Authors

The INES project has been running since 2014 and requires more working capacity, time and costs than initially planned. Sometimes people ask us how we can tell that all the work and time pays off. This question is justified (also because of all the donations) and since we are part of the project implementation team of INES we are challenged to give answers. We too ask ourselves: Should we count teachers? If we measure success with the number of trained teachers, should we count the number of trainees or those who have actually started their own mobile school? Should we count school children? If we measure success with the amount of school children, should we count all children who have spent time in a mobile school, have participated in assemblies and started their learning journey with the Introduction ladder of learning or only those who can read their first words in Daasanach? Which criteria do we use to measure that the INES project pays off?

From our observations we say: If one child moves one step towards maturity all the work pays off. If two learners support each other to reach the very best of their potential, the effort was worth it. If one mobile teacher provides a prepared learning environment in the stock camp, nothing was wasted.

We are one learning community.

Padmanabha and Rama Rao, RIVER chief executives

6. What Is the Pedagogical Perspective on Development?

6.1 Changing Concepts and Definitions

Cooperation advocates values such as equality, solidarity, social responsibility, work for mutual benefit and the common good, trusting and viewing situations from all perspectives (Johnson & Johnson 1999). Cooperation assumes that every human being has the strength to help himself, that external impulses and the exchange with each other are the essential aspects for common learning processes. However, in the context of cooperation between the *Global North* and the *Global South* we all too often remain in post-colonial thinking that there are clear donors and recipients in a one-sided transfer of resources from *North* to *South*. This thinking can be traced back to the fact that we stick to old definitions of development and maintain concepts of the past, even though they have undergone fundamental changes.

The concept of development assistance goes back to the colonial era at the turn of the 20th century in particular with the British policy of colonial development that emerged during that period. For a long time, the term development assistance described the cooperation between institutions from donor and recipient countries for the purpose of local and national promotion of development.[43] The progressive-optimistic concept of development of the 19th century contributed to creating a quasi-rational basis of legitimation for European colonialism and imperialism by seeming to justify the violent transfer of its own economic, cultural and political forms of life and organisation to non-European societies (Sangmeister 2009). Tetzlaff and Jakobeit describe the education efforts of European colonists and missionaries as being the most important positive legacy of colonialism (Tetzlaff & Jakobeit 2005).[44]

During the decolonization processes, the concept of development took on a new, more concrete meaning. The former colonial powers chose to support the *underdeveloped* to create autonomous *developed* states with social and economic systems that are as similar as possible to the former colonial powers. To set this development in motion, assistance from outside was given through the transfer of material (e.g. medicine, food and equipment) and non-material services (capital, knowledge and skills) (Sangmeister 2009). In the 50s and 60s, many non-governmental and Christian development organisations were founded in Europe as a result of the horrors of World War II that were still vivid to the people. As the *Global North* faces the shocking news of poverty and misery in the so-called post-colonial *Global South*, women and men want to pass on the help they themselves had received during reconstruction in post-war Europe (Steeb 2019). The massive criticism of the paternalistic and hierarchical undertone in the word assistance, being raised by development groups and by the participating countries themselves since the 1960s, led to a search for alternative formulations. Under the premises that both sides want to benefit and learn from each other, why not talk about cooperation between countries, organisations, groups and individuals? In

---

43 Especially in the 19th century, a progressive-optimistic concept of the term development came up: development was understood as a positively evaluated process of change, as movement and liberation. Development symbolized the prospect of a better future in this world that can be shaped by people themselves (Sangmeister 2009).

44 For more information on the pre- and post-colonial development of the Kenyan school system see chapter *2.1 Kenyan Primary Education System*.

the 1990s, development cooperation replaced the term development assistance or aid, however, the idea of advancing in development was still noticeable. In 2011, with the conference in Busan, the *North-South paradigm* in the context of development cooperation was dissolved for the first time but a real paradigm shift was initiated with the *Global Agenda* (2030) for sustainable development. It emphasises that major global challenges such as climate change, growing numbers of refugees and out-of-control financial markets require transnational responses and alliances (Kude 2019). Today, development cooperation, therefore, describes a partnership which targets a common task for the future and is based on mutual learning. The term development assistance is only used to describe short-term measures to bridge an acute shortage of infrastructure of food or medical supply. Humanitarian aid in conflict, post-conflict or disaster situations (man-made or natural, avoidable or not) is a classic example for development assistance. The German federal ministry for economic cooperation and development (BMZ) emphasises that the term development cooperation describes this intensive partnership much better than the formerly customary terms of aid or assistance as it does not regard the countries and organisations with which it cooperates as recipients of aid but as equal partners (BMZ).

Even if the term development assistance has been replaced with development cooperation, the question arises why not also dissolve the term development since there are persistent negative connotations that still resonate in the context of projects in former colonies. The term development, as shown before, is not generally definable, nor value-neutral, but depends on space and time, and in particular on individual and collective values (Nohlen 1991). In the past years, there has been a revival of the term due to the etymological origin of *develop*, which comes from the 16th century and means *emerge (unfold), progress in a process* (Sangmeister 2009). Since cooperation, as describes above, ideally involves a learning process, unfolding of one's own abilities, dispositions and potentials, profit and ownership on both sides, the term cooperation suffices. If international personnel is involved in the project, the prefix *international* is commonly added (Lücking-Michel 2019).

6.2 International Cooperation of INES

The history and structure of the INES project is an example of transnational knowledge transfer: The project idea is based on the wish of Kenyan-Daasanach parents for flexible, mobile education provided for their children, avails itself on pedagogical experiences from the rural school reform in South India and Germany and is implemented by a Kenyan-German project team. The following passage outlines the course of the INES project and consequently begins with the Indian developments 30 years ago.

The MultiGradeMultiLevel-Methodology with its ladder of learning, which presents the pedagogical foundation of INES, was developed by Padmanabha and Rama Rao, an Indian couple in Andhra Pradesh, India for the application in rural village schools.[45] After reforming thousands of rural schools in India, the RIVER-team was given the *Global Development Award* for the *Most Innovative Development Project* in 2005. Since then the interest and the demand for presentations, workshops and teacher training programmes on the MGML-Methodology and its ladders of learning have increased nationally and internationally.

---

45 For more information see chapter *8.1 Ladders of Learning Come from India*.

Governmental organisations and educational institutions from across the globe contact RIVER, visit the *Satellite Schools* in Andhra Pradesh to learn about the methodology and participate in workshops. As a result, variations of the MGML-Methodology and its ladders of learning were started in Nepal, Pakistan, Bangladesh, Thailand, Bhutan, the Maldives, Peru, Columbia, Cambodia, Ethiopia, Sierra Leone, Ivory Coast, Spain, France, Germany and Kenya.[46]

Around the globe, the design and concept of the adapted ladders of learning vary strongly depending on the culture of the individual country or region, as well as, the required subject, age group and school type. The variations of the MGML-Methodology have led to different forms of cooperation making use of synergy effects. In February 2016 the first MGML-World conference was held in Chennai, India with representatives and presentations of different countries, organisations, schools and universities where the global MGML learning community was celebrated. Collectively in these countries, if you will, one speaks of a transfer of knowledge from *South* to *South* and from *South* to *North* in this global learning process.

Since 2002, Father Florian OSB has been living and working with Daasanach pastoralists hearing the constant pleads of the parents for a mobile school system which led to his eventual nomination as an elder. Together with local teachers and a small project team he performed a survey to analyse the enrolment of Daasanach pastoralist school-aged children in ten semi-permanent settlements of the Daasanach and assess the relevance of a mobile school system.[47] Based on these results INES was founded in 2014 and the development of first learning materials took place in Illeret. Father Florian OSB contacted the Indian and German colleagues for MGML expertise and soon after the personnel cooperation with a small team from the University of Regensburg was started in 2015. Father Florian OSB decided to make use of support through personnel cooperation for the following areas:

– Support in developing ladders of learning for Literacy, Mathematics and Science
– Support in developing a teacher education programme
– Training of mobile teachers, a teacher trainer and an INES management
– Development, consultation and monitoring of the mobile school system
– Building an APME structure and reinforcing APME capacities
– Fundraising and public relation work in Germany

For the Kenyan-German project team, it would have not been appropriate to simply import and translate Indian or German ladders of learning and teaching curriculums. Instead, the INES team drew on the Indian expertise on how to transform teaching curriculums into ladders of learning and how to educate basically trained villagers to organise and support multi-grade and multi-level learning groups. The German expertise consists of developing flexible learning materials, setting up APME structures and tools, as well as, drawing upon

---

46 Since 2002, RIVER has closely cooperated with the University of Regensburg (Girg & Lichtinger) and the University of Würzburg (Müller), Germany. Research teams around Müller, Lichtinger and Girg initiated, student and teacher exchange programmes organised and project cooperation started (e.g. URC-INES (2015 – 2018); URC-PLCC (2015 – 2016). In 2015, a private school, the Pangani Lutheran Children's Centre (PLCC) in Nairobi developed first sequences of ladders of learning for various subjects in cooperation with the URC-PLCC team (Böcker, Girg, Lichtinger, Schaller & Würzle) of the University of Regensburg. Between 2015 and 2017 the two scientific assistants Schaller and Würzle regularly visited both projects to work with the local teams.

47 For more information see chapter *2.5 Fixed Schools for Mobile Communities* and chapter *4.1 Which Form of School Service Is Desired?*.

donations due to high interest from Germany. The INES Kenyan staff are experts of their language, customs, learning culture, curriculum and mobile lifestyle. Also, the analysis of existing concepts for mobile schools from Iran, Mongolia, Somalia and Kenya helps INES to fall back on common features which seem to complement or promise success.[48] Most importantly, the Daasanach pastoralists are experts at organising the livelihood of individuals and groups, as well as, shifting the production team and livestock in harsh, remote areas. The concept and setup of a mobile school system with rotating schools, teacher and/or learners can only be developed, tried out and reviewed by mobile pastoralists themselves. In summary, mutual development within the international setup of INES takes place drawing upon the knowledge, skills and abilities of all women and men involved in this international cooperation.

6.3 Participation and Partnership Approach

There are numerous principles, structures and models that support communication and promote successful cooperation. International cooperation projects such as INES aim at achieving intended positive developmental impacts on situations that have been assessed as negative. These positive impacts should be observable and measurable. In those international cooperation projects, which have achieved intended positive change, there is a broad range of principles and key concepts which can be observed. Terms such as participation, partnership and right-based approach, resource and impact-orientation, do-no-harm, empowerment and ownership are defined in the relevant literature. Experience has shown that these principles increase the effectiveness of cooperation projects, make efficient use of available resources and reduce costs (Sangmeister 2009).[49] Below, the focus lies on the principles of participation and partnership approach.

Participation. Participation generally means that people (population groups, organisations, associations, political parties) participate actively and decisively in all decisions that influence their lives. Therefore, it is important to involve all direct and indirect partners in decision-making processes to facilitate and promote sustainability. Participation and taking over of responsibility ultimately creates a breeding ground for sustainable development. Participation of people is achieved when the target groups and partners are empowered to articulate and assert their interests. It also means that men and women contribute their experiences and values to the joint development of international cooperation. In this way, they make the projects their own and assume responsibility for their success (ownership) (BMZ).

To empower local Daasanach men and women to lead mobile schools and to assume responsibility for the education of their children, INES offers a specialized teacher education programme with as little theory courses but as much practical support as possible.[50]

---

48 See chapter *3.What Are International Approaches to Mobile Education?*.
49 At the federal state level, for example, "donor and recipient countries" committed themselves for the first time to principles of impact-oriented development cooperation with the Paris Declaration on Aid Effectiveness and the Accra Agenda for Action in 2005. The Declaration sets out five core principles for increasing the effectiveness of development cooperation: Ownership, Alignment, Harmonisation, Managing of development results and Mutual Accountability (Organisation for Economic Co-operation and Development 2012).
50 For more information see chapter *12. How Does INES Empower Mobile Teachers?*.

Participation (empowerment and ownership) does not reflect a linear process. Every person and group of people goes through their own process of change. Some might go faster, some slower; some changes might be observed earlier, others later, other simultaneously (Kuijstermans 2019). A simple example of participation is the opening and closing assembly in the mobile schools. In interviews with Daasanach men, women and children it became clear that they not only wanted the school to teach literacy, numeracy and languages but also that the teachers create a culturally sensitive school atmosphere without fear. INES recommends that teachers perform certain rituals and routines in the opening and closing assemblies of their daily school schedule to create structure, security and a feeling of togetherness. During the first workshop with a group of Daasanach teacher trainees, appropriate rituals were determined and a schedule for the opening and closing assembly was developed.

The initial theory and planning of these opening and closing assemblies in the teacher education workshops are then practised by the teacher trainees during the workshop. They take turns copying the facilitators in their behaviour by welcoming the group into the workshop and also close the session with reflection and feedback. In the beginning, they may read out the steps of the assemblies as compiled in their manuals and act exactly according to the schedule. This first reactive behaviour slowly evolves to active behaviour when the teachers conduct the assembly without the schedule and in their own words. Proactive behaviour is overserved when the individual teacher has obviously internalized the schedule of the assembly, applies components according to the current circumstances and necessity and extends or shortens special elements depending on the current requirements. Ownership evolves when the teachers have started their own schools, can make adjustments, share their experiences and even assist colleagues in how to organise their assemblies.

Partnership approach. Partnership approach is a widely used term in international cooperation because it affirms the underlying principle that all progress begins and ends with people and is success through interaction, dialogue and mutual learning (Kuijstermans 2019). In order to find solutions for the common future it is essential for all men and women involved, locals and expatriates, to build trust in and solidarity with one another and to engage in mutual learning. The mutual attitude of partnership and communication skills, such as, active listening which is required to share knowledge and experience and to work towards new, creative and lasting solutions. As simple as it seems, partnership approach remains highly complex, because it demands women and men to look beyond cultural, educational, religious, political and social differences and, for example, talk openly about requirements, wishes and problems. Only in partnership-based communication can a common vision be developed, strategies planned and all available resources optimally integrated.

An open approach for all patrons of INES (members of the project implementation team of INES, direct partners, indirect partners, as well as, strategic partners) is an essential component of sustainable management. For this reason, INES places great value on building trust and a good communication culture (discussion rounds, feedback sessions, and teambuilding activities).

Personal Notes of the Authors

When people hear that we cooperate with local teachers in Northern Kenya, they often ask what German pedagogy we contribute. We then explain that the development of the INES project draws upon Indian, Kenyan and German ideas.

We are a learning community. This philosophy of Rama and Padmanabha Rao impressed both of us during our stays in South India. In the *Satellite Schools* of the Rishi Valley Institute of Educational Resources (RIVER), we saw that joyful, activity-based and individualized learning is possible. As German student teacher doing internships at RIVER, we were encouraged by the Indian couple to develop our own Milestones and activity pools, which RIVER then used to develop their next ladder of learning in our case was the first English ladder of learning. We came to learn from them and in the end, we were asked to share and teach. From our present position and experience with teacher training in the INES project, we are highly impressed by how Rama and Rao were able to break down the complexity of differentiation and individualization in such a way that teachers even without many years of experience could enable flexible learning for children of mixed ages and abilities and still keep the overview in the school.

As student teachers, we both had the great privilege of being a part of Dr. Ralf Girg's team which pursued the question: What are good schools? We were able to observe and reflect on teaching-learning processes in innovative schools such as the Ilztalschule, Germany. Through various internships, we were able to try out our work with ladders of learning not only in India but also in Tanzania and Germany. Being learners ourselves, we were asked to give impulses in workshops and seminars to other educators. We fondly remember workshops, for example, at the Massai Vision English Medium Academy in Tanzania, the Mittelschule Parsberg and the University of Dortmund in Germany, the Pangani Lutheran Children Centre in Kenya and, of course, at RIVER in India.

In the global debate on education, international organisations and experts from various backgrounds and countries exchange ideas and concepts on how to offer good learning settings to develop schools and to create sustainability in education. We profit so much from this global network of educators and the various forms of cooperation that we can only agree: *We are one learning community.*

People want big things to happen and very fast but they do not have the patience to go small steps. Perseverance is a measurement for success.

Edwin K Changamu, educational manager of INES

7. What Is the Plan of the INES Project?

The project landscape of INES covers a spectrum of national and international actors and partners among which are personnel from AGIAMONDO.[51] In this intercultural set up of the INES project implementation team, it is essential that everyone understood as a partner.[52] Since there are no examples that can be copied, finding educational solutions for the Daasanach pastoralist children in Northern Kenya is a process. Learning takes place through interaction and mutual questions between the persons involved. Change is a complex process undergoing several stages that are not linear. School development projects, such as INES, are by nature complex projects which involve many actors and factors that cannot be described linearly or mechanistically by a simple cause-effect model (Rolff, Buhren, Bank & Müller 2000).[53] Human interaction and learning is a circular way of development and therefore also needs a suitable circular concept for analysis, planning, monitoring and evaluation which is flexible to changes and further developments.

Since 2007, AGIAMONDO supports local partners in Civil Peace Service (CPS) programmes with *Managing Outcomes*, a methodology for outcome-focused analysis, planning, monitoring and evaluation (APME).[54] Managing Outcomes puts behavioural change people's actions and interactions at the core of the project's change process. In other words: sustainable change of negative situations (e.g. conflicts) only takes place when people start behaving differently. The following chapter makes brief references to analysis and planning tools of Managing Outcomes (Kuijstermans 2019) and describes the INES project.

7.1 Central Issue

After initial interviews and the problem analysis of the educational situation of the Daasanach pastoralist children in Northern Kenya, as depicted in the first part of this book, the foundation of an INES project plan was needed.[55] Since school development projects, such

---

51 AGIAMONDO (formerly Association for Development Cooperation AGEH) is a German Catholic agency which mainly develops and implements peace building programmes in cooperation with local partner organisations aimed at preventing violence and promoting peace in crisis zones and conflict regions. The international personnel of the agency supports its local partner organisations in over 60 countries.
52 The INES project implementation team comprises of Father Florian OSB, Edwin Changamu, Eveline Momanyi and Bonaya Yierar as permanent local staff, Goosh Kwanjang, Daniel Losit, Lydia Lokademo, Rose Hitler and Munan Long'ayie as temporary workers, Theresa Schaller and Ruth Würzle as expatriate staff and consultants and Bärbel Löffler is a senior volunteer (as of 2019).
53 School development and consulting always includes personnel, teaching and organisational development (Rolff, Buhren, Bank & Müller 2000).
54 Managing Outcomes is based on Outcome Mapping, a methodology developed by the International Development Research Centre in Ottawa, Canada with a manual provided by Earl, Carden and Smutylo (2001). However, Managing Outcomes is adapted to the special needs of international partners with special attention to the aspect of Personnel Cooperation. The editorial responsibility lies with Kuijstermans, while contributions were also made by Bash-Taqi, Blenig, Irmscher, Laker, Lombo, Ngassa, Nkurunziza, Pacheco, Picott, Pino, Pires, Prieto, Sandouka and Willmutz.
55 The problem analysis in the first part of this book focuses on the complex issue of education provision for pastoralist children (chapter 2), how many Daasanach pastoralist children visit a school and/or want an alternative system with mobile schools (chapter 2 and chapter 4) and what experiences and expectations Daasanach girls, boys, men and women have in regard to education (chapter 4). The specific information was

as INES, are part of an interconnected system of actors, factors and relationships. Not only are different ideas for desired outcomes apparent but also the project, as such, influences this system and is influenced by it. The methodology of Managing Outcomes describes this as an inherent complexity of change (Kuijstermans 2019). The INES project implementation team needed to collect and define the desired behavioural changes of those targeted by the educational system. In interviews with Daasanach parents and INES team members in 2017, 2018, 2019, as well as, in internal INES leadership meetings, these questions were addressed and the desired change of behaviour of the direct partners (mobile teachers) was formulated.

The approach of Managing Outcomes is based on the premise that sustainable behavioural change only happens when people experience that their behavioural change has a positive impact on themselves and their environment. In the formulations of the central issue of INES, it was a challenge to move from a problem-oriented approach (e.g. reduction of the marginalization of pastoralist children through basic education) to a more solution-oriented approach that describes behavioural changes of the pastoralist communities, mobile teachers and school children. This change from perspective and formulation was necessary for the whole INES project implementation team because it helped to look not only at the project's (limited) resources, inputs and the INES team's activities but first and foremost at the long-term behavioural changes of the direct and indirect partners.[56]

In summary, the central issue of INES, as depicted in the first part of this book, is: The remote region of the Daasanach pastoralists and their mobile lifestyle pose great challenges to the conventional, settled system of formal education with its fixed school buildings.[57] Daasanach pastoralist want mobile schools which offer their children in Northern Kenya realistic access to basic education. The mobile schools need to be run by trained mobile community members and the children need a flexible system which allows them to live with their family, attend school and support their family with livestock production.

7.2 Forces and Actors

The problem analysis focuses on the views and perspectives of Daasanach women, men and children who are concerned about the central issue, as well as, the conventional, settled system of formal education. It is important that the problem analysis also identifies the key factors and actors through which INES hopes to positively influence the central issue. The tabular overview (*Forces and Actors of INES*) provides a brief insight into the driving and restraining forces as well as the key actors of INES. Driving forces are actors and factors that already have a positive influence on the central issue while restraining forces describe aspects and/or actors, which cause problems or work against the central issue. An integral part of the problem analysis is to assess the capacity and strength, as well as, areas for improvement of

---

collected with two different methods (surveys and interviews).
56 INES's direct partners are the mobile teachers, the indirect partners are the Daasanach communities (elders and parents) and the (future) learners. Read more in *7.4 Partner Landscape*.
57 The starting point of any project is a specific issue an organisation wants to address by creating Change through cooperation with stakeholders. Therefore, according to Managing Outcomes, the first step of the analysis stage is to agree on this central issue. The central issue comes from various sources and is linked to the experiences an organisation has had from working in similar situations.

the organisation to contribute to the central issue.[58] In the beginning, the small INES project implementation team analysed their capacities and strengths and chose to make use of support through personnel cooperation with members of the Chair of Education of the University of Regensburg.

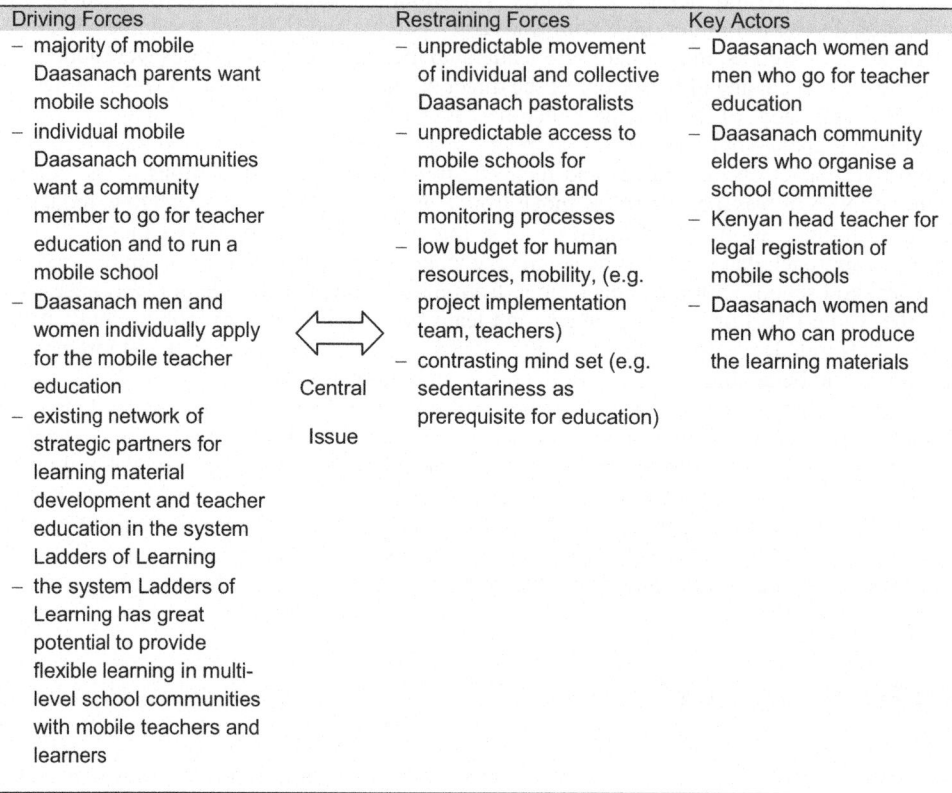

Driving Forces	Restraining Forces	Key Actors
– majority of mobile Daasanach parents want mobile schools – individual mobile Daasanach communities want a community member to go for teacher education and to run a mobile school – Daasanach men and women individually apply for the mobile teacher education – existing network of strategic partners for learning material development and teacher education in the system Ladders of Learning – the system Ladders of Learning has great potential to provide flexible learning in multi-level school communities with mobile teachers and learners	– unpredictable movement of individual and collective Daasanach pastoralists – unpredictable access to mobile schools for implementation and monitoring processes – low budget for human resources, mobility, (e.g. project implementation team, teachers) – contrasting mind set (e.g. sedentariness as prerequisite for education)	– Daasanach women and men who go for teacher education – Daasanach community elders who organise a school committee – Kenyan head teacher for legal registration of mobile schools – Daasanach women and men who can produce the learning materials

Fig. 7.1: Forces and Actors of INES (Source: own illustration).

7.3 Project Vision and Mission

The project vision represents the ideal long-term changes that should be contributed to and it focuses on the central issue. It describes concrete and visible changes, describes both the general situation, as well as, changes in the behaviour of women and men or groups affected by the central issue. According to Managing Outcomes, the project vision looks at the central

---

58 Managing Outcomes suggests the following categories to assess the strengths and capacities of an organisation: (1) Knowledge and experience of the organisation, (2) Organisational structure & culture, (3) Access to people in the communities, (4) Resources of the organisation, (5) Networking and communication and (6) Learning as organisation (Kuijstermans 2019).

issue beyond the timeframe of the project.[59] In several interviews with Daasanach men, women and children and in internal meetings of the project implementation team, long-term changes and goals of the INES project where collected.

By 2027, their own children will be teachers and their own children will not be separated from them. By 2027, we should have the first graduates of the INES system who will make the INES system and work suitable.
Edwin K. Changamu, pedagogical manager of INES

The answers were compiled, evaluated and then a common vision was formulated:

Project Vision of INES. Daasanach pastoralist children live and shift with their mobile families, support in the family in livestock production and participate in educational activities in the mobile schools. Daasanach men and women, who are mobile pastoralists themselves, visit the INES mobile teacher education programme and gradually expand with various subject ladders of learning in their mobile schools. The mobile Daasanach communities form a school committee and ensure fair participation of children, as well as, parents in school administration decision making processes. The Kenyan government registers the mobile teachers, supports with administration, teacher salaries and school meals and offers mobile learners access to national exams in registered governmental schools.

Secondly, the project mission describes how the organisation contributes to the vision and defines which resources the organisation has at its disposal. The project mission details working areas that will be focused on, where the project will be implemented and which women and men the project will work with to achieve its desired outcomes (Kuijstermans 2019).

Project Mission of INES. In order to contribute to the project vision, INES develops ladders of learning for pre-school (Introduction), literacy (Daasanach), Mathematics, as well as, Environmental, Religious, Hygiene and Nutrition Activities (Life Studies) and produces first sets of materials. INES develops additional supportive tools for the learning environment and teaching practises (daily schedules, organisers, registers, assessment forms, teaching aids etc.). INES develops teacher education modules and facilitates workshops for mobile teachers in Illeret. Five mobile communities chose women and men who will be trained and supported to start and run mobile schools in their communities. INES will collaborate with the local elders and the five mobile school committees to participate in this piloting phase of a mobile school system for pastoralists. INES will offer information and observation possibilities for other educational stakeholders to support the implementation in other projects of pastoralist education.

---

59 Managing Outcomes defines the following characteristics of a project vision: "The project vision is an ideal. The project vision is long-term and describes changes that the project is contributing to beyond the timeframe of the project. The project vision identifies observable conditions relating to problems or conflicts that women and men would like to see changed. The project vision describes the ideal and improved lives for those women and men affected by the Central Issue" (Kuijstermans 2019: 30).

7.4 Partner Landscape

Besides the project implementation team, various other actors support INES. Since the relationship with these individuals, groups and organisations is one of giving and receiving Managing Outcomes refers to the actors as partners. Figure 7.2 shows the partner landscape of INES. Each of these partners has a specific role and function in the project. Based on the role they play in the project, three different types of partners can be identified: Direct, indirect and strategic partners.[60]

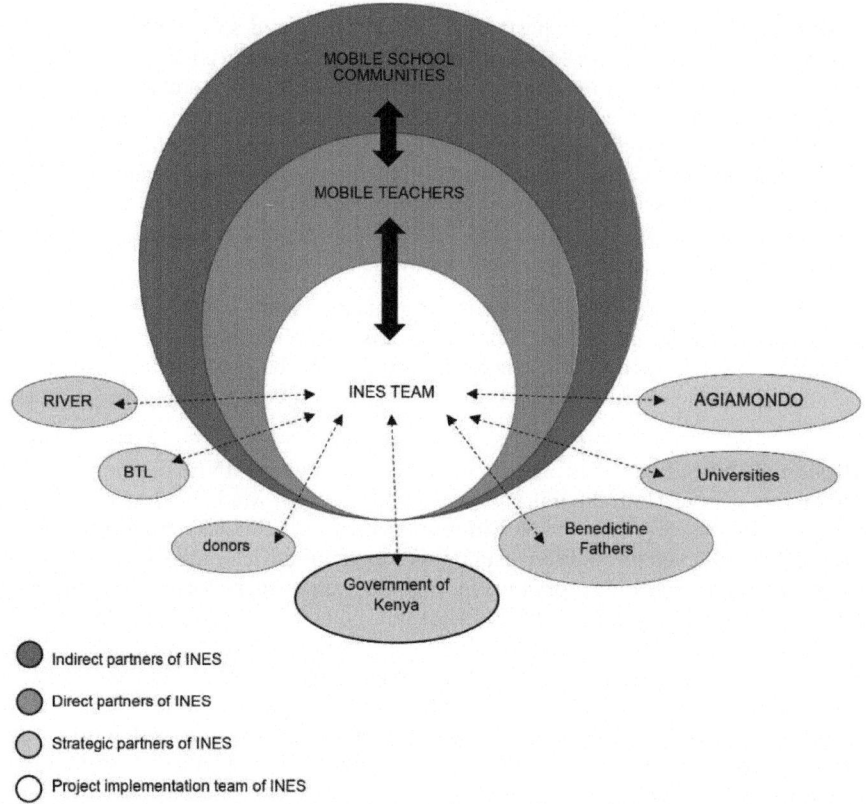

Fig. 7.2: Partner landscape of INES (Source: own illustration).

---

60 Indirect partners are those women, men or groups who are affected by the central issue the project is dealing with and those who experience the change to which the project contributes to. However, the project cannot influence them, or all of them, directly. Direct Partners are the women, men, groups or organisations the project interacts with directly to contribute to a change in the situation of the indirect partners. Strategic Partners are organisations or individuals that share, or already contribute to, the project mission and/or vision. For this reason, the organisation interacts and cooperates with them while the project is being implemented (Kuijstermans 2019).

7.5 Desired Outcome and Progress Markers

Desired outcomes of a project ideally describe behavioural changes that enable a direct partner to influence an indirect partner. In the context of INES, the desired outcomes refer to the desirable and possible behavioural changes of the mobile teachers that consequently influence their learners and mobile school communities. In practice, these behavioural changes are presented, addressed and discussed in the teacher education programme of INES. It is always the aim of the facilitated teacher education workshops that the mobile teachers understand, experience and agree upon how they can offer a fearless and well prepared learning environment for their learners and how they can support them in their individual learning processes. INES uses monitoring and observation tools, such as observation sheets, personal interviews with the teachers and analysis of photographs and films to assess these behavioural changes of the teachers.

Progress markers describe the change process that leads to the behavioural change described in the desired outcome. They allow us to measure the progress of the change process of a single direct partner towards the desired outcome. This can be a direct partner's behavioural change, actions, relationships and interactions. Progress markers are a tool to describe and monitor the change process over time and the progress towards the desired outcome. Regular reviews subsequently allow for possible changes in the project planning, inputs and activities. Managing Outcomes suggests to divide each progress marker into three phases: 1) expect to see/reactive behaviour; 2) like to see/active behaviour; 3) love to see/proactive behaviour[61]

As mentioned above, INES uses observation tools which refer to the desired behavioural changes of the mobile teachers. Since the three phases and the position of the progress markers do not reflect a linear process, INES needs to look at each teacher individually in her or his own process of change. INES has developed observation sheets, which state progress markers in the behavioural change of the mobile teachers, one for the school start (with new learners) and one for daily school (with regular learners). Since the teacher always begins and ends the school day with an assembly, the observation questions on the teacher's behaviour are the same, whereas, the questions on the introduction phase and learning ladder time are different. Weekly observations provide the basis for the feedback talks together with the teachers, planning sessions of future teacher education workshops and project internal monitoring and evaluation talks.

---

61 "The first progress markers [expect to see] show early responses to the project. They capture initial engagement, or participation in activities. Direct partners participate in activities initiated by the organisation as part of the project and which contribute towards the desired outcome. The next phase [like to see] contains progress markers showing changes relating to first engagement by the direct partner, or learning or commitment towards the desired outcome. The last phase [love to see] describes progress markers that demonstrate the direct partner taking initiative, sharing expertise or assisting others in reaching the desired outcome. This is where sustainability of the change becomes visible" (Kuijstermans 2019: 47).

7.6 Strategy Map and Tasks

The last steps in the project planning stages are developing a strategy map, defining tasks and responsibilities. The strategy map is an instrument that ideally shows the relationship between different strategies and fields of work and how they complement and relate to each other. This implies a close review of progress markers, partner landscape, factors and actors that could have a negative influence and the organisational capacities. Tasks and responsibilities refer to the project implantation team and therefore also specifies the role of personnel cooperation and their added value (if this is the case in a project).

SCHOOL	MATERIAL	TEACHER	ORGANISATION
1. Mobile School Development − review of mobile school experiences worldwide − development and revision of a mobile school system with ladders of learning − life-related and cultural know-how of the mobile pastoralists	**1. Learning Material Development** − review of Kenyan lower primary school curriculum and school books − development and revision of subject ladders of learning, learning materials and bags	**1. Teacher Curriculum Work** − review of Kenyan ECD teacher curriculum and college books − development and revision of modularized teacher education and teaching aids	**1. Analysis Planning Monitoring Evaluation** − building an APME structure and reinforcing APME capacities in the organisation
2. Mobile School Foundation − building mobile community learning groups and school committees − concept for mobile school start − start of mobile schools	**2. Learning Material Production** − purchasing of local and imported raw materials − training for local learning material production − large scale local production of learning materials with printing, cutting, laminating, binding, tailoring, carpeting, crafting of learning materials and material bags	**2. Teacher Education** − foundation of teacher education centre − modularized qualification of mobile teachers in the form of practical school studies (didactically reduced theory, practice, reflection)	**2. Leadership** − training of local organisational management: communication, APME structure, pedagogical concept, quality of learning materials − training of local teacher educators: communication, teaching didactics, mobile school system, content of ladders of learning − training of local material developer
3. Mobile School Routine − observation and assessment of learners and school routine	**3. Learning Material Logistics** − learning material service	**3. Teacher Supervision** − observation of and feedback for mobile school teachers	**3. Governance** − building local organisational management − building local school administration structures
4. Monitoring & Evaluation	**4. Monitoring & Evaluation**	**4. Monitoring & Evaluation**	**4. Monitoring & Evaluation**

Fig. 7.3: INES strategy map with the four working fields (Source: own illustration).

Figure 7.3 shows a strategic map of the four working areas of INES (school, material, teacher, organisation) and the tasks which generate and grow within these fields. Since INES has included personnel cooperation, the tasks and responsibilities of INES were developed together with input from all project implementation team members and also redefined during the project years. A clear advantage of this step is that a discussion on the tasks and responsibilities of the project implementation team, including the tasks and responsibilities of personnel cooperation, helps to create a shared understanding between all those involved.

Personal Notes of the Authors

Our usual working days in Illeret are filled to the brim with appointments, tasks and travelling and therefore it is often a great challenge to pause and reflect. We have learned, however, that it is these moments that lead to ideas and suggestions, respond to challenges and in general improve the way INES is implemented. Of course, this happens when we write our reports, but most importantly, we particularly cherish the "leadership sessions" with Edwin Changamu, where we break from the day's demands, sit together and reflect on the past work. We reflect to ensure our activities have served those women and men which INES has been designed to support. We are grateful for the past years of mutual learning, the talk rounds where we share knowledge and experience and encourage each other to continue towards new and lasting solutions.

Part III Learning System and Teacher Education

Today, I learned there is a journey of learning.

Neete Anyder, learner in Bonaya's INES school

8. What Is the System Ladders of Learning About?

The starting point of the system Ladders of Learning is the idea of activity-oriented learning. The learners – not the teacher – organise their learning process with the help of so-called ladders of learning. When the curriculum and lesson plans of a given subject are transformed into activities and learning plans, learners are empowered to organise their own learning process.

The visualization of this learning plan is called a ladder of learning. With an elaborate logo and colour system the sequence of activities on this learning plan, guide the pupils through the learning process of one or several forms of a subject. In the learning system, learners of multiple grades and levels meet in a well-prepared learning environment (with one or more ladders of learning) and work at their own pace. They do the activities either alone, with a partner, in a group or with the teacher – depending on the didactical design of the given activity. An integrated help system with self-evaluations and feedback secures the self-regulated learning progress and achievement of each learner.

The natural heterogeneity of learning groups and the widespread phenomenon of dropouts is no longer an insurmountable problem for schools, because the learning environment is systematically, methodically and materially so well equipped that it allows learners to interrupt and resume their learning according to their personal need.

The learning process is no longer bound to the teacher alone because the ladders of learning are the guardrails to which the learners can orientate on their learning path. All learners go step-by-step in their own pace, so they can step in and out without missing subject matters, which in turn often leads to the high dropout rates in conventional schools around the globe. In India, children might have to interrupt schooling for some weeks due to harvesting whereas, in Kenya, children might have to resume schooling to support livestock production. Finally, it is entirely normal that all over the world, some children simply need more time for learning than their schoolmates need. For whatever reason, the reality of heterogeneity in schools calls for learning opportunities that adequately address the diversity of children and consistently provide heterogeneous learning opportunities.

The system Ladders of Learning not only allows multi-grade and multi-level pupils to learn together but also allows teachers to spend less time teaching and more time supporting their learners individually. The learning system therefore also offers new teaching opportunities. Ladders of learning redeem the teacher of the conventional task of constant instruction. Instead, teachers are organisers of the learning environment; they can focus on being a role model and supporter of the individual learners.

8.1 Ladders of Learning Come from India

Fig. 8.1: Classroom of the MGML-school Sundravanam, Andhra Pradesh, India (Source: Ruth Würzle).

This approach is not new. In the 1980s, an Indian teacher couple developed the MultiGradeMultiLevel-Methodology with its ladders of learning. The learning system brakes with traditional conventions of teacher-centred instruction and thinks the learning process from the individual learner's point of view. With a child-friendly pedagogy – the motto is *the child in the driver's seat* – learning is initiated through joyful, meaningful, manageable and small activities, which are systematically structured with colours, symbols and numbers.[62]

---

[62] As described in the picture of the learner in the driver's seat of a car, the role of the teacher is less important (even though vital). Depending on the learner and the given situation, the teacher either drives along as a passenger, simply accompanying and experiencing the development of the pupil. A second possible role could be that of a driving instructor, providing the learner with skills and supporting the pupil during exercises. Finally, the teacher's task could also be to guides the learner from outside the car – literally handing over the whole responsibility to the learner, yet supporting with guidelines and necessary information for the pupil to drive on (Lichtinger & Höldrich 2016).

Padmanabha and Rama Rao, today the chief executives of the Rishi Valley Institute for Educational Resources (RIVER), started by deconstructing the national curriculum and transforming the teaching plans into learning plans.[63] Teacher instructions and textbook activities were rearranged with a series of graded cards, pictorial graphics and multisensory learning materials. A well thought-out symbol and colour system guides the pupils within the learning environment of grade ladders, material shelves, learning zones, graded cards, multisensory materials and activity types.

Through collaborations with distinguished educators, writers and artists, RIVER has developed a comprehensive educational programme for primary schools up to class 5. Each subject provides an assortment of three-dimensional learning aids, a large collection of illustrated learning cards and a Teacher's Manual (Rishi Valley Education Centre 1999).

Fig. 8.2: Indian ladders of learning; learners and teacher in MGML-school Sundravanam, Andhra Pradesh, India (Source: Ruth Würzle).

Design and concept of the numerous national and international adaptions may vary strongly depending on the culture of the individual country or region, the requirements of subject, age group and school type. The flexibility of the field-tested system explains the popularity of the MGML-Methodology with its ladders of learning around the globe at times when there is a call for new learning opportunities that adequately match the diversity of children, adolescents and adults and consistently offer heterogeneous learning opportunities.

---

63 Rishi Valley Institute for Educational Resources (RIVER) is the teacher training and resource development wing of Rishi Valley Rural Education Centre (REC) which also runs a residential Middle School for students from the immediate neighbourhood and *Satellite Schools* which are located in nearby hamlets. In the beginning, there were 16 of these *Satellite Schools*. To date, there are seven and two pre-schools run by RIVER. RIVER calls the series of cards and the ladder of learning *School in a Box*. In classrooms, these are supplemented with puppetry, books and study of village life and the natural environment.

8.2 Mobile School Concept with the System Ladders of Learning

The Kenyan mobile schools with the system Ladders of Learning rely on the highly flexible methodology of MGML with its ladders of learning, milestones and activities, as well as its concept of an integrated support system. Nevertheless, a comparison of the Indian *Satellite Schools* with the Kenyan mobile schools shows that concept and appearance are quite different due to the respective requirements of the cultural contexts. As the rural population of Andhra Pradesh, India live sedentarily and mainly of agriculture, schooling is meanwhile offered in permanent buildings, whereas the Daasanach pastoralists, who are constantly on the move, require mobile schools which move with the learners and their communities. This difference affects on the one hand the possible furniture of the school and the amount of learning materials, and, on the other hand, the steadiness of pupil enrolment. Since the rural population in southern India are mainly day workers for landlords, the composition of pupils in the *Satellite Schools* is quite stable. Pastoral production in Northern Kenya, however, forces the Daasanach families to migrate regularly, which not only requires school mobility but also learners' mobility. The learners have to be able to switch between mobile schools as well as leave and (re)enter mobile schools, whenever the pastoralist production team splits and/or (re)joins.

Furthermore, language, culture and the guidelines of the national curricula require the *Satellite Schools* in India and the mobile schools in Kenya to focus on different subject matters and to choose a well-balanced selection of suitable activities types and materials. The system Ladders of Learning takes into account all dimensions of learning at the same time: age and stage of development, construction and co-construction, the associated different learning pathways, activation of all senses, action orientation, mimesis and own creativity, both halves of the brain, corporeality and performativity, tension and relaxation, structure and freedom. In the following chapters, the mobile school concept with the system Ladders of Learning is explained in detail. Even though all components are closely linked to each other, the complex system is clustered into the following topics and components for the sake of clarity and legibility:

- (de)construction of learning contents
- support system for the learning and teaching practice
- daily school schedule
- learning space
- monitoring tools

8.3 (De)Construction of Learning Contents

The major rethink and achievement of the system Ladders of Learning is that conventional teaching and lesson plans are converted into learning plans. From an educator's point of view, ladders of learning break the annual or biennial teaching curriculum of a subject down into a learning curriculum for pupils. (De)Construction of learning contents means for the education providers to analyse the (national) curriculum and conventional textbooks of a given subject and level and to (re)arrange the existent tasks into a systematized learning plan.

The development of ladders of learning is comparable to the challenges and processes of school textbook providers. Since learning is always about constructing knowledge for oneself, sometimes, conventional, deductive and teacher-centred approaches, as given in the lesson plans and exercise books, need to be changed.[64] Learners need to start their construction process where they are. The most important and pervasive question is what learners need to construct an own understanding of a given subject matter and in how far the content is or can become of significance for the learners.

The learning system pays close attention to ensure that learning impulses are primarily based on life-world phenomena, problems or questions, to which the learners have to find answers, generate or check hypotheses. It does not make sense to offer Daasanach children a picture of an apple to teach them the initial sound and grapheme A as most Daasanach children have never eaten nor seen an apple. For this reason, ladders of learning offer inductive learning processes.

Fig. 8.3: Two Daasanach girls are attaching their nametags on the Introduction ladder of learning (Source: Ruth Würzle).

The providers of ladders of learning often need to delete activity suggestions from the national textbooks and replace them with new, more appropriate ones. The MGML postulate *the child in the driver's seat,* which was coined by Padmanabha and Rama Rao, understands pupils and also teachers as autonomous and self-responsible. In the sense of constructivism,

---

64 Constructivism (largely by Jean Piaget (1896 - 1980) and Lev Vygotsky (1896 - 1934)) suggests that learning is an active process. When knowledge is presented it has to be constructed in a social and emotional context first and is then appropriated by individuals. Learners compare their version of the truth with that of the instructor and fellow learners to get to a new, socially tested version of truth (Reich 2012).

learners steer their own learning processes, educate themselves and exploits the opportunities provided for this purpose. Ladders of learning offer the learners an activity plan, which they follow in their own pace. Wherever possible, variations of construction processes are offered to address various learning types. The learners may decide upon how much time they want to spend with a given topic according to their abilities and interest.

Ladders of Learning. In the mobile schools of INES, ladders of learning are the largest structuring unit of the learning system. With an elaborate logo and colour system the ladders of learning display the sequence of activities, which guide the pupils through the learning process of one or more forms of a subject or subjects of a grade. In India, there are four ladders of learning in four colours for the first four grades. Hereby, each of the colourful ladders of learning covers the subject matters of Languages and Mathematics. INES constructs ladders of learning for each subject and assorts the colours to a subject – Introduction: grey; Daasanach: red; Mathematics: blue; Life Studies: yellow. A ladder of learning in INES can cover all subtopics of a subject class (e.g. number concept, arithmetical operations, measurements and geometry in Mathematics Class 1) or it can cover two grades of a subject (e.g. literacy acquisition in Mother Tongue Class 1 and 2).[65]

Fig. 8.4: Indian systemic ladder of learning for EVS (RIVER) (Source: Ruth Würzle); Linear ladder of learning for preschool in Northern Kenya (INES) (Source: own illustration).

---

65 There are also possible larger structural variations. The Ilztalschule, a German primary school, uses a Learning Atlas to display all subject matters of all primary school levels and subjects. The Learning Atlas of the Ilztalschule helps learners and educators to comprehend what the primary education is about and gives freedom to develop apt learning plans for each child. (For more information: www.ilztalschule.de) It is also possible to combine several ladders of learning into a Learning Landscape. Some German primary schools use the so-called *Buchstabenberge* (literally letter mountains) as a Ladder of Learning for literacy acquisition in Class 1 and 2. The *Buchstabenberge*, however, is one of three ladders of learning for the subject German in the primary school. The so-called German learning landscape for the Primary School also includes a Ladder of Learning called *Königreich der Wörter* (literally kingdom of words) as well as *Lesewiesen* (lit. reading pastures). (For more information: Lichtinger & Höldrich 2016).

Regardless of whether in India, Kenya or Germany, ladders of learning have a starting point (somewhere down below) and guide the learners upwards towards a definite end.[66] Since the learning path is finite, pupils are constantly aware, where they are, how far they have come and how far the journey is ahead of them. Generally, ladders of learning can be of two types: linear or systemic. Linear ladders of learning guide the pupils on a linear learning path. The learners set the pace while the sequence of activities is clearly defined. A systemic ladder of learning on the other hand displays small, interconnected units that represent epoch-like topics.[67] The next smaller (de)construction units in a ladder of learning are milestones.

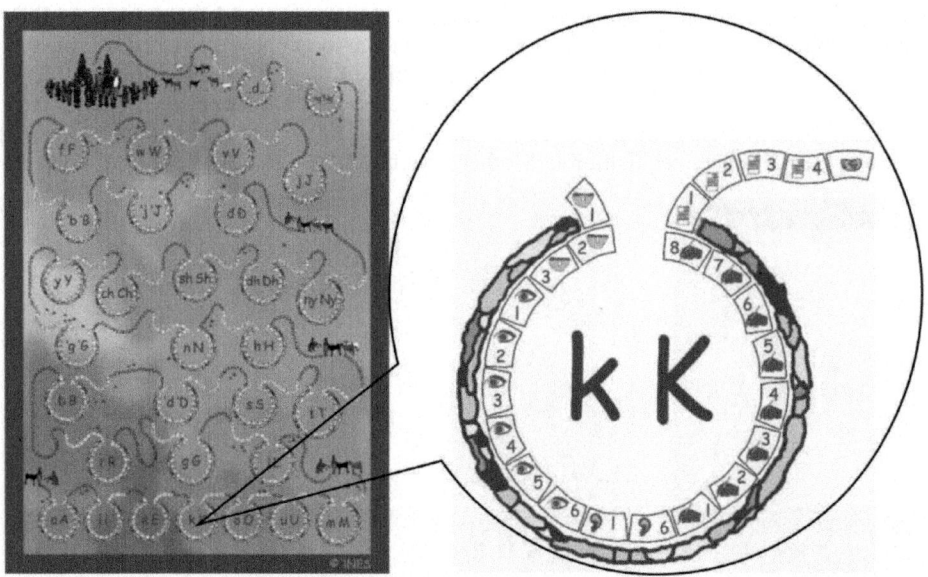

Fig. 8.5: Linear arrangement of the milestones in the INES Daasanach ladder of learning; Linear arrangement of the activities in the milestone kK of this ladder of learning (Source: own illustration).

Milestones. Milestones are self-contained, content related sequences or units of a topic on a ladder of learning. A milestone sequence in the mobile schools in Kenya is divided into introduction, reinforcement and evaluation activities. The Indian milestones offer further remedial and reinforcement activities after the evaluation. With the integrated evaluation, which are always teacher-based, the milestone materials offer adequate feedback on the learning process of each learner. Depending on the learning outcome in the evaluation, respective reinforcement activities are chosen as remedial activities, before the learner

---

66 The Introduction ladder of learning of INES has an exceptional character: It has a clear starting point at the lower left corner. However, the learning path has no definite end but a junction with two paths. One leading out of the ladder of learning and one returning to the starting point. For more information see chapter *9.2 Linear Structure of the Ladder of Learning*.
67 RIVER uses liner ladders of learning for Languages and Mathematics, systemic ladders of learning for EVS (Environmental Studies) and mixed milestone arrangements for English.

proceeds to the next milestone. Each of these activity phases within a milestone are realised by different activities types, which are explained in more detail in chapter 9 and 10, which focus on the Introduction and the Daasanach ladder of learning.

Care is taken that milestones offer inductive learning. The level of abstraction increases within the milestones – learners are lead from the known to the unknown, from the concrete to the abstract. The learners are given tasks such as analysing real situations or life-oriented stories. Many activity types, especially in the early stages, involve all senses, are experimental and thus provoke the learners to provide and test hypothesis. If necessary, some milestone types also follow simple structures such as teacher demonstration in the beginning and subsequent practices thereafter.

As with the sequence of milestones on the ladder of learning, also the activities in a milestone can be structured linearly or systemically, leaving the learner subject-related larger and smaller freedoms of choice. In India, the systemic EVS (Environmental Studies) ladder of learning arranges the activities within a milestone also systemically. There is a clear introduction to an EVS-related topic, but then the learners chose, which activities they want to do and also in which order (Müller, Lichtinger & Girg 2015). For English, RIVER has chosen mixed forms of arranging the activities in a milestone – the activities within the milestone allow the learners to choose between two possible paths to achieve the evaluation.

The activities in all milestones of the Introduction and the Daasanach ladder of learning are arranged linearly, even if the design of each milestone draws an almost circle, with the milestone logo in the centre. Each milestone has a clear beginning and end. The path between the milestones is indicated through footprints. For the sake of simplicity and concerning unexperienced young children in the mobile schools as well as the relatedness-oriented background of the Daasanach, INES has previously only developed milestones, which offer a linear arrangement of activities within the milestone, just as the milestones on the ladder of learning are also arranged linearly.

Activities. All learners follow the learning path from one activity to the next and after successfully passing through all activities of one milestone they follow the path to the next milestone. In the Kenyan ladders of learning, each activity is visualized by a white field with a logo and a number. Each of these steps induces specific learning materials and a specific task. It is up to the individual learners, how much time they need and want to spend for each of the materialized activities.

The more senses are involved in playing and learning, the more valuable and intense is the experience. While some perceive and learn more through perception, others prefer listening. Because human beings perceive differently, there are also different types of learning. Nevertheless, it can be said generally that the proportion of what has been learned increases when more senses are involved in the learning process.[68] Thus, care is taken that the learning tasks activate as many senses as possible and that they have a playful character. Since games usually involve many senses, human beings learn much faster through playing. Learning playfully is not only easier it is also much more fun and more successful. In the system Ladders of Learning each activity should meet the following five criteria.

---

68 According to the rule of thumb, approximately 10% of what is read can be kept, the rest is forgotten. However, if something is heard and seen, the kept content increases to about 50%. When listening and seeing is additionally combined with action, the chance of really learning and remembering something lies at 90% (Lübben-Chambí & Jackson 2001).

They should...

- allow active handling of a learning aspect;
- be manageable, so possible without much further guidance by a teacher;
- be meaningful because they are created from the life context of the learner or refer to it;
- be joyful to support learning motivation;
- be small and appropriate according to the ability of concentration of the age group. Small also implies that the process of abstraction should be small enough to allow complete understanding.

Since there is a large pool of demonstrably good learning activities worldwide, the system Ladders of Learning does not claim to have invented all types of activities. The Indian and Kenyan ladders of learning implement appropriate activity types and adapt them to age, culture and the given technical and organisational preconditions of the educational provider. It is particularly motivating for the children if they already know activity types from their free play. Therefore, INES consciously integrates traditional Daasanach songs, rhythmic clapping and game forms such as a wide range of skill and sorting exercises with pebbles and sand. During the development process of the learning materials, INES not only tests the activity types with particular respect to the given culture but also to compatibility in the context of mobile schools of Kenyan savannah. Besides the criteria small, manageable, meaningful, joyful and active, the following criteria also have to be taken into account with regard to the learning materials:

- extreme robustness
- lightness
- reusability
- local manufacturability

8.4 Support System for Learning and Teaching

When learners work mostly individually in open learning arrangements, they depend – to a varying degree – on support. Therefore, the system Ladders of Learning needs an integrated support system to ensure that learner can solve learning activities on their own yet know where and how to get support if necessary. The support system relies on three different components: firstly, the teacher helps single learners or a group, or secondly, learners help themselves by using additional or explanatory materials, or thirdly, learners help each other (Bohl 2010). To relieve the teacher of permanent instruction, various support tools are integrated into the system Ladders of Learning. Colours, logos and numbers systematize the series connection of activities and empower the learners to understand the instruction on the given ladder of learning as well as the activity cards. The symbols direct the learners to the required learning materials in the material pool and into the assigned learning cooperation, which happens in a specified learning zone. Learning and teaching practice happens in various social forms, thus a form of cooperative learning takes place. The provision of solutions enable learners to regulate their learning process more autonomously and trains them to take over responsibility for themselves.

Colour, Logo and Number System. In the Indian MGML-Methodology as well as its adaptations in the Kenyan mobile schools, individual learning materials induce the learning and teaching activities. The learning materials are mainly cards but also various three-dimensional learning materials are incorporated. Each activity with its prerequisite learning materials carries a unique logo and number and is associated with a colour. All materials are labelled with the colour, logo and number system to assure order and directions for work. Children can read logos and colours from an early age (numbers are initially also only read as symbols) and with a little practice can organise their learning process autonomously.

Each learning system can choose its own system of colours and logos. As explained in chapter 8.2, the Satellite Schools of RIVER use colours to show the grade, whereas animal logos are associated with a specific activity type of a subject. Hereby, mammals are assigned to Telugu (Language), birds to Mathematics and insects to environmental studies. This allows the Indian ladders of learning to incorporate milestones for Languages and Mathematics into one grade. In Kenya, each subject receives a colour:

- Preschool – grey
- Daasanach – red
- Mathematics – blue
- Life Studies – yellow
- Swahili – purple
- English – pink

In India, the learners have to look up which activity type is done in which social form, whereas, in Kenya, each activity and material card carries one of the four social form logos.[69] In the INES mobile schools, each milestone is also given a logo, which hints at the content of this learning phase. This supports the arrangement of learning materials and allows that the learning materials of one milestone are stored in a unique bag of the mobile schools. In the mobile schools in Kenya, each activity of a given subject has a unique logo and a number.

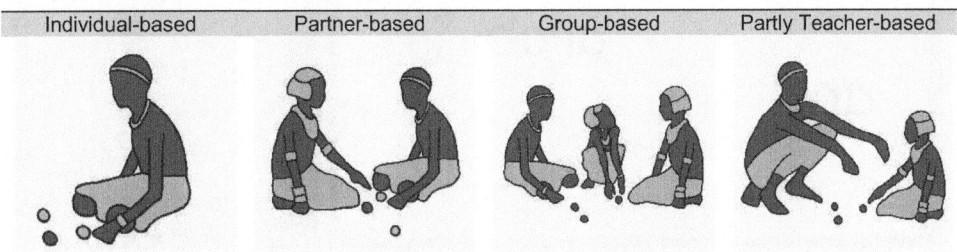

Fig. 8.6: The activities are realised in one of the four social forms (Source: own illustration).

Together with the milestone logo, this system allows learners to redo activity types for each milestone even though the subject matter, content and level increases with each activity. The learning activity *il* 5 (eye 5) of the Daasanach ladder of learning, for example, asks the learners to place stones on the newly learned letter (e.g. milestone aA). In the following milestones, learning activity *il* 5 (eye 5) always asks the learners to do the same task, however, focusing on the respective letter of the given milestone.[70]

---

69 All logos within INES are designed by Ruth Würzle.
70 A detailed explanation of the colour, logo and number system and how they are used in the Introduction and the Daasanach ladder of learning can be found in chapter 9 and 10.

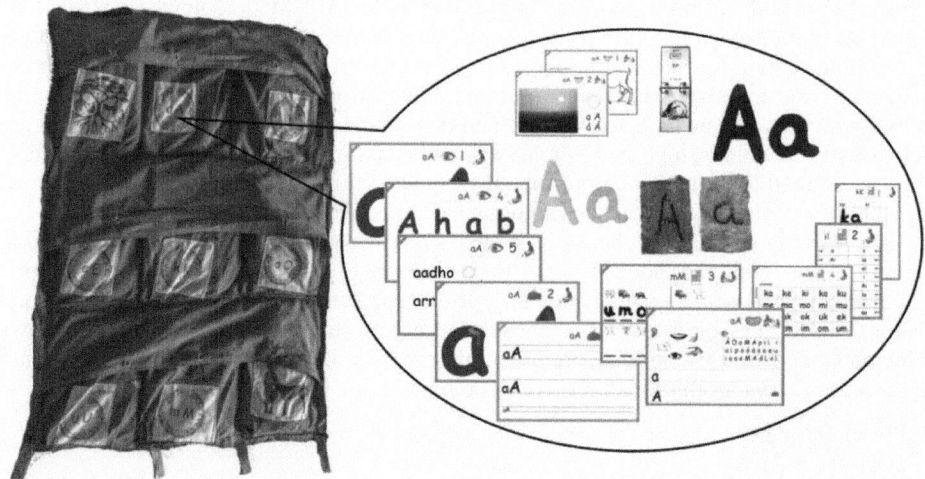

Fig. 8.7: The Daasanach bags have compartments for each milestone, which carry the milestone materials (Source: own illustration).

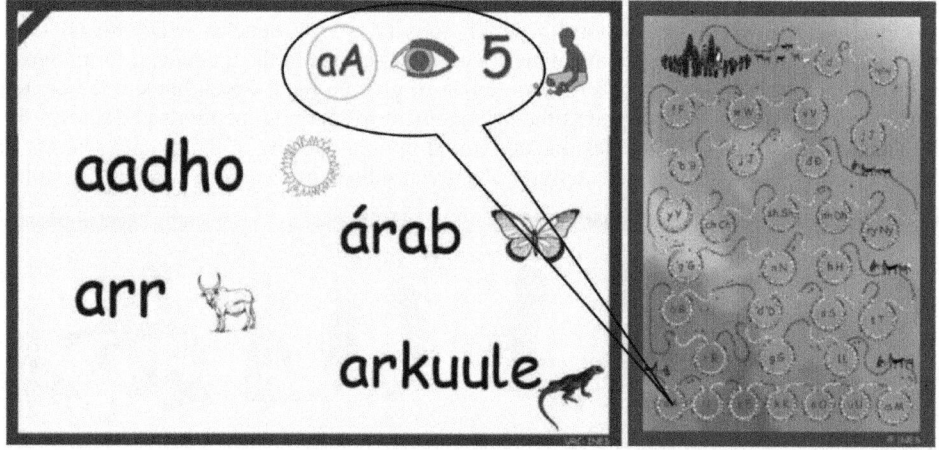

Fig. 8.8: Each activity is associated with a colour, a milestone logo and an activity type logo and number (Source: own illustration).

Activity Cards and Learner's Activity Booklets (LAB). The support system in the mobile schools heavily relies on so-called activity cards.[71] INES distinguishes between material and activity cards. Material cards are learning and content-based whereas activity cards are instruction-based. The outline refers to the required learning materials, social form and the task of the specific learning activity. Using the same cohesive colour, symbol and number system as the learning materials, the activity cards give the following information about the activity:

---

71 Activity cards are not found in the Indian MGML-Methodology.

- The colourful border of the activity card indicates the subject of the ladder of learning (grey: Introduction; red: Daasanach; etc.).
- There are three symbols at the top right corner, that have to be read from left to right as follows: In the first position is the symbol for the activity type, in the second position the respective number for the activity and in the third position the logo for the recommended social form.
- Under the headline *hééllá fe'dé* (lit. you need), photos show which materials the learners need for the activity.
- Under the headline *hééllá tágkok* (lit. you do), one or two pictures hint at what the learner should do.

The milestone logo is not depicted on the learner's activity cards since they are used universally for all milestones. For example, the activity type *il* 5 (eye 5) in the Daasanach ladder of learning is always the same activity only with different content. Therefore, the learner's activity card for *il* 5 (eye 5) provides non-content-oriented guidance to the learners.

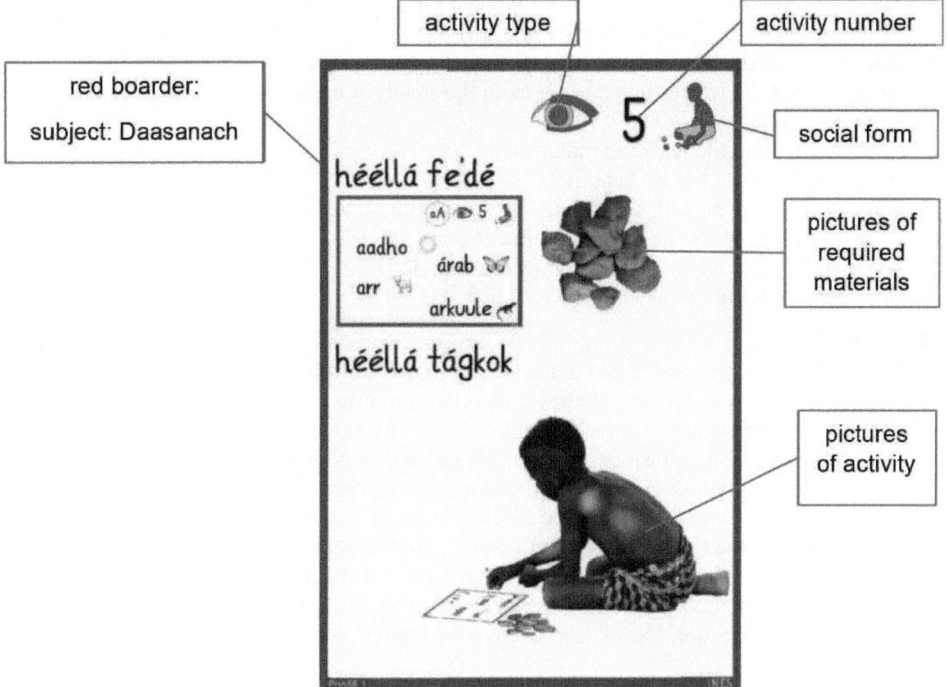

Fig. 8.9: Outline and information of a Daasanach ladder of learning learner's activity card (Source: own illustration).

The first ladders of learning (Introduction, Daasanach and Mathematics) only use pictures for the activity instruction and serve the learners as a reminder to the activity training which they did beforehand. The activity training is necessary to learn the correct performance of all activity types. With increased reading ability on the side of the learners, the activity cards may also include short explanatory texts.

The activity cards are bound together to phased booklets and thus serve as a summary of all the activity types, which occur in one milestone or milestone phase of the ladder of learning. If learners cannot remember a specific activity type, they look up the respective card in the learner's activity booklets (LAB) for support.[72]

Activity Training. Since each ladder of earning (or milestone phase on a ladder of learning respectively) uses the same set of activity types for the gradual development of learning content, learners have to complete an activity training with the teacher before they start the self-directed learning. To facilitate the entry into independent work, it is recommendable to train the activity processes with each learner. It is also possible to train smaller groups, to support newcomers with a tandem partner and to have learners start at staggered times, to avoid crowding (Lichtinger & Höldrich, 2016). In the mobile schools in Kenya, the activity training is scheduled at the school start, when new groups of learners are enrolled.[73]

Moreover, activity training takes place when the learners have advanced to a new milestone phase on the ladder of learning.[74] After the activity training the learners have to be able to answer the following questions for each activity type:

- What do I have to do on the ladder of learning?
- Where do I find the required learning materials?
- How do I get the learning materials from the material bags?
- How do I do the activity?
- How do I handle the learning materials?
- When am I finished with an activity?
- What do I assess myself, when I am finished with an activity?
- How do I clear up the learning materials?
- Whom can I ask, when I do not know what to do?
- How can I help others, when they ask me?

Solutions. The materials are designed in various forms so that the learners can control themselves. Many individual based material cards offer solutions on the flipside for ultimate self-control. Children learn self-control and self-regulation gradually. These are important features, which help young learners to listen to and trust themselves, which are necessary to acquire problem-solving abilities. Partner-based and group-based activity types support cooperative learning, which means that the learners need each other to find a solution.

Finally, there are tasks which have to be presented to the teacher in order to be prove-read. Especially for the evaluation of a milestone, the learners present their learning outcome to the teacher and do the activity with the supervision of the teacher. There are also activity types which are designed in a manner that it is up to the learner to decide upon how the learning output should look like. These forms may include arts and crafts but also short plays,

---

72 An equivalent to the learner's activity booklets (LAB) are the teacher's activity booklets (TAB) which describe in detail how an activity is done, what the teacher has to take care of and how the teacher can support the learners if they have problems with this certain activity. These TABs are also bound together to flipbooks and are stored separately in the teacher's bag. More information on the Teacher Activity Booklets can be found in chapter 11.
73 Activity training with the learners is a fixed component in the so-called Steps of Introduction of the different ladders of learning. INES provides a manual, which supports the teachers when they introduce new ladders of learning in their mobile schools. Extracts of this manual and a more detailed description can be found in chapter 12.6. *Phase 3 – Start of the Mobile School*.
74 On the teacher's side, there are similarly structured activity trainings as fixed components of the INES teacher training as presented in detail in chapter 12.5 *Module 2 – Introduction Ladder of Learning*.

self-written stories and other forms of presentations. Immediate feedback on the learning output is not only important to ensure correctness but also to keep up learning motivation. The process of taking control of and evaluating one's own learning emphasises autonomy and responsibility, which in return are core goals of the learner's development process.

Advanced Learners. In heterogeneous (multi-grade, multi-level) learning groups, it is natural for some learners to advance on the ladders of learning faster than others.[75] If learners have successfully completed a milestone, they are well placed to help others to achieve the same. Based on a constructivist-interactional understanding of learning, learning primarily takes place in the debate and exchange with others. Therefore, it can be said that learning is socially constructed. So, the teacher is not the only source of help, or instruction, when learners need support or input from outside. In the Indian MGML-schools, advanced learners, who have passed a certain point on the ladder of learning, wear a paper crown, equipped with a logo to signalize they can support co-learners with a specific subject matter as *king/queen of learning*. In the INES mobile schools, advanced learners are assigned the temporal task of tutoring co-learners. Either the teacher announces the tutor of the day, usually, however, the learners check on the ladder of learning and may ask advanced learners, who are ahead of them, to support them. Even if the right form of tutoring must be learned first (the motto is: *I do not do the activity for the others; I show others how to do it themselves*), children may explain matters to other children much more comprehensible than teachers.[76] Therefore, the advancement on the ladder of learning is connoted with personal success but with it comes the responsibility to tutor others. As with relatedness-oriented contexts, children learn to take over responsibility from an early stage. The older ones support the younger ones, the younger ones learn from the older ones, whereby in the system Ladders of Learning older and younger is defined according to their position on the ladder of learning.

In a multi-grade multi-level learning group, the interaction between the learners gets a special quality due to the deliberately induced heterogeneity. Of course, the teacher will have to take care, that tutoring tasks rotate in order not to place a too heavy burden on individuals and not to hinder the learning progress of advanced learners. Experience has shown that the milestone level of an individual learner in different subject ladders of learning can vary strongly, which ensures a natural change of the tutors anyway. Overall, advanced learners helping others often offers more practical support since learners do not necessarily need to wait until the teacher has time. This brings discharge to the teachers since they have more time to observe and to focus on those learners who really need special help. Advanced learners also benefit from their support, since the task of explaining something deepens their own understanding of the content. Finally, mutual help not only has positive effects in the cognitive area but also in the social area. Consideration, acceptance and understanding of one another's needs are developed and the learning community takes over responsibility for one another (Bohl 2010).

---

75 According to an evaluation of six-grade learners in a German school already after a four week teaching practice with a milestone arrangement in English, the level of performance varied strongly, due to internal factors such as competency and motivation but also external factors such as absence or crowding (Würzle 2014).

76 A German study (JÜLiSA study by Kucharz & Wagener 2007) has shown that mutual help has to be learned and that the teachers needed discuss the topic of how to help each other well in plenary sessions or with individual learners (Bohl 2010). The desirable assistance, of course, is indirect support where the learners who need help get encouragement and support so that they can actively continue working by themselves. When receiving direct support on the other hand (for example receiving the solution without an additional explanation) the learner who is supported remains passive (Kucharz & Wagener 2007).

8.5 Daily School Schedule

The daily school schedule in the mobile schools with the system Ladder of Learning is divided into plenary time and individual ladder of learning time. While the plenary times are rather teacher-centred the learning times are learner-centred. Both forms of teaching serve different objectives and are clearly structured through ritualization to reduce the complexity of the learning system and to provide security for the learners. The deliberate celebration of rituals in the system Ladders of Learning creates special moments in the daily tasks of teaching and learning, gives rhythm to the learning processes, contributes to a good learning atmosphere and makes all participants feel community spirit (Deal & Peterson 2009).[77]

Plenary Time. Plenary sessions are an important and necessary tool for groups to experience the feeling of connectedness. Activities that are done in plenary strengthen the community spirit. Moreover, the learners establish close relationships with one another as well as with the teacher and experience appreciation as well as attention from the whole group. The goal of plenary sessions is to establish a positive atmosphere where everybody feels secure, seen, heard, appreciated and as an essential part of the group (Chen 2016). In the Indian *Satellite Schools* of RIVER, plenary sessions are an important part of each regular school day: there are opening and closing assemblies and many milestone introductions are presented in plenary sessions with the whole learning group taking part.

In the mobile schools in Kenya, the plenary times may serve different objectives. Within INES, obligatory plenary sessions at the beginning and the end of each school day (so-called opening and closing assemblies) give teachers the time to create a sense of community. Mindful rituals such as saying hello and goodbye, singing, praying, discussing events that affect the entire learning community and their families and celebrating learning success are part of these assemblies. In the protected and trusting environment of the closing assembly in mobile schools, learners are encouraged to reflect upon their own learning process and to practise communication. Reasons for communication can be special events of the day as well as the reflection of the day's work. The closing assemblies offer the possibility to give and receive feedback as an essential driving force for continuous development. Further, plenary sessions allow topic presentations by learners or the teacher and whole group-activities to evoke co-constructions of a given or freely chosen topic.

All plenary sessions within INES – whether in the running mobile schools, in the INES office with the material production team or teacher training sessions – follow a fixed structure and have a ritualised start, a central part with different contents and a ritualised phase-out.[78] Hereby, the contents within the central part of a plenary session can comprise:

---

[77] A ritual is an action that follows a set pattern and has a symbolic character. The ritual creates a framework of orientation, it provides support and it reduces the complexity of life to an easily comprehensible level. Through repeated succession and certain words or gestures closely linked to the ritual, a routine emerges that makes the coexistence manageable and strong. Rituals and ritualization give rhythm to the everyday school life by setting accents at striking, difficult points – such as the beginnings or end points of a session, the school day, the week –, which become distinctive through a recognizable arrangement. This highlights a beginning or an ending of a certain time period. Time as such is more consciously experienced. The deliberate celebration of rituals in the classroom gives rhythm to the learning processes, contributes to a good class climate and enables the communal examination of the basic questions of human existence. If everyone is used to it, the procedure can increasingly be used independently and be filled creatively (Petersen 2001; Deal & Zurbriggen 2011).

[78] The detailed structure of opening and closing assemblies within INES schools and also INES teacher training sessions can be found in chapter *12.4 Module 1 - Basics*.

- presenting results
- planning the day
- reflecting on different learning processes
- giving feedback
- posing and discussing open questions
- introducing new contents, activities or methods
- celebrating achievements

Ladder of Learning Time. Embedded between the opening and the closing assembly, the learners continue on their individual learning paths during the ladder of learning time. Even though the system can be characterized as an open and flexible learning form, during the ladder of learning time each learner follows a fixed procedure for every activity:

1. Attach the name tag on the ladder of learning.
2. Get the activity booklet from the material bag.
3. Open the page of the activity booklet.
4. Identify which materials you need *(hééllá fe'dé)*.
5. Get the materials from the material bag.
6. Go into the correct learning zone.
7. If needed, look for a partner or a group.
8. Identify how the activity is done *(hééllá tágkok)*.
9. Return the activity booklet into the material bag.
10. Do the activity.
11. Return all materials into the material bag.

This fixed procedure serves as a guideline in which self-regulated learning is made possible. Self-regulation is the ability to identify and modulate emotions and control impulses. According to Maria Montessori and many other educators and psychologists, self-regulation is a vital competency that is at the core of all success in learning and life. It is the ability to acquire knowledge and skills independently because choosing their own goals, making thoughtful and conscious choices and selecting learning strategies which are needed to reach these goals are self-motivated. The learners are responsible to evaluate the efficacy of the chosen learning strategies by themselves and – if necessary – to modify and optimize them (Hall & Goetz 2013). As referred to beforehand, the MGML-Methodology puts the learners with their emotions, abilities and goals on the driver's seat of the individual learning process.

When learners need a break the system Ladders of Learning provides clearly defined possibilities for a so-called time-out. Learners may pause between two activities. They may decide how long they want to spend with one activity and advanced learners may even choose which subject ladder of learning or systemically arranged milestone they would like to work on a respective day. The learners take one or more control measures (cognitive, meta-cognitive, volitional or behavioural) and monitor the progress of the learning process themselves (Lichtinger & Höldrich 2016).

The ladder of learning time can offer the learners one or different subject ladders of learning. In the Indian *Satellite Schools*, the learners work on the Telugu and Maths ladder of learning during the morning hours, while EVS is done in the afternoon. In the mobile schools, which use more than one ladder of learning,

a) the ladder of learning time can be divided into different phases for the different subjects or
b) the ladder of learning time leaves it up to the learners to decide for themselves (together with the teacher) on which subject they want to focus for the day or
c) the ladder of learning time focuses only on one ladder of learning for the respective day/week.

Experience has shown that the mobile teachers have to decide for themselves what they and their learners can handle.

Fig. 8.10: Joshua Esho conducting an opening assembly in his mobile school (Source: Ruth Würzle).

8.6 Prepared Learning Environment

Similarly, as in Montessori pedagogy, the system provides a so-called prepared learning environment with materials that stimulate the senses and draw the attention of the learners.[79] The environment should be aesthetic and must be adapted to the proportions of the children, e.g. the bags have to hang at a tangible height. In a wider sense, learning environment does

---

79 In the pedagogical context, the term learning environment is closely linked to different reform pedagogical approaches and is a spatial description of the learning location as such. Particularly in the pedagogy of Montessori, the prepared environment is an integral part, but also other reform educators, such as Freinet and Steiner, also developed concepts about the design of the learning environment (the classroom, the schoolhouse, etc.) (Bohl 2010).

not primarily – and exclusively – mean the spatial design but rather the didactic preparation of the learning object. This includes the task, the material supply and the support, for example, by the teacher.

A prepared learning environment, therefore, provides coherent and clearly structured learning opportunities for learners so they get the chance to work independently and according to their level and needs (Bohl & Thorsten 2010).

School Tree. The mobile schools in the *fora* take place under a school tree. Besides the small non-permanent round huts of the stock camps (which give room for not more than five to seven people) bushes and small thorn trees are the only sources of shade. The teacher and the local community choose the school tree as early as they migrate to this spot since during schooling it cannot be used by other community members or livestock. The material bags can either be attached directly to the branches of the tree or are they spanned with the supported of extra sticks which are fixed into the ground.

Fig. 8.11: Material bags on a complex carrier system made from sticks; Jeremiah Teete fixing the material bags in the school tree by means of ropes (Source: Ruth Würzle).

Material Pool. Another prerequisite for successful learning with the system Ladders of Learning is an organised material pool. The immanent colour and logo system is used to direct the learners from the ladder of learning to the material bags which serve as fabric-shelves. The material bags are divided into smaller bags which carry the logo of single activity (Introduction ladder of learning) or a whole milestone (Daasanach and Mathematics ladder of learning). The graded learning material cards and three-dimensional learning materials are stored inside the bags. These fabric-shelves have various advantages in a mobile school:

– Each learning material has its storage location. This ensures order.
– The fabric-shelves are portable. This allows the schools to be mobile and not to lose time to assemble and disassemble the learning environment.
– Only one set of each learning material is provided because the learners are at different learning levels anyway and it helps to learn social behaviour and consideration. This reduces weight and costs.

- Switching between getting up (going to the ladder of learning and the material bags), sitting down (doing the activity) and getting back up (bringing the learning materials back to the material bags) promotes the concentration of young learners as their natural urge to move is met.
- The learners organise their learning since the material pool is accessible for each learner. This promotes self-regulation.

The *Satellite Schools* in India have fixed school buildings and can therefore offer a wider range of (bulky) learning materials. Each learner has a personal blackboard section along the lengths of the classrooms and folders to store written paper, whereas the mobile learners in Kenya have to do with a limited amount of light learning materials and a small personal whiteboard card. The fixed shelves in the Indian schools store the multiple labelled boxes with graded cards, three-dimensional learning materials and exercise books, whereas the mobile schools require portable organisers.

Fig. 8.12: Jeremiah Teete (left); Bonaya Yierar (right) (Source: Ruth Würzle).

Also low tables, colourful mats as well as arts and crafts of the learners structure and decorate the classroom in India, whereby decorations, heavy learning materials and furnishing are out of place in a mobile school. The learning environment of the mobile schools has to be transportable and also the fact that pastoralists have few possessions and little or no craftsmanship must be considered in the school concept.

Teacher. The system Ladders of Learning seeks to provide a learning environment in which learners actively do joyful, meaningful, manageable and small learning tasks. Joy and meaning are not only generated through the tasks but as much as through a school atmosphere of mutual appreciation and mindfulness, which is expressed both in the interaction with one another and in the sensitive design of the learning environment. Primarily, it is the teacher's responsibility to generate an attentive, appreciative attitude towards the learners and their individual learning processes and to create a positive atmosphere of openness, friendliness and self-confidence. Teachers are role models for their pupils. The apprenticeship of learners not only happens on the cognitive, subject, knowledge and skill but also on the behavioural level.

The teacher-learner relationship is vital and requires the teacher to respect all learners for what they bring to class (from home, culture, peers). Developing relationships requires many different skills by the teachers – such as the skill of listening, empathy, caring and having positive regard to others (Hattie 2009). If teachers speak kindly, accept and do not judge, handle learners as valuable fellow human beings and support, learners will most likely follow this behaviour with their peers. Further, the teachers have to develop skills in observation as well as didactics to perceive various processes in class and to competently manage and guide these situations for the advancement of learning. The teacher as a role model also meets the general perception of many Daasanach when they were asked in interviews how a teacher should be and behave according to their view.

The teacher should be a role model and properly lead the children. The teacher should show good practice so that the children can copy that.
Joshua Esho, elder

To sum up, the teacher has the following different roles:

– activity partner
– evaluator of the learner's progress
– helper
– provider of the learning environment
– presenter
– observer
– cultural ambassador

With less qualified teachers the role of designing and developing (additional) learning materials may be less realistic. In the case of the mobile schools in Kenya, the teachers are asked to give the INES team feedback on learning material designs and during the teacher trainings ideas may come up but it is up to the educational provider to develop and design the learning materials.

Plenary Circle. During the plenary time, the learning group meets below the school tree between the material bags. Care is taken that the whole group (including the teacher) forms a neat circle so that all meet at eye level and have an equivalent place. The learning zone poster caries the four social form logos and is placed in the middle of the learning area to serve two purposes. Firstly, it shows the directions for the four different social form areas (individual based, partner based, group based and teacher based). Secondly, it marks the centre of the plenary circle.

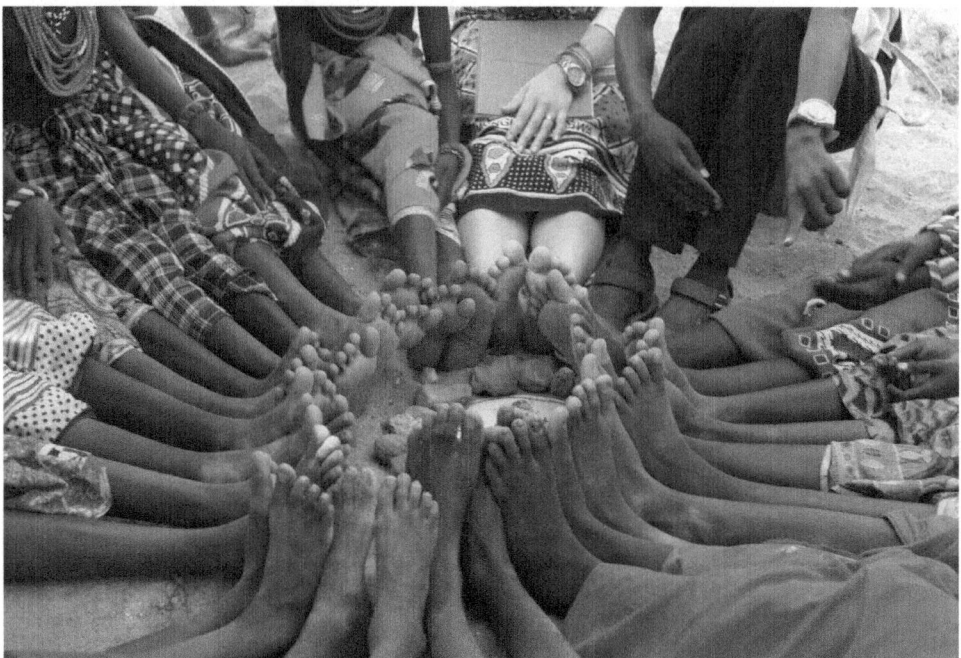

Fig. 8.13: A group of learners gathering around the learning zone poster for plenary time in the model school 2017 (Source: Theresa Schaller).

Learning Zones. A prerequisite for successful learning with the system Ladders of Learning is the deliberately planned design of the learning environment with zones for various forms of cooperative learning. Clearly defined learning zones enable and support dynamic learning in different social forms. The mobile schools provide four learning zones for individual, partner, group and teacher based learning. These are clearly indicated through a chart, which not only marks the centre for the plenary circle during the assemblies but also shows the extended learning zones in all four directions below the tree.[80] Each activity type has an assigned social form logo, which directs the learner into the correct learning zone and indicates whether the learner should work alone or cooperate with a partner or a group. While each learner is responsible for their learning process, the system Ladders of Learning constantly demands pupils to go into cooperation with other pupils to fulfil the learning tasks. Cooperative learning has been an established concept in school pedagogy and didactics since the 1970s.

Cooperative learning is the instructional use of small groups so that students work together to maximize their own and each other's learning. It may be contrasted with competitive (students work against each other to achieve an academic goal such as a grade of "A" that only one or a few students can attain) and individualistic (students work by themselves to accomplish learning goals unrelated to those of the other students) learning (Johnson, Johnson & Smith 2013: 3).

---

80 In the *Satellite Schools* in India, four large tables in the classroom are labelled with the respective social form. In German classrooms, various rooms of sets of tables are arranged to support learning in the various social forms.

Cooperative learning not only improves the learning acquisition of different contents but also progresses the social, personal and cognitive skills of pupils because these learning environments allow learners to capitalize on one another's resources and skills. These are asking one another for information, evaluating one another's ideas, monitoring one another's work, etc. (Johnson, Johnson & Holubec 1994).[81] Ross and Smythe (1995) describe successful cooperative learning tasks as intellectually demanding, creative, open-ended, and involve higher order thinking tasks. In the system Ladders of Learning it can be discussed, how open-ended the individual activity types are but the five essential elements, which are identified for the successful incorporation of cooperative learning in the classroom are also prerequisite in the various activity types in the system Ladders of Learning:

- positive interdependence
- individual and group accountability
- promoted interaction (face to face)
- teaching the students the required interpersonal and small group skills
- group processing (Johnson & Johnson 1975)

Fig. 8.14: Two girls working together on a learning activity in the partner based zone; A girl working individually (Source: Ruth Würzle).

The activity type might also direct the learners to the teacher who will introduce them to a new concept, show them a new method or assess their learning progress. Since learning and teaching are parallel worlds of experience it is vital for educators to have the mind-set, readiness and time to respond to their pupils, their individual learning processes and needs. While mind-set and readiness have something to do with the teacher's personality, his experience and his teacher education, the system Ladders of Learning provides the time for the teacher, to work with individual learners.

---

81 Compared to individualistic or competitive learning settings, cooperative learners not only achieve more and learn individual as well as group accountability but also gain higher self-esteem through social support.

8.7 Monitoring Tools

The learning success immediately shows itself with the progress of the personal name tags which is attached on the current activity field on the ladder of learning as well as through the teacher's entries in the assessment forms and registers.

Name Tag. The very first activity of the Introduction ladder of learning implies creating a personal name tag with the help of a security peg, arrangements of beads and a piece of plastic reading the name of the learner. From then one, the learner attaches the name tag for each learning step to the respective activity fields on the ladder of learning which is printed on fabric. This allows learners (parents and the teacher) to maintain an overview of the progress and to step in and out of schooling. If a learner has to interrupt the learning progress for some days or even weeks, the name tag on the ladder of learning will help them to keep track of where they left off. If there is a comprehensive mobile school system, it is also possible for learners to take their name tag along with them when they switch between different mobile schools.

Assessment Form. In the system Ladders of Learning, evaluations are always teacher-based to make sure the learners receive qualified feedback on their learning progress and are (if necessary) directed to remedial tasks. The teacher documents the learner's successful completion of the milestone with a respective entry in the so-called assessment form. Only if the individual learners pass an evaluation, can they continue with the next milestone.

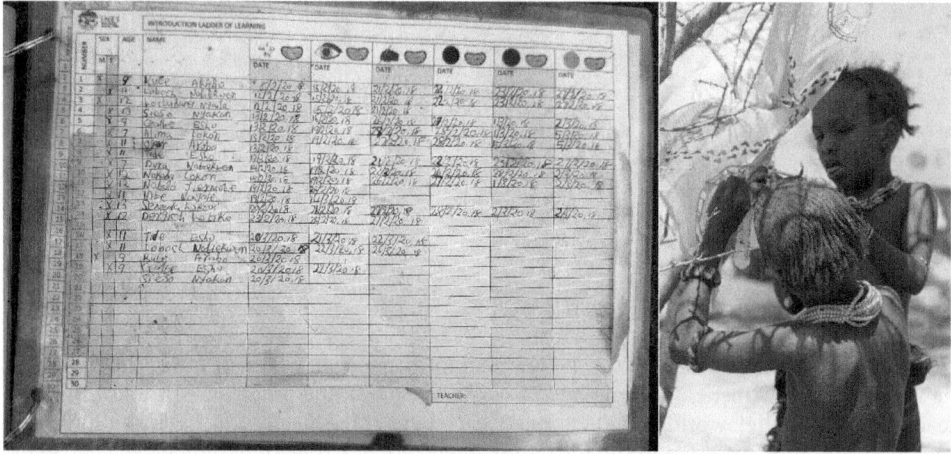

Fig. 8.15: The assessment form of one of the mobile teachers; Two girls attaching their name tag on the Introduction ladder of learning (Source: Ruth Würzle).

Register. Together with the name tag on the ladder of learning, the assessment form and the entries in the daily register, the teachers are permanently oriented about the progress and performance of each learner. During the morning assembly, the teacher takes the register and maintains an overview of the fluctuation in the mobile school.

Personal Notes of the Authors

The development of ladders of learning and its learning materials needs close interaction between cultural and pedagogical experts. The Daasanach pastoralists are experts of their culture and language and school developers for planning, implementing and evaluating mobile schools with the system Ladders of Learning. In the last four years, we had the privilege to grow into this exciting field of school development and truly enjoy the close cooperation with Daasanach pastoralists. Several Daasanach INES team members provided background information on culture, language, stories, perspectives and everyday situations, while we provided the pedagogical and technical knowhow to develop and design the ladders of learning and the respective learning materials. The idea of mobile schools with the system Ladders of Learning developed in the close interaction of Father Florian OSB who has been living with and serving the Daasanach for many years. The pastoralists repeatedly asked Father Florian OSB to help them and after some months of cross-continental e-mail correspondence with RIVER in India and the University of Regensburg and Würzburg, Father Florian OSB started the project cooperation with us.

During the past four years Father Florian OSB, Edwin Changamu, Eveline Momanyi and the INES team have repeatedly invited us to closely consult and support the cooperative development of mobile schools with the system Ladders of Learning. This would not have been possible without the support, encouragement and innovative ideas by many different people. Padmanabha and Rama Rao and their RIVER team have repeatedly welcomed us in India and helped us to see, experience and understand the MGML-Methodology in theory and practice. We are truly grateful for these experiences and the ongoing dialogue. Thomas Müller, Ralf Girg and Ulrike Lichtinger are the first German MGML experts and have contributed their expertise and supported INES and us at various points in time. Their voluntary commitment reached from offering strategic options of project management to scientific research methods and practical learning material aids. We are grateful for all they have done for us and taught us.

The dialogue with experienced scientists, school developers and teachers who work with the MGML-Methodology is always very inspiring and it is amazing to see the different variations and adaptions of this methodology in various school forms and countries around the globe. The development of ladders of learning and its learning materials is always different – based on the different cultures, contexts, etc. – often challenging, yet always highly interesting. We are glad to work as pedagogical experts with the system Ladders of Learning, especially on this task of developing a mobile school system together with Daasanach pastoralists, many of them we call dear friends today.

My favourite activity in the Introduction ladder of learning is acting out animals because it makes me and my friends laugh together.

Kamate Longaye, learner in Bonaya's INES school

9. How Do the Learners Start Schooling?

Learners in a mobile INES school start schooling with the Introduction ladder of learning. This first ladder of learning introduces the learner to various contents, which are part of the Kenyan pre-primary syllabus of early childhood education. Hereby, the focus lies on the core competencies of communication and collaboration, critical thinking and problem-solving, learning to learn and self-efficacy, creativity (Kenya Institute of Curriculum Development 2017). Care is taken, however, to adapt the contents to the Daasanach pastoralist context and their special needs.[82] It is the aim to establish a curriculum for early childhood education, which is activity-based and child-centred. For this reason, six milestones with a total of 49 joyful learning activities focus on important pre-school competencies, as well as, prerequisite skills for the individualized and highly flexible learning within the system Ladders of Learning. This simplified Introduction ladder of learning teaches the school starters how to move about in the prepared learning environment, how to read the logos, where to find the learning materials, how to learn cooperatively and how to follow the procedures of individualized learning in this system.

Even very young children and new learners can structure their own learning processes by the means of ladders of learning, as experiences in Rishi Valley, India and Würzburg, Germany have shown.[83] The Introduction ladder of learning marks the starting point of schooling in the INES mobile schools in Kenya and provides the basis for the following subject ladders of learning.

9.1 Relatedness-oriented Background

The idea of how children should play and therefore how the design of playful situations should look like to support early childhood education processes varies widely depending on the cultural context (Borke & Keller 2014). While in comparison, German children are more used to object play and free play, these forms of play are much less common with Daasanach children. Some Daasanach children report object play while making different items out of clay or crafting with beads.

I enjoy making livestock out of clay and water.
Helekua Nyabatang', boy

Daasanach children often imitate their parents' daily chores in their play. Girls, for example, can often be found building miniature round huts with small sticks just as Daasanach women set up the traditional houses (lokool).

---

82 For more information on how INES develops ladders of learning see chapter *11. How Does INES Develop Ladders of Learning?*.
83 Prof Dr Müller and his students from the University of Würzburg (Temper, Müller, Enders, Hörning, Vaas, Reithmeier, Bausenwein, Hanf, Alles, Stier, Würpel) developed ladders of learning for children from 3 to 4 years old and for children from 5 to 6 years old. In 2017, they published an explanatory teacher's manual. These ladders of learning for early childhood development are used in the *Satellite Schools* in India, Rishi Valley and are constantly revised by RIVER.

Fig. 9.1: Daasanach children building play huts (Source: Theresa Schaller).

Depending on the cultural context, different socialisation goals and different theories about what is a *good and beneficial interaction* of children are existent.[84]

There are different, culturally-related notions on what is considered important, desirable and beneficial. While some behaviours and manners are emphasised, others are rather neglected or even suppressed (Keller 2007). All of these conscious (and partly unconscious) expectations and theories have an important impact on children's development (Borke & Keller 2014). In general, culturally sensitive early childhood education differentiates between autonomy-orientated backgrounds and relatedness-oriented backgrounds. Both needs, autonomy and relatedness, are important for all people but in quite different forms and significance. The central point of reference within a prototypical autonomy-oriented context is the individual itself. A stable ego boundary, differentiation from other people and individualism are important for the health and well-being of a child. This is accompanied by a self-perception that refers to the ideal of freedom and individual independence which is a typical philosophy of life in large parts of the Western world. The socialisation goals in this prototype of an autonomy-oriented culture are self-realization and self-confidence (Borke & Keller 2014). The prototypical autonomy-oriented background regards children as (almost) equal partners to adults whose personality and wishes should be included in decision-making

---

84 Socialisation prepares people to participate in a social group by teaching them its norms and expectations so that the children can meet these respective socialisation goals. This includes ideas about what children should develop, what matters, what is unimportant or even harmful and also at what age they should have acquired certain skills. Depending on the cultural context, different perceptions may exist (Keller 2011). Hence, different convictions of how children can be supported by *good and beneficial* interactions are described (Borke & Keller 2014).

processes (Keller 2003). In relatedness-oriented contexts, however, these socialisation goals of development towards a creative and self-actualizing child have subordinate roles. The prototypical relatedness-oriented backgrounds esteem respect, obedience and cooperativeness as the most important socialisation goals. According to this differentiation, Daasanach pastoralists have a strong relatedness orientation.[85]

I learned from my mother when I was young. Now I teach my daughters. First, I talk to them and then I show them.
Lokolom Long'ada, mother

The child is an apprentice and adults, or older people in general, pass the knowledge to the child (Borke & Keller 2014). For this reason, children start to participate and eventually take over tasks within the family's everyday life at a very early age and through these chores are integrated into the community.

I have learned from my mother and my father. My mother was the one who taught me to respect those who are not my age mates. I also saw it from the neighbours.
Felicitas Muer, young woman

Forms of free play, as stated above, are much less common and are sometimes even consciously prevented in relatedness-oriented cultures (Gaskins 1999; 2006) because children are supposed to be introduced to the actions and demands of the adult's world. Interactions are often not child-centred, but rather adult-centred. Therefore, freedom of choice and self-determination may be unfamiliar to children with a relatedness-oriented background, since they are more used to a structured style of interaction (Borke & Keller 2014).

This explains why existing ladders of learning with its learning activities and materials from one context cannot necessarily be transported into other backgrounds without being aware of the comprehensive and complex cultural differences. The background orientation, as well as, the development goals have to be considered to develop culturally sensitive ladders of learning.

---

[85] Borke and Keller state that all different cultural models can be arranged through the interaction of two central human needs: autonomy and relatedness. Autonomy is defined as the ability to gain control over one's own life, as well as, one's own decisions and actions. Relatedness is defined as the psychological and/or economic interconnectedness between persons. Autonomy and relatedness mutually reinforce one another (Borke & Keller 2014). Of course, hybrid forms also exist and occur probably more often than the prototype. However, here the prototypical form of the two cultural models (autonomy-oriented and relatedness-oriented) is described.

9.2 Linear Structure of the Ladder of Learning

Fig. 9.2: Introduction ladder of learning of INES (Source: own illustration).

Since children with a relatedness-oriented background are used to a highly structured style of interaction marked by older people's guidelines and choices, the structure of the Introduction ladder of learning is linear without the freedom to choose between milestones or sets of activities. Free choice or different options are characteristics of systemic ladders of learning which may overwhelm and intimidate Daasanach learners at this early point. A linear path on the ladder of learning, however, provides a clear guideline which the learners can follow at their own pace. Eventually, the learners are introduced to more open learning processes.

The learners start their journey on the grey framed Introduction ladder of learning on the lower left-hand corner where a teacher is depicted next to the learner. The two face each other. Before the learner starts there is a teacher based input in the form of an introductory unit. During this teacher based introduction, the learner listens to the story framework of the ladder of learning. Further, the learner is introduced to the different milestones with their topics, the material pool, the social forms and the learner's activity booklet. Moreover, there is a first activity training to empower the learners to do the first activities on their own. This teacher-guided start in the mobile schools takes several days and can be clustered into 50 introductory steps.[86] During the introduction, all learners make their own name tags with the

---

86 For more information on these Steps of Introduction on the Introduction ladder of learning see chapter *12.6*

help of an individually chosen amount and order of colourful beads, a wire, a safety pin and a piece of plastic with their name written on it. These name tags will accompany the learners on their individual learning path which they start after this first activity. The experience has shown that especially relatedness-oriented children like to move their name tags as a group or partners (autonomy-oriented children more often like to *outrun* others in the ladder of learning). In both cases, the teacher faces the challenge to maintain the focus on the core ideas of the learning system right from the beginning. Each learner sits in the driver's seat of their own learning process. Each learner drives at their own pace and it is not important to drive fast but to keep moving.

Fig. 9.3: The Introduction ladder of learning in the campus school with the nametags of all learners attached (Source: Ruth Würzle).

The Introduction ladder of learning has six milestones as depicted above. The ladder of learning, as seen from a bird's eye view, forms six thorn hedges within a secure *forich* (literally stock camp) in daily life and the design secures the circular milestones. There is an opening to enter each temporary settlement and the activities offered inside. Inside the *forich* are several steps with symbols and numbers on them. The centre of the *forich* is the meeting place in a temporary stock camp and depicts the milestone logo. Footprints connect the six milestones of the Introduction ladder of learning with each other and guide the learners on this linear path. Unlike other ladders of learning, the Introduction ladder of learning in the mobile schools does not have a clear end on the top of the fabric but rather offers two options at the top left corner. One path leads back to the initial starting point and the other path upwards. After passing through all six milestones of this first ladder of learning, the learners

---

Module 3 - Start of the Mobile School.

have the chance to redo the Introduction ladder of learning until they feel prepared and qualified enough to continue with the second ladder of learning. INES advises the learners to go through this first ladder of learning at least twice. Experience has shown that after the second round they are familiar with the system and the different activity types, which are a prerequisite for the following subject ladders of learning. The teacher monitors the individual learning progress and after assessing and advising the learner whether to redo a milestone, to start a second round of the Introduction ladder of learning or to continue with the Daasanach ladder of learning. The teacher and the learner meet again after the first round of the Introduction ladder of learning as visualized by the graphic of the teacher and the learner right before the crossroads and make the decision together.

9.3 Each Milestone Introduces a Different Domain

The Introduction ladder of learning is arranged linearly, meaning that the learners follow the ladder of learning step by step, visiting six different forich, alias milestones. Each milestone focuses on important pre-school competencies and trains different skills. Each milestone offers between four and eleven different learning activities. Besides, there is an evaluation at the end of each milestone which determines whether the learners may continue with the next milestone or should do remedial activities. The learning activities of the Introduction ladder of learning are chosen from different categories such as the motor domain and the cognitive domain. At the same time, the social forms, new activity types and a basic introduction to the Daasanach language, Mathematics and Life Studies are introduced. Additionally, the domains of language and social development are integrated into the activities (Müller et al. 2017).

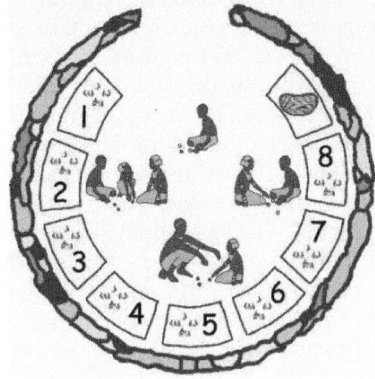

Fig. 9.4: Milestone Learning Together, Introduction ladder of learning (Source: own illustration).

Milestone: Learning Together. The learners who start schooling with the system Ladders of Learning have to get introduced to the different social forms and practise cooperative learning in the respective learning zones which are linked to the social forms. The learners realise that activities can be done individually, with a partner, in peer groups or with the teacher. Even if their learning process is highly individualized they are strongly integrated and supported by peers and the teacher. Moreover, in this initial milestone, they learn and practise the organisational procedure within the system Ladder of Learning (e.g. how and where to find the respective materials for an activity and how to use the learner's activity booklet, when and where to move and settle down for an activity etc.). The learners practise these overall goals in the milestone Learning Together using activities of the gross motor domain.

Motor skills are divided into gross motor skills and fine motor skills. Gross motor skills are used to coordinate the movement of the entire body, which enables children to maintain their balance, to move against gravity, body tension and coordination (Tröster, Flender,

Reineke & Wolf 2016). The gross motor skills include, for example, running, jumping, throwing and balancing. The learning activities in the milestone Learning Together joyfully train gross motor skills in different social forms, taking into account that motor skills are well trained with most Daasanach children already at a very young age.[87]

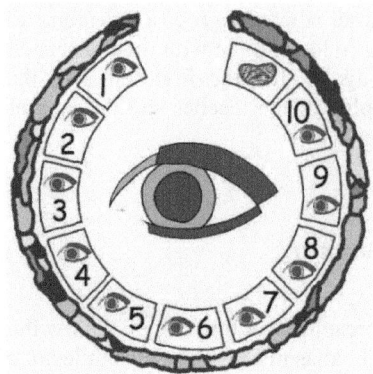

Fig. 9.5: Milestone Eye, Introduction ladder of learning (Source: own illustration).

Milestone: Eye. The activities of the milestone Eye of the Introduction ladder of learning are mostly chosen from the cognitive domain. The learners are asked to identify equal objects, to build different categories and to distinguish items along with a specific feature. From the perspective of the learning system, the main focus of the milestone Eye lies on introducing the learners to ten different activity types which will recur in the following milestones and also ladders of learning. Activity types such as domino, clip cards or Bandolo slowly introduce the Daasanach learners to concepts of pictures, colours and shapes. They are also taught to handle these different learning materials, such as picture cards, bead sticks, clip cards and other materials. Particular attention is paid to the gradual introduction to drawings and pictures since these are quite unfamiliar to traditional pastoralists of the Daasanach. For many learners at this stage, it is the first time looking at pictures.

Fig. 9.6: Milestone Hand, Introduction ladder of learning (Source: own illustration).

Milestone: Hand. Fine motor skills are one of the two components, next to gross motor skills, which make up the motor domain. Fine motor skills are based on the eye-hand coordination and include the control of the hand and finger movements, which is required, for example, for painting, writing and crafting (Tröster, Flender, Reineke & Wolf 2016). Big and small movements of the hands, as well as, the production of graphic signs using a finger or a writing instrument tool, a stick or a pencil on different surfaces (e.g. sand or paper) is practised in this milestone. These are the motor prerequisites for fast writing later. At this stage, it is rather a slow, faithful "painting" of shapes and letters with visual control. The form control is the focus here. However, the transition to writing motor skills is fluid and dependent on the abilities of the individual child (Pauli & Kisch 2016). The milestone Hand slowly prepares the learner for the writing process also because most Daasanach children have never used a pen or pencil on paper before.

---

87 An overview of all activity types of the Introduction Ladder of Learning is given in chapter *9.4 Joyful Activities.*

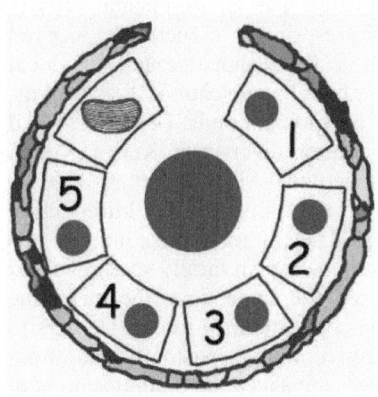

Fig. 9.7: Milestone Daasanach, Introduction ladder of learning (red circle) (Source: own illustration).

Milestone: Daasanach. One of the basic prerequisites for literacy learning is the phonological information processing skill. Learners must be able to pick out and reproduce individual elements (words, syllables, phonemes) and memorise them.[88] To be able to assign phonemes to graphemes, children must be able to detach themselves from the meaning content of the language. Learners must develop phonological awareness and be able to direct their attention, irrespective of the content, to the phonetic structure of the language (Tröster, Flender, Reineke & Wolf 2016). The milestone Daasanach of the Introduction ladder of learning sharpens the phonological awareness of the learners and thus prepares them for the Daasanach ladder of learning. The learners are introduced to the five vowels and they practise important acoustic activities with focus on the phonetic structure of a set of simple words. They practise hearing and pronouncing the vowels using the culturally adapted initial sound pictures and the respective chart (*'bil 'Daasanach*). On various levels, the learners are introduced to the main tools of the Daasanach learning materials (singing the initial sound chart song, identifying the initial sounds and pictures, identifying graphemes of the five vowels etc.).

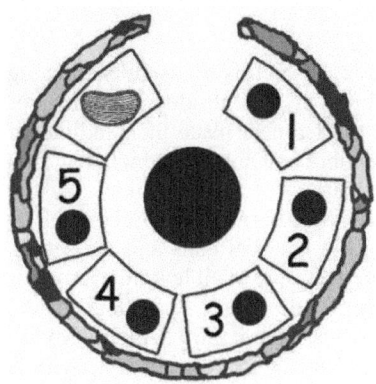

Fig. 9.8: Milestone Mathematics, Introduction ladder of learning (blue circle) (Source: own illustration).

Milestone: Mathematics. At pre-school age, learners acquire different basic skills which are prerequisites for understanding Mathematics. To impart mathematical knowledge and competencies in primary school, the teacher and the learning materials need to build on these previously acquired skills. These precursor skills can be subdivided into pre-numerical and numerical concepts (Tröster, Flender, Reineke & Wolf 2016).

The Introduction ladder of learning focuses on basic numerical skills, especially on the understanding of numeral series and counting skills: counting rhythmically, counting rhymes in Daasanach, counting fingers, beads, stones, etc. In the milestone Mathematics, the learners are also introduced to different learning materials (e.g. colourful bead sticks) along with the pre-numeric concepts which will be part and practised in detail in the Mathematics ladder of learning later on.

---

[88] Additionally to phonological information processing skills, basic language skills build the basis for literacy learning which means that children must master basic grammatical structures of the language, understand the meaning of words and sentences and have sufficient vocabulary, in order, to be able to learn to write and to read (Tröster, Flender, Reineke & Wolf 2016).

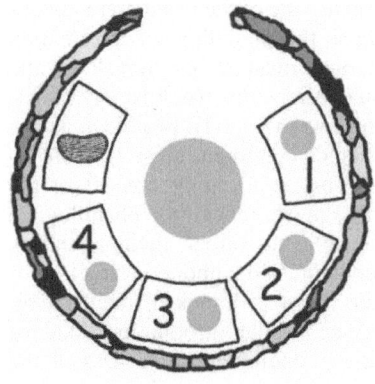

Fig. 9.9: Milestone Life Studies, Introduction ladder of learning (yellow circle) (Source: own illustration).

Milestone: Life Studies. The environmental activity area is important for pre-primary learners. The Kenyan syllabus states that it EVS should entail the local natural environment, how to take care of it, as well as, social relationships and social bonds. Learners should appreciate the rich cultural diversity in Kenya (Kenya Institute of Curriculum Development 2017). Therefore, this final milestone of the Introduction ladder of learning (Life Studies) encourages the learners to think about their own family structures and their surroundings. At the same time, the milestone Life Studies provides opportunities for the learners to reflect on their daily routine as pastoralist children. Moreover, the learners are asked to communicate with one another by posing and answering questions. This milestone also prepares the new learners for the subject ladder of learning Life Studies which focuses on learning modules of the Kenyan syllabus such as hygiene, water, peacekeeping, livestock husbandry, cash economy etc.

9.4 Joyful Learning Activities

In the Introduction ladder of learning each learning activity, which is realised by learning materials, has its own bag in the grey set of material bags of the Introduction ladder of learning. The first step in the learning system is where the learners place their individual name tags on the ladder of learning. The combination of symbol and number, which they find on each activity step is identical to the symbol on the learners' activity booklet and the material bags.[89] Necessary stones and sticks are not stored in the learning material bags. The learners collect them when needed to avoid overloading the material bags and the school donkey when shifting. The tables 9.10 and 9.11 provide an overview of all learning activities of the Introduction ladder of learning. Each activity is designed according to the MultiGradeMultiLevel-Methodology criteria for activities, these are small, joyful, meaningful and manageable. The table shows in which milestone the respective activity is placed, wherein the milestone the activity is found and in which social form the activity should be conducted.

---

[89] Later on, in the subject ladders of learning, all the learning materials of one milestone are stored in one bag in the respective material bags. The system in the Introduction ladder of learning is more simple because each learning activity has its own small bag with the respective materials. This makes it easier for new learners to find the correct materials, to practice the identification of symbols and numbers and not to be overwhelmed by the large amount of learning materials in one bag.

Milestone Learning Together		
	1	Name Tag
	2	Describing Picture Cards
	3	Singing & Dancing
	4	Looking at & Touching Materials
	5	Rope Forming & Tiptoeing
	6	Jumping on Right & Left Foot
	7	Hopscotch Drawing & Jumping
	8	Animal Acting & Guessing
Evaluation		Social forms and zones
Milestone Eye		
	1	Looking at and Touching Shapes
	2	Placing Shapes
	3	Lokode Forming & Tiptoeing
	4	Matching Picture & Graphic
	5	Dominos
	6	Bead Sticks 1-5
	7	Clip Cards
	8	Felt Bag
	9	Matching Big & Small Picture Card
	10	Spotting Errors in Picture Cards
Evaluation		Clip Cards
Milestone Hand		
	1	Banner Sticks
	2	Stringing Beads
	3	Bead Lines on Lokode
	4	Placing Stones on Lines
	5	Correct Hand Posture with a Stick
	6	Following Lines with a Stick
	7	Following Paths with a Stick
	8	Writing & Guessing on the Back
	9	Forming Shapes with a Rope
	10	Drawing Shapes into the Sand
	11	Copy Shapes on Whiteboard Card
Evaluation		Copy Shapes on Whiteboard Card

Fig. 9.10: Activities milestone Learning Together, Eye and Hand Introduction ladder of learning (Source: own illustration).

Milestone Daasanach		
	 1	Initial Sound Chart Song (Vowels)
	2	Initial Sound Picture Naming
	3	Matching Initial Sound Pictures
	4	Placing Rubber Letters
	5	Initial Sound Chart Song (All)
Evaluation		Initial Sound Pictures & Sound
Milestone Mathematics		
	 1	Maths Song
	2	Counting 10 Stones
	3	Counting 10 Fingers
	4	Numeric Sticks
	5	9 Colourful Bead Sticks
Evaluation		Matching Bead Sticks & Stones
Milestone Life Studies		
	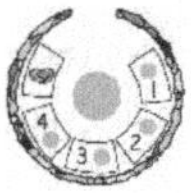 1	Matching Picture & Graphics
	2	Objects in my House
	3	Family Fan
	4	Daily Schedule
Evaluation		Copy Shapes on Whiteboard Card

Fig. 9.11: Activities milestone Daasanach, Mathematics, Life Studies Introduction ladder of learning (Source: own illustration).

Personal Notes of the Authors

School development is a triad of personal, lesson and organisational development, whereby, learning material development in the INES project belongs to the area of lesson development. It is rather uncommon for pedagogical consultants to be in charge of all three areas especially because of the tremendous workload of learning material development. The Indian RIVER team comprises school developers, teachers, artists, writers and designers. Since INES is a low budget project and due to the lack of resources and personnel in Illeret, the INES team was forced to choose rather unusual paths for the project. Since there were no national textbooks in the local language, the development of learning materials of the Introduction and the Daasanach ladder of learning took more than three years. Especially the Introduction ladder of learning had to be revised several times and many initial learning activities were replaced to cover the national syllabus, fit the pastoralist background and match the design and the activity types to the Daasanach ladders of learning. The parallel development of these two ladders of learning required close coordination. It was quite challenging to find a common system for all subject ladders of learning and, at the same time, satisfy the different subjects and their contents. Of course, we always focused on making the ladders of learning and their learning materials as similar as possible in order to help the learners and teachers handle the learning system which heavily relies on symbols; however, it was not possible on all levels. In the case of the Introduction ladder of learning it was extremely challenging to reduce the complexity of the system and the symbols to a minimum so that young learners without (pre)-school knowledge would manage to learn individually. Since the INES teacher education programme was started during the production phase of both ladders of learning, the trainees were the first to pretest the Introduction ladder of learning and provided valuable feedback for necessary changes. The version presented in this chapter is the fourth revision and it might well be that further revisions follow, after the piloting of the first groups of mobile learners.

I want to help and support the Daasanach children to learn how to read and write in their mother tongue.

Jakob Lon'gada, elder and mobile teacher trainee

10. How Do the Learners Acquire Literacy?

Learning how to read and write is a complex process also known under the term literacy acquisition. Literacy, as a school subject, addresses the ability of learners to make meaning of letters and sounds, thus making sense of written codes. Reading and writing ability consists of a bundle of sub-skills, which begin well before the start of school.[90] Just as frequent addressing and communication are important for children to acquire language, so all types of print (storybooks, bulletins, signposts, packages etc.) are important for the acquisition of literacy.

Even if mobile phones and prints on packages and signposts gradually enter the pastoralist environment in Northern Kenya, the nomadic children are rarely exposed to concepts about script and print. For children with fewer prior experiences, initiating them to the alphabetic principle will thus require more focused and direct instruction, since a conceptually written language can only be produced and received if all information contained in the linguistic symbols is completely and correctly recorded.[91]

Scientific recommendations and the Kenyan national curriculum for the primary school require that literacy acquisition should happen in the learners' mother tongue to build on a rich vocabulary basis (Kenya Institute of Curriculum Development 2017). For the development of phoneme-grapheme-correspondence, so-called initial sound charts with pictures and names of the cultural surrounding of the children are highly recommendable. Overall, educators are advised to drive a flat progression, they should repeat vocabulary and sentence structures frequently and it is recommendable to design writing tasks reproductive.

10.1 Literacy in the Mother Tongue

It is hardly surprising that teaching pupils in their mother tongue has a demonstrable impact on improving the quality of education (Komarek 2006). According to the Kenyan Institute of Curriculum Development which published the latest national syllabus in August 2017, literacy shall be taught in the language of the catchment area of the learners.

The knowledge of literacy which includes the ability to understand, respond to and use forms of written language to communicate in varied contexts, are important to facilitate the learners' understanding of English as a second language. With the Daasanach ladder of learning the learners acquire literacy (reading and writing) in their mother tongue. Since the process of acquiring strategies for literacy is comparable with early childhood primary

---

90 The acquisition process takes place in three stages in which logographic, alphabetical and orthographic strategies are developed (Frith1986; Brügelmann 1998). The *logographic strategy* of children implies they realise that letters have something to do with language, even if this involves a purely visual mode of operation. Children identify script or words by referring to the salient features such as connected lines and signs or they capture specific characteristics of words (word length, eye-catching letters, and word beginnings). Gradually capturing grapheme-phoneme-correspondence is the core of the *alphabetical strategy*. The children become aware that there is a mutual relationship between the visual units and their phonological meaning. The *orthographic* strategy implies the understanding that orthographically correct spelling is mainly ruled by morphological, syntactical and semantical relationships.

91 The *alphabetical principle* states that a limited set of letters comprises the alphabet and that these letters stand for the sounds (phoneme-grapheme-correspondence) that make up spoken words (Sousa 2005).

language acquisition, listening and speaking activities are interwoven into the Daasanach ladder of learning at various levels.

To assess the reading and writing abilities of nomadic Daasanach school-age children, the INES team tested 32 nomadic Daasanach children living with their families and their livestock out in remote stock camps. The children between the age of 6 and 12 years were tested with different small and self-contained activities which reviewed previous knowledge in literacy. Among other tasks, they were given, for example, five wooden letters and were asked to name them. Besides, visual-construction exercises were part of the test. The children were asked to follow and copy lines, shapes and letters on a whiteboard card to test fine motor skills as well as eye-hand-coordination.[92] The Daasanach school-age children were also asked to identify the corresponding letter to a given sound. Finally, they were given syllables for reading.

The diagnosis showed clearly that the participating children could not establish meaning of the written codes (grapheme-phoneme recognition: non-existent; reading ability: non-existent) but showed great motivation to copy letters on a whiteboard using a pencil (pencil-hold, writing-speed and direction: medium level) and often they assigned arbitrary English terms to the wooden letters.[93]

The order of the milestones and the establishment of the Daasanach alphabet in the Daasanach ladder of learning is based on the frequency and importance of the various phonemes in the Daasanach language. An analysis of traditional, orally transmitted stories, which were written down by BTL and INES, as well as, the BTL Daasanach Dictionary determined, which phonemes are used more frequently than others and should therefore be learned first. INES developed an initial sound chart in the form of a traditional round hut.[94] The five vowels are positioned at the bottom line, near the entrance of the '*bil* (round hut). The consonants and double-consonants are presented along the arc of the '*bil*, beginning with K and finishing with NG' and D – two graphemes which only occur at word-middle or the final position in the Daasanach language. All initial sound pictures are taken from the nomadic context of the Daasanach. The phoneme A is introduced with *aadho* (sun) and not with an apple as many Kenyan textbooks and initial sound charts do.

---

[92] Fine motor components and eye-hand-coordination represent an important basis for visual-construction and/or visual-spatial perception (Daseking & Petermann 2009). The visual-construction describes the ability to recognise and reproduce complex shapes or patterns and is particularly important in the school context, as it is directly related to reading, writing and calculating (Jacobs & Petermann 2008).

[93] In Part A of the test (grapheme-phoneme recognition they obtained only 4%; In Part B (pencil-hold, writing-speed and direction) almost half of the points were achieved (47,5%); In Part C (phoneme-grapheme recognition) they achieved an average of 27,5% (due to a high hit rate); Part D (reading ability) clearly showed they were not even able to read syllables (0 %).

[94] A first initial sound chart was developed by BTL (Bible Translation and Literacy) in 2010. INES changed the character of the chart, put the letters into the order of establishment in the Daasanach ladder of learning and also included the letters, which later on will be introduced through Swahili and English foreign language acquisition. The subsequent adoption of Swahili and English graphemes and double graphemes are literally flown in by birds. The *'bil 'Daasanach* exists as printed fabric and is part of the material pool in the mobile schools.

10.2 Pastoralist Lifestyle in the Design

The design of the Daasanach ladder of learning deliberately takes up the nomadic lifestyle of pastoralist communities. The background is earthy, brown-beige like the savannah planes with occasional tufts of grass. From a bird's eye view, thirty-one, almost circular, thorn hedges, which protect the *forich* (temporary stock camp and settlement), lie dispersed across the high-rise format. A beaten path with footprints connects the various fora. Inside each camp is a grapheme written into the sand. Along the inner fringe of the thorn hedges are neatly lined-up white fields – like huts – carrying various symbols. The Daasanach ladder of learning is printed on special flag fabric to be light, foldable and robust enough to be hanged in thorn bushes and to carry numerous name tag pins.

The learning path starts in the lower left-hand corner of the red framed ladder of learning. A young child, representing the learner, together with a black and white goat starts the learning journey. In the beginning, a teacher sits next to the learner. They meet at eye level and hold hands. Following the footprints of the learning path from one milestone to the next, repeated meeting points between learner and teacher occur. Initially, there is only a single goat accompanying the learner. Gradually, the number of goats increases, however. The growing herd represents the increasing abilities and literacy skills of the learner on the journey. At the upper left-hand corner, there are two, elaborately embroidered learners – a boy and a girl – who are surrounded by mixed aged members of their community. The special hair dress, clothes and accessories show that the learners have completed the Daasanach ladder of learning and are thus in the limelight of the celebration.[95] The learning path is finite and the achievements of this learning journey are celebrated extensively.

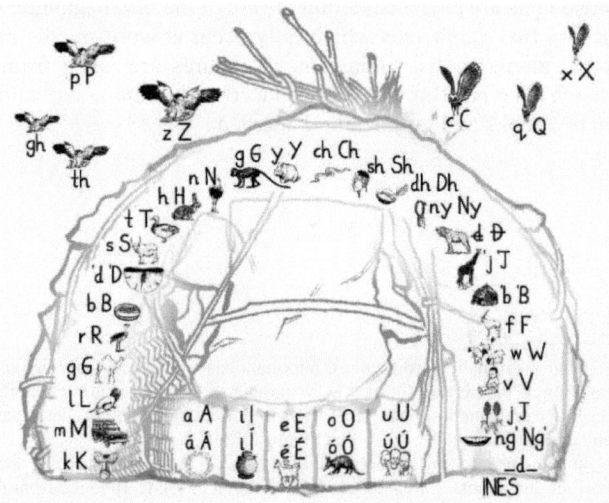

Fig. 10.1: *'Bil 'Daasanach* – Daasanach initial sound chart of INES (Source: own illustration).

---

95 As described in chapter *1 How Do Daasanach Pastoralists Live?*, a big white ostrich feather in the hair dress indicates in Daasanach culture that a celebration is held on behalf of the person wearing it. The feather can be worn by males and females.

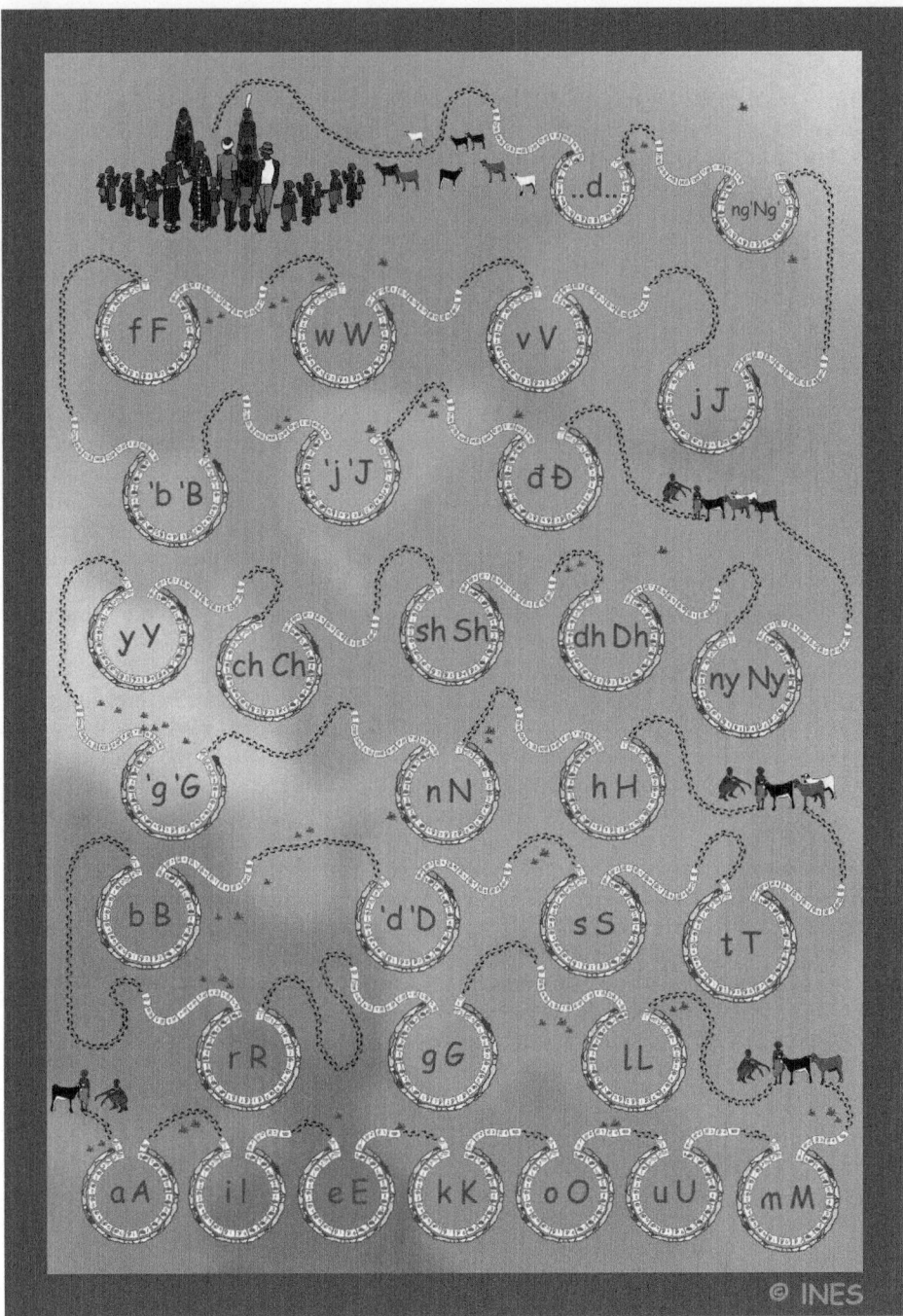

Fig. 10.2: Daasanach ladder of learning of INES (Source: own illustration).

10.3 Guidelines for the Learners

The learning path of the Daasanach ladder of learning starts from the bottom left and in a linear order leads upwards. The linear structure is twofold, to support and relieve young learners. The sequence of milestones is linear and the activities within each milestone are in ascending order.[96]

Fig. 10.3: Milestone K, Daasanach ladder of learning of INES (Source: own illustration).

Each milestone introduces and analyses a grapheme or grapheme combination of the Daasanach alphabet, progressively practises reading and writing skills and provides an assessment of the learning progress. When the learner enters the thorn crest of a milestone, there are introductory activities, followed by visual, acoustic and fine motoric activities of the respective sound and grapheme (letter/ letter combination). Stepping out of the thorn crest, the learner practises the newly acquired literacy skills with reading and writing activities. Each milestone ends with an evaluation. The results of the evaluation help the learner and teacher to decide whether the learner proceeds on the learning path or should do specific remedial activities beforehand.

The introductory activities carry the symbol of a *'daate* (hollowed-out calabash). This utensil is used in the traditional tea ceremony of the Daasanach and metaphorically depicts the first encounter with something or someone new. The day starts with tea. Visitors are welcomed with tea. Meetings start with tea. Here, the learner is introduced to the learning subject of this milestone.

The symbols for the reinforcement activities show the focus of the three different activity types. *Il* (eye) stands for visual analysis. *Nete* (ear) stands for acoustic analysis and *gil* (hand with a pen) for fine motoric analysis of the respective phoneme and grapheme. The symbol for reading and writing activities is *war'gat* (a lined piece of paper). The symbol for the evaluation is a *noono* (donkey carrier basket). These stick-woven baskets are used to store household stuff in the traditional round hut and as carriers when migrating to the next camp. The *noono* metaphorically depicts the storage of newly acquired skills and knowledge. Figure 10.4 provides the definition of the symbols.

---

96 As explained in chapter *9 How Do the Learners Start Schooling?*, freedom, choice and self-determination may be unfamiliar to children with an affinity-oriented background since they are usually used to a more structured style of interaction (Borke & Keller 2014).

Name	Symbol	Explanation
Calabash *'daate*	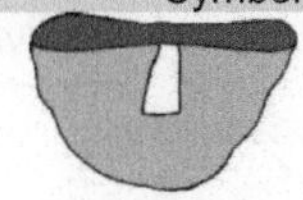	Introduction to the new grapheme / grapheme combination (*introduction*)
Eye *il*	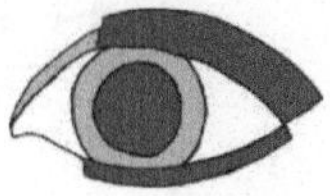	Visual analysis of the grapheme / grapheme combination (part of *reinforcement*)
Ear *nete*		Acoustic analysis of the phoneme (part of *reinforcement*)
Writing hand *gil*		Fine motor skills and writing analysis of the grapheme / grapheme combination (part of *reinforcement*)
Written page *war'gat*	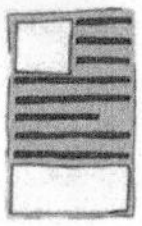	Reading and writing exercises with a special focus on the respective grapheme / grapheme combination (part of *reinforcement*)
Donkey carrier *noono*	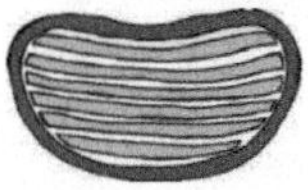	Evaluation of grapheme-phoneme correspondence, as well as, the reading and writing skills (*evaluation*)

Fig. 10.4: Names and definition of the activity type symbols of the Daasanach ladder of learning (Source: own illustration).

As mentioned in chapter 7, the learners pass through an activity training at the beginning of the Daasanach ladder of learning, as well as, follow-up trainings at the beginning of the second, third and fourth phase. Only when the learners know how to do every activity type (as in broad cases of activity types) and also how to assess themselves, they may continue the learning journey. The activity cards are tied together in activity booklets for each phase. These activity booklets (LAB) support the learners to do the activity types all by themselves despite the increasing level of difficulty and literacy content. The teachers have an additional version of the activity booklet (TAB), which explains the activity, what they have to take care of as teachers and how to react when the pupils face problems.[97] Figure 10.5 shows the structure of a learner's Daasanach ladder of learning activity card (LAB).

---

[97] For an example of a teacher activity booklet (TAB) see chapter *12 How Does INES Empower Mobile Teachers?*.

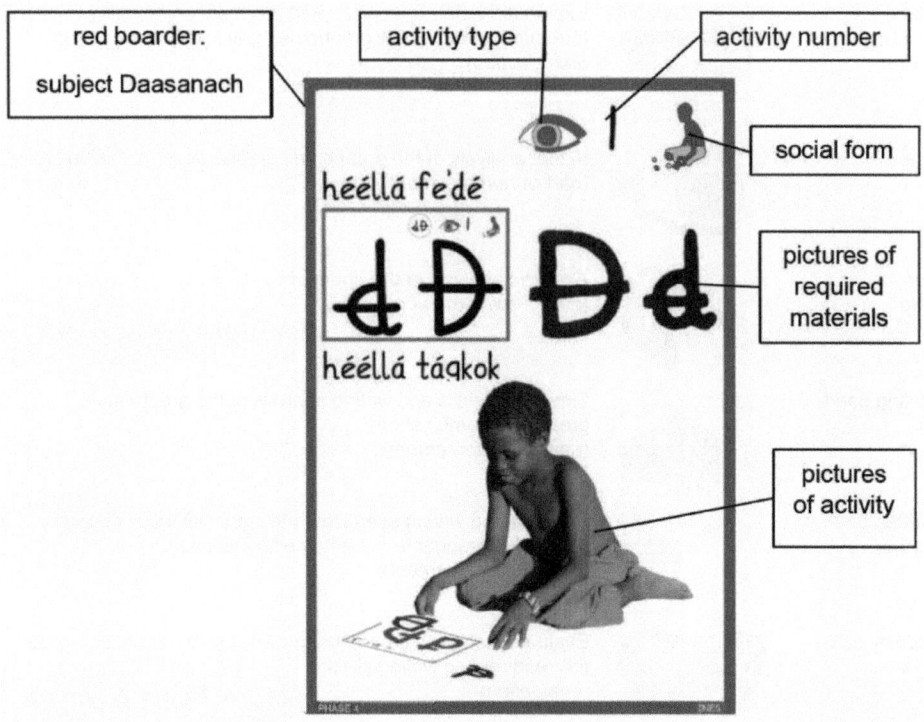

Fig. 10.5: Structure of a Daasanach ladder of learning learner's activity card (Source: own illustration).

Fig. 10.6: Learning materials for the milestone mM of the Daasanach ladder of learning (Source: Ruth Würzle).

Type + Symbol	Number	Desription	Social Form
Introduction Activities	1	Introduction Story	
	2	Initial Sound Chart	
	3	Other Initial Sound Pictures	
Reinforcement Activities (Visual Analysis)	1	Big Rubber Letter	
	2	Felt Bag	
	3	Lines & Bows	
	4	Bead Rings around Letters	
	5	Stones on Letters	
	6	Small Rubber Letters	
Reinforcement Activities (Acoustic Analysis)	1	Finding Words with the Sound	
	2	Finding 3 Initial Sound Pictures	
	3	3 Sound Position Boxes	
	4	Free Word Search	
	5	Syllable Clapping	
	6	Sound Couplet Search Box	
	7	Domino	
Reinforcement Activities (Fine Motor Skills)	1	Bead Letters on Skin	
	2	Follow Letter on Card	
	3	Follow Letter in Sand with Finger	
	4	Write Letter in Sand with Stick	
	5	Write Letters on Whiteboard	
	6	Big Help Lines	
	7	Small Help Lines (Teacher)	
	8	Small Help Lines (Individual)	

Fig. 10.7: Introduction and Reinforcement activities (Visual Analysis, Acoustic Analysis and Fine Motor Skills of the Daasanach ladder of learning (Source: own illustration).

Type + Symbol	Number	Description	Social Form
Reinforcement Activities (Reading & Writing Practice) 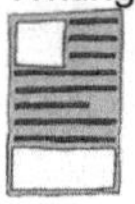	1	Rubber Letters into the Boxes	individual
	2	Bandolo Frame	individual
	3	Initial Sound Pictures & Rubber Letters	pair
	4	Speed Reading	individual
	5	Clips Card	individual
	6	Bottle Top Bingo	pair
	7	Reading Stripes	individual
	8	Gap Reading	individual
	9	Reading Together	group
	10	Window Copying	individual
	11	Connecting Syllables	individual
	12	Connecting Sentence Elements	individual
	13	Self-Dictation	individual
	14	Partner-Dictation	pair
	15	Word-Search-Box	individual
	16	Story Writing	individual
	17	Story Reading	individual
Evaluation 		Evaluation of visual and acoustic recognition and reading and writing skills	group

Fig. 10.8: Reading and Writing Practices and Evaluation activities of the Daasanach ladder of learning (Source: own illustration).

10.4 Learning Activities

Care is taken that the learning tasks allow active handling of a learning aspect making it *manageable* without much further guidance by a teacher. Even if some activities are teacher-based, they are conceptualised in a manner that the learners are actively involved. The activities should be created from the life context of the learners or should refer to it in order to be *meaningful* to learners. They should be *joyful* to support learning motivation and *small*. *Small*, in the sense of short, implies the length of performing an activity, which should be appropriate according to the ability of concentration of young learners. At the same time, the different learning activities should build on one another in short and consistent distances so that the learners can achieve the handle the increasing demands. INES developed and tested several fun learning materials and activities, which are related to traditional games and involve stones, beads, singing, jumping, clapping etc., but has also chosen concepts of learning activities which in this or similar form are known in schools around the globe (e.g. activities like Bandolo, Bingo, Domino etc.). As mentioned in chapter 5, INES also designed the activity types with particular respect to compatibility in the context of mobile schools of Kenyan savannah so that they withstand heavy wind, strong sunlight and rain.

The figures 10.7 and 10.8 provide an overview of the 41 activity types of the Daasanach ladder of learning. Each activity type has a symbol, a number and the associated social form in which the activity is carried out.

The Daasanach ladder of learning is composed of 31 milestones. Each milestone offers between 19 and 32 activities so in total, the learners have to do at least 848 to complete the Daasanach ladder of learning. Depending on the learner, literacy acquisition may require doing further remedial activities or repeating reading and writing tasks for practice. The learning path of the Daasanach ladder of learning is divided into four phases. Each phase includes seven or eight milestones. The symbol of the learner (with one, two, three or four goats depending on the phase) at the beginning of each phase indicates to the learner, as well as, to the observing teacher that they have to meet. At the meeting they will reflect on the acquired knowledge of the previous learning progression and the teacher will give important information about the next phase. This also includes the activity training. As far as possible and didactically reasonable, all milestones of one phase use the same set of activity types.

Fig. 10.9: Phase 1 logo of the Daasanach ladder of learning (Source: own illustration).

In phase one, the learners are introduced to the five vowels which in Daasanach may be short (spelling with a single vowel) or long (spelling with double vowels) and the two most frequent consonants K [k] and M [m]. Since Daasanach children hardly encounter script outside of school, this phase puts a strong focus on the visual analysis, as well as, writing practices of the respective grapheme.

In phase two, additional acoustic activity types are added to train the learners' detailed analysis of the pronunciation of words. The acoustic analysis supports learners in their writing skills because the Daasanach language uses phonetic spelling. With the introduction of the next seven consonants, the learners also build up the pool of words they are able to read and write. For this reason, the first reinforcement activities of reading and writing are left out and six new activity types are added to train reading and writing skills.

In phase three, the three double graphemes CH [tʃ], SH [ʃ] and DH [ð] are introduced towards the end of the phase. These characteristics are the reason why visual activity types are not consistent in this phase. Otherwise, the first four reading and writing reinforcement activities are taken out and instead, three new ones are included.

In phase four, further acoustic activities support the learners in analysing the structure of sounds in words to practise correct phonetic spelling. Since the learners have repeatedly worked on motor skill activities throughout the last three phases of the Daasanach ladder of learning, there is no need for all fine motoric activity types for these last milestones. The reading and writing activities in this phase focus on phrases, whole sentences and short stories. Figure 10.10 shows the characteristic features of each of the four phases of the Daasanach ladder of learning and the implemented activity types.

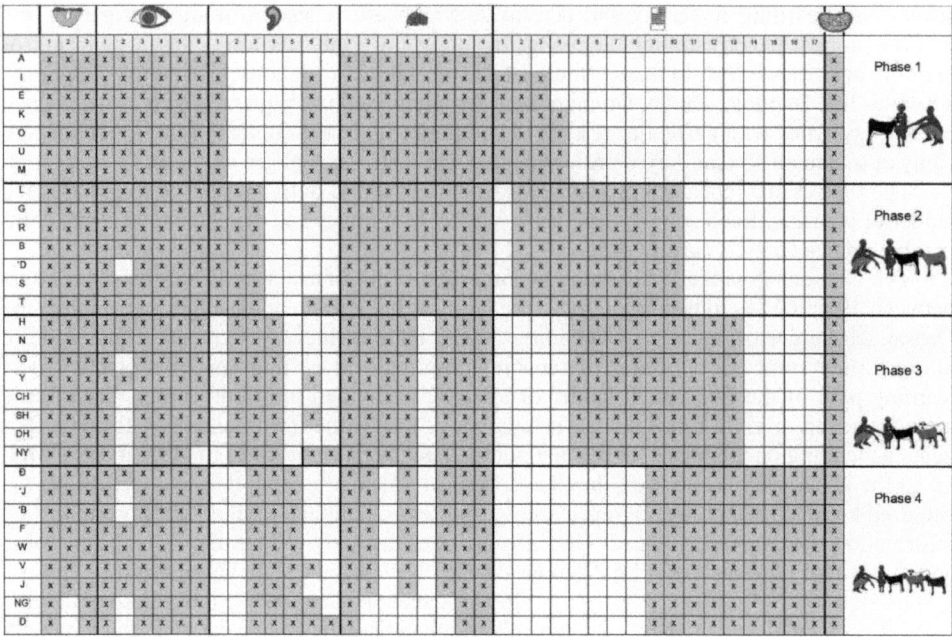

Fig. 10.10: Distribution of activity types in each milestone of the four phases of the Daasanach ladder of learning (Source: own illustration).

10.5 Development Process

The total development process of the Daasanach ladder of learning took three years. In the first phase (February 2015 - August 2016), the Kenyan INES team was composed and was trained in the MultiGradeMultiLevel-Methodology and its ladders of learning.[98] With the help of illustrative materials of German milestone arrangements, initial milestones for Daasanach literacy acquisition were developed.[99] During this time the Kenyan INES team wrote simple stories for children (which stress a certain sound or use a specific set of graphemes) and they established Daasanach, Swahili and English word lists with the help of the recently published Daasanach Dictionary and literacy primers for adults by BTL. These first texts in Daasanach served as a linguistic guide (Nyingole & Kwanyang 2013). Further, orally transmitted Daasanach stories were analysed to determine which phonemes are used more frequently in Daasanach and how to set the sequence of milestones in the Daasanach ladder of learning. Besides the language analysis and graphic design work, Daasanach men and women were trained in woodwork and crafting. They supported the production of literacy

---

[98] These first cooperation and training steps were inspired and supported by the German project cooperation manager from the University of Regensburg Girg (2015-2016).

[99] A team of German teacher trainees under the supervision of Lichtinger from the University of Regensburg developed the first milestone arrangements for literacy acquisition in German: *Buchstabeninseln* (lit. letter islands). The first groups of German primary school pupils acquired literary with them starting in 2014.

learning materials such as wooden and rubber letters cut out of recycled materials, as well as, bead letters on goatskin, which use a colour-coding to train the writing direction of graphemes.

The process of writing, editing, translating and recording songs and stories was demanding and time-consuming since even literate Daasanach are not acquainted with the written form of their mother tongue and correct spelling of all words is ambiguous. Besides, the process of finding culturally appropriate pictures and designing the graded learning material cards, charts and the ladder of learning itself was challenging, since the Kenyan INES team has no qualified artists or graphic designers. Also, designing learning materials on the computer was a challenge due to the lack of technical equipment and knowhow. Therefore, the two consultants Ruth Würzle and Theresa Schaller had to take over the graphic design of all the learning materials with the cultural and linguistic support of local elders and the Kenyan INES team. Moreover, finding an appropriate script for the learning materials in which all letters and graphemes of the Daasanach alphabet are available according to the Kenyan syllabus was time-consuming.[100]

During the development process, all activity types were tested with Daasanach children in pre-tests. From September 2016 to December 2017 under the cooperation management of Dr. Ulrike Lichtinger from the University of Regensburg, the first version of the Daasanach ladder of learning was implemented in a model school on the INES campus with illiterate women. The observations and experiences gained during the pre-tests, the INES model school, as well as, the implementation results of the German ladder of learning on literacy acquisition, led to the first great revision of the initial concept of the Daasanach ladder of learning in 2017.[101] Finally, in 2017 Edwin Changamu and the INES team were trained in producing and storing all learning materials.

10.6 Differences and Similarities of the First Two Ladders of Learning

As displayed in chapter 9.5, INES seeks to develop ladders of learning for all subjects that have as many common features as possible to make the learning system as easy as possible. To reduce the complexity and training of the system the first two ladders of learning have in common:

− Both ladders of learning begin in the lower left corner.
− Both ladders of learning have 14 activity types in common.[102]
− A logo in the middle of the milestone hints at the learning objective and content.

---

100 The problem was solved in 2018 through the voluntary help of Ludwig von Bayern, Jan-Marten Veddeler and the Learning Lions, who designed a new computer script (Dassanech Sans) for the INES project. Learning Lions – Fighting Poverty with Digital Opportunity, is a non-profit organisation dedicated to digital vocational training in rural Africa. The goal is to enable young adults in impoverished rural areas of Eastern Africa to work, and to live a life full of opportunity while remaining in their home area. Therefore, the students are equipped with IT and media skills and are encouraged to become entrepreneurs (http://www.learninglions.org/).
101 In 2016, the milestone arrangements of the *Buchstabeninseln* were revised under Lichtinger and Höldrich. In 2016 they published the German ladder of learning *Buchstabenberge* (lit. letter mountains), which also influenced the concept of the Daasanach ladder of learning.
102 Further activity types are taken up in the Mathematics ladder of learning.

- Both ladders of learning use the circular shape of a *forich* to visualize a Milestone.
- Both ladders of learning use the depiction of a *noono* to illustrate an evaluation activity.

Nevertheless, the framework also has to fit the curricular conditions and skills of the learners. Thus, there are several structural differences between the Introduction and the Daasanach ladder of learning. Table 10.11 shows the most important differences in a brief overview.

Introduction Ladder of Learning (ILL)	Daasanach Ladder of Learning (DLL)
The ILL comprises 45 different activity types.	The DLL comprises 41 different activity types.

Milestone Learning Together of the Introduction ladder of learning	Milestone A of the Daasanach ladder of learning
The learning activities within a milestone, visualized by consecutive steps, carry the milestone logo and the activity number (except the evaluation).	The learning activities within a milestone are subdivided into introductory activities and reinforcement activities (visual, acoustic, fine motoric and reading and writing activities). The activity steps on the ladder of learning carry the respective symbol and the activity number. They hint at the didactical concept behind the activity type.
e.g. 2nd activity of the milestone Learning Together	e.g. 5th fine motoric activity in of the Daasanach milestones
The ILL consists of 49 activities.	The DLL consists of 848 activities.
The learning material for each activity is stored in an extra bag.	The learning materials for one milestone are stored in one bag.
In the ILL content and activity types of each milestone is completely different.	The DLL is divided into four phases. The milestones of each phase contain the same learning activity types (as far as possible) to establish a routine. The learners can focus on the content and are familiar with the tasks.

Fig. 10.10: Differences and similarities of the Introduction and the Daasanach ladder of learning.

Personal Notes of the Authors

The development process of the Daasanach ladder of learning took the Kenyan INES team (Edwin Changamu, Bonaya Yierar, Paul Lokono and Paul Gosh Kwanjang') and us three years. Recalling these three years (2015 - 2018) from the start of development to the first real implementation of materials in a mobile school, it feels like the INES team, as well as ourselves, were travelling on the desert paths of the Daasanach ladder of learning. The road leads through stretches of conceptualization of a linear ladder system, linguistic analysis and language work, computer design, pre-tests of prototypes, various revision, trials in a campus school, printing and local large-production of learning materials, storage and training of teachers. On our journey, we were often overwhelmed by challenges such as fluctuation or unannounced absence of dear team members, power cuts and disputes over spelling and word meaning. It was not easy to train pastoralists, who are not acquainted with books or paper, how to cut, laminate, compile and order card based language materials. It was also a challenge developing literacy learning materials of an indigenous, oral language, which was put into writing by BTL only recently. Because there was no possibility for us to take language courses, we had to rely fully on local translators, which had experience with the transcription of the New Testament of the Holy Bible, the compilation of a first dictionary and were part of the editorial team of two adult literacy primers. Analysing the language with the help of translators and finding didactically meaningful words, phrases, sentence and culturally adequate stories for children proved to be very time-consuming. Various rounds of revisions were necessary due to errors but also spelling disputes and discussions over word meaning.

Nonetheless, the team spirit kept growing on our way and the milestones, which we passed, will never fade. We remember recording all alphabet stories under shady trees in a nearby riverbed, away from the noise of the village. We recall the cheerful discussion about how to visualize a joyful ending on the Daasanach ladder of learning. We celebrated the large-scale productions of the learning materials of phase 1, phase 2, phase 3 and phase 4. It was very exciting for us to train the first teachers on how to use the Daasanach ladder of learning with the learners of their own mobile schools and we will surely never forget packing the first material bags, handing them over to the first mobile school teacher and seeing them in usage with Daasanach children out in the *fora*.

It is important to teach Mathematics with a life reference to the Daasanach.

Bonaya Yierar, INES campus teacher

11. How Does INES Develop Ladders of Learning?

When the curriculum and lesson plans of a given subject are transformed into activities and learning plans, learners are empowered to organise their own learning process. The visualization of one of these learning plans is called a ladder of learning.

The curriculum of a subject and a grade published by the national Ministry of Education defines the contents and learning objectives and is thus the basis of a ladder of learning for the school context. As broached in chapter 8 the development process of the various subject ladders of learning for the mobile schools is lengthy. The development of each subject ladder of learning involves a similar procedure.

Step	Field of Work	Questions in the Development Process
I	Analysis of the curriculum and the textbooks	– Is a curriculum provided for the subject? – Which general learning objectives does the curriculum target for the subject? – Which core and sub competencies does the subject entail? – Which topics does the curriculum provide in order to put the learning objectives into meaningful contexts? – Which specific learning objectives does the curriculum target for each topic? – Which learning activities does the curriculum suggest? – Which tasks do learners have to perform according to the national examinations?
II	Tests with children in the catchment area	– What are the cultural, linguistic, cognitive characteristics of the learners in the catchment area?
III	Field research in the catchment area	– Which important topics does the curriculum not cover? Which topics should be included?
IV	Preparations and development of the subject ladder of learning	– Which activities can be reused for the subjects? – How can the basic concept of the ladder of learning look like? – How can the basic concept of the subject milestones look like? – How can the corporate design look like? – Which skills and resources does the development team bring along? With whom can the team cooperate? – (see figure 11.6)

Fig. 11.1: Steps, field of work and questions in the development process of ladders of learning (Source: own illustration).

Firstly, the basics provided by the national curriculum and textbooks are analysed. The Kenyan national curriculum and textbooks are the basis for all subject ladders of learnings of INES, however, as described in chapter 2.3 many presentations of learning contents in the regular textbooks are alien to children from a pastoralist context. This is why in a second and third step the INES development team considers research and field studies within the catchment area of the learners as a major component within the development process. Lastly, the construction, design and actual production of learning materials are started. Step by step, the INES development team poses the following questions and generates a solution for a specific subject.[103] This chapter gives an insight into selected questions, tools and materials of the development process of the Mathematics ladder of learning.

---

[103] Schaller and Würzle have developed a series of workshops and a manual which trains educators to develop and produce own subject ladders of learnings and its materials.

11.1 Analysis of the Mathematics Curriculum and Textbooks

The latest national Kenyan Curriculum Design (2017) seeks to reform the learning experience and outcome in all state schools and universities in Kenya because the prevailing reality in Kenyan national schools is teacher centred classrooms with educators mainly using methods such as repetitive speaking and memorizing answers for multiple-choice assignments. The targeted paradigm shift implies moving from a teacher to a learner centred and from a content to a competency based curriculum.

The Lower Primary Level Curriculum Design (grade 1-3) uses operational verbs to formulate nine general learning outcomes in the early years of education and explicitly underlines the necessity for learners to develop key competencies such as communication or problem-solving. A great deal of emphasis is placed on teaching appropriate etiquette in social relationships, offering a surrounding which promotes emotional, physical, spiritual and moral wellbeing and appreciation for the own culture, as well as, the diversity of cultures and peoples within Kenya. Sense of belonging with the own culture, as well as, appreciation for cultural diversity are considered as basics for the harmonious coexistence in Kenya (National Curriculum 2017). Examination of the latest Curriculum Design – Pre Primary 1 and 2 (2017) for Mathematical activities and the subject Mathematics of the Lower Primary Level Curriculum Design (2017) – show clear statements on what contents should be offered, which skills should be trained and how teachers can deliver the curriculum. In Kenya, Pre Primary is divided into two school years and Lower Primary comprises grade 1, 2 and 3. Figure 11.1 shows the repetitions of Mathematical strands in the first five years of schooling which focus on classifications, numbers, measurements and geometry. Building upon the knowledge skills from the previous year the spectrum of numbers increases and operational tasks become more advanced. In the reformed curriculum, a great deal of attention is emphasised on the delivery methods of teachers and how learning materials should be designed to offer active learning experiences. Teachers are expected to actively "engage the [learners] into the learning process" and to offer more "practical experiences that will help learners to retain more" (National Curriculum 2017: iii). The curriculum instructs teachers to enable self-reliant and joyful learning in order to nurture the potential of every learner. The curriculum emphasises didactical approaches that provide a learner-centred, competency based, resource-oriented and interactive lesson design. The construction process of each learner is put into focus. This demands high pedagogical and didactical skills and for learning material providers, as well as, teachers to include the social and cultural context of the learners.

Mathematical Strands in Pre Primary		Mathematical Strands in Lower Primary		
Pre Primary 1 (PP1)	Pre Primary 2 (PP2)	Grade 1	Grade 2	Grade 3
1. Classification 1.1 Sorting & Grouping 1.2 Matching & Pairing 1.3 Ordering 1.4 Patterns	**1. Classification** 1.1 Sorting & Grouping 1.2 Matching & Pairing 1.3 Ordering 1.4 Patterns			
2. Number 2.1 Rote Counting 2.2 Number Recognition 2.3 Counting Concrete Objects 2.4 Number Sequencing 2.5 Symbolic Representation of Number 2.6 Number Puzzles	**2. Number** 2.1 Rote counting 2.2 Number Recognition 2.3 Counting Concrete objects 2.4 Number Sequencing 2.5 Number Value 2.6 Symbolic Representation of Number 2.7 Number Puzzles 2.8 Putting Together 2.9 Taking Away	**1. Numbers** 1.1 Number Concept 1.2 Whole Numbers 1.3 Addition 1.4 Subtraction	**1. Numbers** 1.1 Number Concept 1.2 Whole Numbers 1.3 Fractions 1.4 Addition 1.5 Subtraction 1.6 Multiplication 1.7 Division	**1. Numbers** 1.1 Number Concept 1.2 Whole Numbers 1.3 Fractions 1.4 Addition 1.5 Subtraction 1.6 Multiplication 1.7 Division
3. Measurement 3.1 Sides of Objects 3.2 Mass (Heavy and Light) 3.3 Capacity (How Much a Container Can Hold) 3.4 Time (Daily Routines) 3.5 Money (Kenyan Currency) 3.6 Area (Surface of Objects)	**3. Measurement** 3.1 Sides of Objects 3.2 Mass (Heavy and Light) 3.3 Capacity (How Much a Container Can Hold) 3.4 Time (Daily Routines) 3.5 Money (Kenyan Currency) 3.6 Area (Surface of Objects)	**2. Measurement** 2.1 Length 2.2 Mass 2.3 Capacity 2.4 Time 2.5 Money	**2. Measurement** 2.1 Length 2.2 Mass 2.3 Capacity 2.4 Time 2.5 Money	**2. Measurement** 2.1 Length 2.2 Mass 2.3 Capacity 2.4 Time 2.5 Money
		3. Geometry 3.1 Lines 3.2 Shapes	**3. Geometry** 3.1 Lines 3.2 Shapes	**3. Geometry** 3.1 Position and Direction 3.2 Shapes

Fig. 11.2: Mathematical strands of Pre Primary 1 and 2 and grade 1, 2 and 3 of Lower Primary (Source: own illustration).

11.2 Mathematical Test with Daasanach Children

To assess which skills and abilities are prevailing among Daasanach pastoralist children between 5 and 7 years of age, INES applies field research before developing learning materials. INES is interested in the unique skills and abilities of pastoralist children to encourage these in school and use them for abstract construction processes for literacy, numeracy or exploration of the environment. Close analysis of the context of Daasanach pastoralists is also necessary to identify concrete concepts, pictures and stories that are familiar to them. These answers support the INES team to develop learning activities and milestones which pick up the concrete environment and context of the learners. For this reason, INES has developed basic field tests for literacy and numeracy which assess the skills and knowledge of pastoralist children who have never experienced schooling.[104]

Basic Mathematical Competencies. Imparting Mathematical competencies in primary school build upon precursor skills which are fundamental for the development of abstract Mathematical skills and are usually acquired in pre-school. These precursor skills are classified into pre-numerical and numerical concepts. Pre-numerical skills comprise the knowledge about quantities and quantity relations (Krajewski 2005; Krajewski & Schneider 2006), which are:

- comparison of quantities according to their size
- arrangement of quantities in decreasing size (seriation)
- sorting and grouping objects according to specific characteristics e.g. colour, form and size (categorization and classification)
- identifying same quantities even if the space between the objects varies (variance)
- Numerical skills focus on knowledge on the numbers:
- understanding of numeral series (sequencing)
- counting skills (rote counting)
- basic arithmetic operations (arithmetic)

In the beginning, pre-numerical knowledge about quantities, quantity relations and counting skills are still independent knowledge systems which are combined at a later development stage (Fritz, Ricken & Gerlach 2007). According to the stages of development by Ricken, Fritz and Balzer (2011) there are consecutive stages which are each characterised by one main concept. The understanding of this concept is pre-conditional for a child to acquire the next.[105]

Diagnostic Objectives. The overall diagnostic question for the Mathematical test is: Which pre-numeric and numeric skills do (approximately) six-year-old pastoralist Daasanach children have who have never experienced schooling before. In western contexts, most children are in stage three (cardinality and disassembly) according to Ricken, Fritz and Balzer (2011), when they enter primary school. Since there was no information and experience on Mathematical skills in the Daasanach context, the INES development team had to assess which stage Daasanach children are in when they start in a mobile INES school.[106] The Mathematical test assesses the basic pre-numeric, numeric and measurement skills, which

---

104 Besides these field researches for Language and Mathematics learning materials, INES targets to develop further field tests for socials, sciences and religion which will be compiled later in the subject Life Studies.
105 In the first stage of development (number counting), numbers are present only as word series. In the second stage (representation of a mental number line), the child has learned that each number occupies a position on the number line and that numbers that follow a number are *bigger* and numbers which come before a number are *smaller*. At this stage, the child can name predecessors and successors of a number and can solve simple addition problems by counting. In the third stage (cardinality and disassembly), a child must innumerate quantities and then emphasise the ending number. The ability to disassemble quantities into subsets allows additions and subtractions without having to count the elements. In the fourth stage (containment), the child understands that numbers are made up of other numbers. This can be used to solve problems of addition and subtraction. In the fifth stage (relationality), the child has understood that intervals between successive numbers are the same so that they can determine and compare differences between quantities of different sizes (Ricken, Fritz & Balzer 2011).
106 The INES development team for Mathematics consists of Löffler, Schaller and Würzle. In 2018, the team was supported by Böcker.

are objectives of the pre-primary Kenyan curriculum (see also figure 11.1 above). For testing purposes, INES has chosen the following classifications:

a) Time Awareness
b) Sorting and Grouping
c) General Visual Simultaneous Perception and Memory
d) Shape and Form Discrimination
e) Counting up to 10
f) Number Recognition
g) Quantity Comparison
h) Addition and Subtraction

Scope of Application. The Mathematical test is conducted in a single setting, there are no technical requirements and the test secretary brings all necessary materials. Since the children are illiterate, the instructions are pre-formulated, read out by the test secretary and then translated into the local vernacular Daasanach. As with the literacy test, the Mathematical test can also be done by repeat measurements to check the learned progress of learners who are in a mobile school and learn with the Mathematics ladder of learning.

Implementation Time. From the first test rounds in July 2018 experience shows that the implementation by a non-local test secretary and a Daasanach translator takes between 45 to 60 minutes. For this reason, the test also offers a variety of physical tasks in between to keep up the concentration and motivation of the test children.[107]

Interpretation of Test Results. All in all, the children tested had a high awareness of time and were able to answer questions about their daily routines. In the conversations with the children, it became clear how strongly the life of the pastoralists revolves around the needs of the animals and the time and seasons are closely linked to the rhythm of the livestock production. This includes time for working and resting, shifting and settling, the intervals of eating and going without food or drink. During games, they showed good memory of real-life objects which were taken away or added. Keeping track of the family's animals and the few belongings seem to be acquired at an early age. Generally, the children showed high skills in sorting and grouping real-life objects in their immediate surrounding but discrimination of shapes and forms was rather weak. The children all showed abilities to count from 1 to 10 and many also beyond but number recognition was missing completely. The numbers which the test secretary presented on paper or cut out from wood conveyed nothing to them. However, many children associated the wooden number 1 with an ordinary stick, the number 5 with a snake and the number 7 with a hunting stick. Comparison of quantities was very high but they had difficulties explaining whether a quantity is *more* or *less* when the test secretary took objects away or added something. Without standardised tests, it can nevertheless be assumed that the Daasanach children tested (and prospective mobile school learners) are at the first (number counting) or second stage (representation of a mental number line) of the mentioned development model.

---

[107] The first test round was carried out by Böcker and Löffler in July 2018 with 37 test children between the age of 6 and 13 years who have had none or very little schooling experience.

11.3 Mathematical Field Researches in the Catchment Area

Besides these field tests, INES conducts interviews with children, adolescents and adults to determine concepts, pictures and stories which can be used for the development of learning materials and activities. Only if the learning materials pick up the real world of the children does it enable inductive learning experiences for abstract concepts (Lübben-Chambí & Jackson 2001).[108] The basis for the acquisition of Mathematical strategies is everyday experiences with quantities, for example, naming, counting, etc. (Fuson 1988). So for the development of culture-sensitive learning materials information about existing Mathematical concepts, terminologies and situations dealing with quantities and measurements have to be gathered. Additionally to the Mathematical tests, the INES development team conducts interviews with Daasanach children, adolescent and adults to create a digital library of pictures and graphics, as well as, songs and stories, which are incorporated into the learning materials. In most cases, the local INES team members function as informants and advisors, however different translators, councils of elders, as well as, children out in the stock camps have to be consulted. During these field researches, the INES development team gains important and content-determining insights used for the development of learning materials. In the Daasanach context, it is, for example, not permitted to count livestock, which presumably could have been a meaningful Mathematical task.

On the contrary, a desirable skill of a Daasanach pastoralist is to *know* the family's livestock, including those of relatives, friends and clan members instead of *counting* them. Goats, sheep, cattle, camels and donkeys are *known* by their outward appearance, behaviour, kinship etc. Having to *count* livestock in order to check on the complete number is considered evidence of inability. Also numbering living creatures downgrades the animals in the Daasanach' sight. During an interview, the Daasanach informant compared this desired behaviour and skill with a good teacher who does not need to count the learners in the class but knows which one is missing by other than counting. This example shows how important it is to do field research in order not to include cultural *faux-pas* into the learning materials. Interestingly enough, in this particular case, it is possible to count a certain type of goats (e.g. brown goat with white ears) which in turn found a place in the pool of learning activities and materials.

Using colour-coding in the learning system Ladders of Learning has strong links to the Daasanach culture.[109] Besides the association of a particular colour for each subject (Introduction grey, Daasanach red, Mathematics blue, Life Studies yellow), the INES development team uses a slightly modified version of Maria Montessori's *Coloured Bead Stairs* for the introduction of the numbers 1 – 10.

The emphasis that certain colours carry meaning is familiar to young Daasanach children. In this particular case, however, care had to be taken not to use blue and green to contrast something, because in the Daasanach language both colours are combined under *gílieb* (Tosco 2001).

---

108 In a question-answer session with Padmanabha Rao of the Indian RIVER team on the MultiGradeMultiLevel-Methodology, he states that within RIVER, only 50% of the wide range of materials needed for a ladder of learning is provided by the project. 30% are created by the teachers while at least 20% need to be generated with help from the community. In India stories, created by parents and children, are included within this 20% of community participation (RIVER 2003). In Kenya, the INES team feels strongly about including ideas of the teachers and the communities and generates activities and materials based on these findings.

109 For more information see chapter *1.3 Social Organisation*.

Language barriers and lack of technical terms are general obstacles when concepts are transferred to another culture and language. Formerly there were no words for Mathematical shapes in Daasanach. In cases such as these, after numerous INES team meetings and consultations with Daasanach elders, the INES development team has to coin a new technical term. For example, the term *amoodsóón* (lit. round) was found for the shape of a circle. For a triangle, the INES learning materials now use the Daasanach term *hé gáás ka yaalká* (lit. something sharp like a horn) which in return is related to the name of a triangular shaped area in the Ethiopian homeland of the Daasanach. Generally, there was also no official Daasanach word for the number zero. After numerous discussions with elders from different communities, the INES development team decided to use the Daasanach word *mán* (lit. nothing) which some years earlier was also used for *tohuwabohu* in the creation story for the Daasanach Children's Bible illustrated by Russ Flint (Sattgast, Kwanyang & Komoi 1995). Special technical term dictionaries evolve in the process of developing learning materials.

Extract of the Mathematical INES Dictionary		
English technical term	Daasanach technical term	Literal English translation
zero	mán	*nothing*
more	hé burnayká	*something many*
less	hé iraamánká	*something less*
big	hé guđoka	*something more*
bigger	hé súm guđoká	*something very more*
biggest	hé súm súm guđoká	*something very very more*
5 is bigger than 4	chen he afur 'dú guđo	*5 is 4 but bigger*

Fig. 11.3: Extract of the Mathematical INES dictionary (Source: own illustration).

In special cases, care has to be taken that inferred meaning is not lost due to abstract constructions of terms. The Daasanach language has words for the terms more *(hé burnayká)* and less *(hé iraamánká)*. However, when saying 4 is less than 5 *(afur hé chen ki ninni)* a different adjective is used, namely *hé ninniká* (lit. small). Often the expressions in Swahili and other local languages have to be taken into account, where possible INES tries not to incorporate poorly adapted foreign words. To analyse and document all these phenomena intense field research is required.

11.4 Development Process of the Mathematics Ladder of Learning

Construction. For the first Mathematics ladder of learning, INES incorporated the curriculum for Pre Primary 1, 2 and aspects of grade 3 (2017), as well as, grade 1 and 2 Mathematics of Lower Primary Level (2017). The reasons for combining pre-primary and grade 1, 2 and aspects of grade 3 are threefold. Firstly, the (pre-school) Introduction ladder of learning of INES does not cover all parts of the Pre Primary 1 and 2 curricula. The main focus of the Introduction ladder of learning, as described in chapter 9, lies on introducing the learners to individualized and active learning with the system Ladders of Learning.[110]

---

110 The Mathematics milestone in the Introduction ladder of learning focuses on basic numerical skills especially

Secondly, the system Ladders of Learning does not reproduce arbitrary level and grade boundaries of the curriculum, rather reinforces that learning is a continuous process for everyone without competition in the lower primary levels. According to the stages of development by Ricken, Fritz and Balzer (2011) there are consecutive stages of Mathematical development which are characterised by one main concept and are pre-condition for a child to acquire the next concept. Thirdly, as shown before, the Mathematical strands in both curricula are similar and repetitive (classifications, numbers, measurements and geometry) even if there is a logical increase of level between pre-primary 1 and 2 and primary 1, 2 and 3. The national curriculum sets the specific learning outcomes for each strand and sub-strand and suggests learning experiences. The INES development team analyses the suggested activities in the curricula, the current pre and primary school textbooks, which are on the Kenyan market and used in the conventional schools and the suggested teaching concepts. In this process, INES also consults international publishers for Mathematical learning materials. A pool of ideas and mind maps for activities and construction processes evolves.

Just as any other educational textbook provider or teacher in the field, the INES development team constructs its own interpretation of the national curriculum which is based on pedagogical and psychological reflections, as well as, scientific and personal experiences. For the subject ladders of learning the INES development team chooses how to arrange the given strands and sub-strands and then conceptualizes topic based milestones. Each milestone defines itself through a single major learning objective. What follows is a first systematical arrangement of topics and milestones which in the process of development are revised until the concept for each milestone is set. For the individual milestones, the activity ideas are put into an order according to the principles of inductive learning. The aim is to find an order which leads the learners from a concrete Mathematical example of daily life to the construction of a specific Mathematical skill. Each milestone begins with introductory activities then offers various reinforcements and finally allows the learners to assess themselves with an evaluation (Müller, Lichtinger & Girg 2015).

Using the framework of introduction and reinforcement activities the milestone objective has to be obtained. The INES development team formulates learning objectives for each activity which helps to assess the development process. If an activity does not meet the ultimate learning objective it is taken out of the milestone. For each activity, INES formulates a learning objective. Simply stated, the *learning objective* gives a summary of the task and with the usage of the modal verb *can* expresses what the learner should obtain in the course of the activity (e.g. can point, can match, can add, can subtract etc.).[111] Based on their practical experience as teachers and field-researchers the INES development team makes sure the activities in the system Ladders of Learning meet the five criteria: active, manageable, meaningful, joyful and small. Care is also taken that:

- as many previous activity types from the other ladders of learning are reused
- milestones are put together in groups or phases to present similar sets of activities
- activities are as simple and self-explanatory as possible.

---

on the understanding of numeral series and counting skills.

111 In educating the teachers, a clear formulation of milestone and activity learning objectives in a very clear and simple language is also of great necessity. Only if the teachers understand the underlying learning objectives, can they assess whether they themselves have understood the aim of the milestone (and each activity) and be of support for their learners. Hereby, the INES team omits technical terms, in order to enable translation into the local vernacular Daasanach without having to invent technical terms or using loan words from Swahili or English.

No.	Milestone Topic	Mathematical Skills
1	Equals	Pre-numeric basics
2	Big-Small	
3	Patterns	
4	Introducing 1	Numerics
5	Introducing 2	
6	Introducing 3	
7	Introducing 4	
8	Introducing 5	
9	More-Less	Pre-numeric basics
10	Addition (1-5)	Arithmetical operation
11	Reverse Tasks	
12	Introducing 6	Numerics
13	Introducing 7	
14	Introducing 8	
15	Introducing 9	
16	Introducing 10	
17	Addition (1-10)	Arithmetical operation
18	Completion Tasks	
19	Subtraction	
20	Introducing 0	Numerics
21	Addition & Subtraction (0-10)	Arithmetical operation
22	Mathematical Stories a	
23	Place Value (20)	Numerics
24	Introducing 20	
25	Addition & Subtraction (0-20) without regrouping	Arithmetical operation
26	Addition (0-20) with regrouping	
27	Addition & Subtraction (0-20) with regrouping	
28	Introducing 100	Numerics
29	Place Value (100)	
30	Introducing Money	Measurements
31	Addition & Subtraction (0-100) without regrouping	Arithmetical operation
32	Goods & Money	Measurements
33	Addition (0-100) with regrouping	Arithmetical operation
34	Addition & Subtraction (0-100) with regrouping	
35	Written Addition (0-100)	
36	Written Subtraction (0-100)	
37	Mathematical Stories b	
38	Introducing 1000	Numerics
39	Place Value (1000)	
40	Shopping & Money	Measurements
41	Multiplication I (factor 1,2,5,10)	Arithmetical operation
42	Multiplication II (factor 3,4,6,7,8,9)	
43	Division I (factor 2,4,5 and 10)	
44	Division II (factor 3 6,7,8 and 9)	
45	Multiplication & Division	
46	Written Addition (0-1000)	
47	Written Subtraction (0-1000)	
48	Addition & Subtraction & Multiplication & Division (0-1000)	
49	Mathematical Stories c	

Fig. 11.4: Milestone topics of the Mathematics ladder of learning (Source: own illustration).

Repetition and simplicity of activities are prerequisites to ensure that the learners receive as much autonomy in their learning process as possible. If the learners know how activities are done and do not need constant instruction from the teacher or advanced learners, they can fully concentrate on the learning objective (instead of also on the procedure of the activity as such) and thus experience a high degree of independence.[112] The experience *I can do it myself* has a positive effect on motivation and learning as such.

As mentioned above, there is a large pool of demonstrably good learning activities worldwide, so there is no need to invent a whole set of new activity types. Nonetheless, care is taken that the activity types are adapted to age, culture and the given technical and organisational preconditions of the local environment of the learners. It is particularly motivating for the children if they are familiar with activity types from their free play. Therefore, the INES development team consciously integrates traditional Daasanach songs, rhythmic clapping and game forms, such as a wide range of skill and sorting exercises with pebbles and sand. At the end of this construction process, there is a milestone concept paper which reminds of a lesson plans in conventional schools.

The development process of each milestone of a subject ladder of learning requires answers to the questions posed in figure 11.6 that also serve as a checklist for the INES development team.

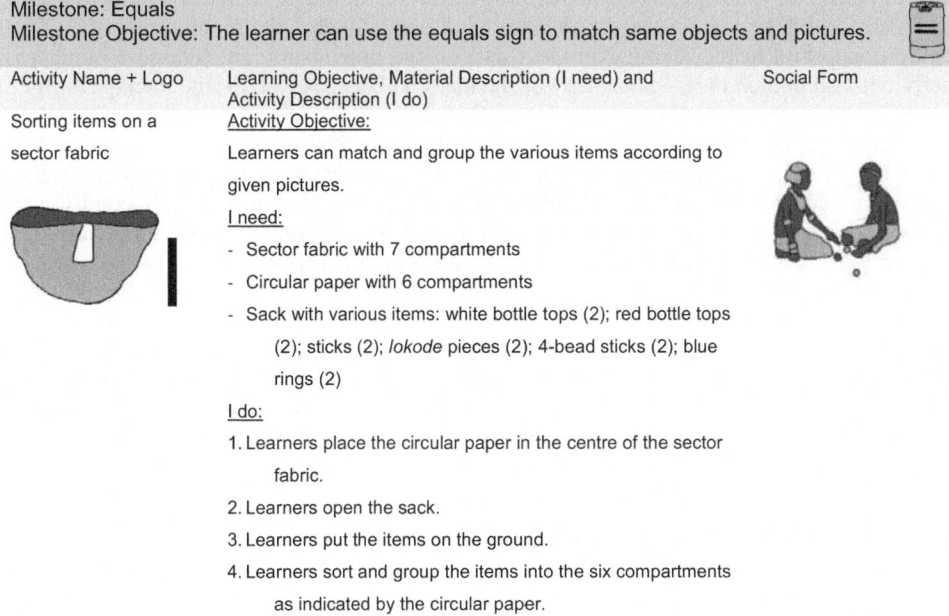

Fig. 11.5: Extract of a concept paper for the milestone *Equals* and activity *Introduction 1* (Source: own illustration).

Design. In the process of constructing the milestone, activities are often added, taken away and shifted between the positions. It helps to have the activities designed on the computer,

---

112 For more information on the system Ladders of Learning, the structure of milestones and the criteria of learning activities see chapter *8. What Is the System Ladders of Learning About?*.

printed, cut and laminated at an early stage to have the chance to try out the activities with these prototypes. The INES development team designs the paper-based learning materials with simple office tools such as Word and PowerPoint which are then put in PDF format, printed, cut, laminated and bound with key chain holders if necessary. Every other learning material prototype has to be crafted in one way or another (tailored, carved, stitched etc.) in order to test their functionality. Concerning the functionality in mobile schools of INES the following criteria also have to be taken into account: extreme robustness, lightness, reusability, local manufacturability and manageability in addition to the other five above mentioned criteria. The learning materials are stored in bags, however, when the learners use them in the mobile schools they are exposed to strong wind and direct sunlight. This means the ink and paper have to be of high quality and every laminated material card smaller than A5 size has to be bound to flipbooks or made of rubber, wood, fabric, beads, goat or cow skin.[113]

Since all learning materials are stored in bags made of cotton fabric which are carried by the school donkeys whenever the school community migrates to the next pasture ground or water hole, the whole school equipment has to be as light as possible. The material bags must also not exceed certain weight to allow the learners to carry them to the school tree, set them up, pack them together and store them in the teacher's homestead. The lightness requirement also implies that, where possible, the learning materials should be reused as often as possible and also for different activities. On the one hand, not enough learning materials should not cause congestion in the learning process and on the other hand, an excessive number of activities will burden the sustainability of the material bags, as well as, the manageability of learners and teachers. Here it is necessary to find the right medium.

There is a large market of international learning materials for the primary school but INES only uses locally produced materials for several reasons: first of all, both local materials and manufacturing, supports the livelihood of sedentary families in Illeret. Secondly, local manufacturing is more favourable than with a publishing house. It allows short runs and frequent format changes of the learning materials which is especially necessary during the piloting phase of the mobile schools but also for future revisions and editions. Thirdly, local production supports sustainability and ownership because the learning materials not only carry local language, pictures and concepts but are also a personal trademark of local Daasanach handiwork. Finally, it is important to highlight manageability of the learning materials at this point once more because, in contrast to other children, young Daasanach school beginners have no prior knowledge of paper, codes (signs, symbols, numbers and letters) and pictures. Handling of cards and pictures, as well as, which side goes up cannot, cannot be taken for granted but has to be taught and practised.

Production. Experience has shown that for the local production of learning materials several preparation steps and support tools are needed. First of all, the local production team leader needs to understand the pedagogical concept behind each learning material. For this, the local production team leader has to undergo similar introductory and practise steps as the future teachers, namely seeing how the activity is done correctly, doing the activity and reflecting on the activity. The INES consultants provide a first complete set of the learning materials, as well as, activity cards for learners and teachers (LABs and TABs) for this initial introduction. When the local production leader is familiar with the learning materials and also understands the learning objectives, he/she will produce one of the respective milestones

---

113 INES calls small self-made booklets, which are bound together with keychain holder flipbooks.

with the help of a so-called quality checklist with written instructions and pictures of the prototypes. The quality checklist consists of all materials needed for this milestone, which materials are a part of previous milestones, who will have to produce which materials (tailoring, carpeting or paperwork), how the materials should be bound, combined and stored and how the final version should look like. The quality checklist also provides an overview of how many sets have been produced. Before the first production runs, the local production team leader will also provide the store with labelled boxes for whole milestones or activity types to file the learning materials appropriately.

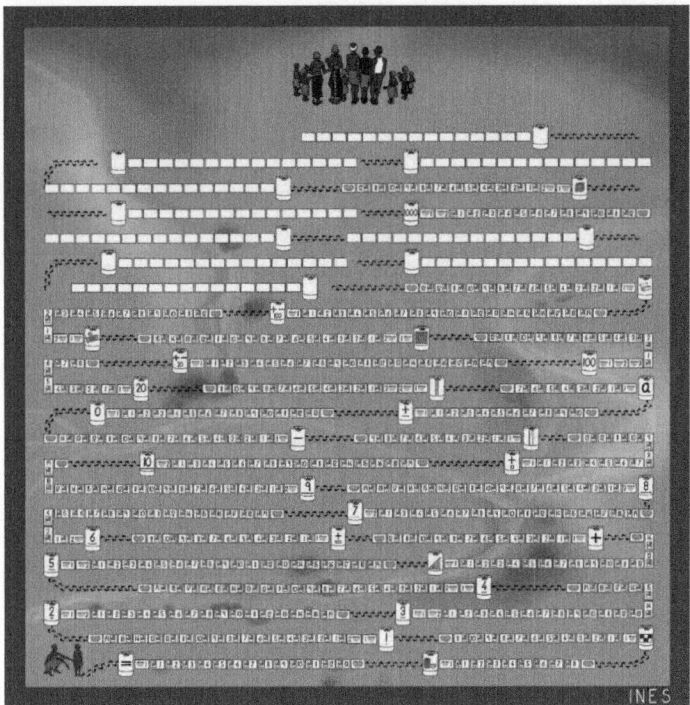

Fig. 11.5: First sketch of the Mathematics ladder of learning (Source: own illustration).

Revision. As in product development, the learning materials must also be repeatedly tested and reworked until it supports as many learners as possible in their individual learning processes. Since the whole concept of mobile schools with the system Ladders of Learning is in the pilot phase it is not yet possible to test whole Mathematics milestones in the mobile schools. To date, the INES development team can only test new activity types with individual Daasanach children and the help of translators, however, during the activity trainings of the teacher education programme, the teacher trainees are encouraged to give feedback on the materials and to propose corrections. The INES development team sees the first edition of a subject ladder of learning and its learning materials as a starting point. After the first experiences in the field, it is to be expected that the mobile teachers will make suggestions for changes and also the INES development team will have collected enough data from their school observations to revise the learning materials.

Checklist of Questions for the Development Process of Each Milestone
– Where in the curriculum is the milestone topic? – What are the learning objectives for the milestone according to the curriculum? – What are the learning objectives for the milestone according to the examination questionnaires? – Which approach does the schoolbook suggest for the milestone topic? – Should the milestone include extra aspects of the topic due to the cognitive, linguistic and cultural characteristics of children in the catchment area? – How many milestones could the topic entail? – What should the learner be able to do at the end of the milestone? – How can the milestone plan look like? – Which activities can the milestone use? – In which order should the activities of the milestone be? – (Which activities are simple? Which activities are more advanced?) – Which activity/ies suit/s as introduction of the milestone? – Which activity/ies suit/s as reinforcement of the milestone? – Which activity/ies suit/s as evaluation of the milestone? – In which social form should the activities of the milestone be done? – Are there too many activities for a single milestone? Should the milestone be split? – How can materials of the milestone look like (sketches of texts, cards, flipbooks, 3D materials etc.)? – Is there a prototype for each activity of the milestone? (hand- or computer made) – What is the task of each activity of the milestone? Which actions are done by the learner or the teacher (TAB)? – What is the learning objective for each activity of the milestone (TAB)? – Are all activity cards of the milestone designed (LAB)? – Do all materials, LABs and TABs of the milestone carry the correct logos? – Is there a prototype for all materials, LABs and TABs of the milestone? – Have the materials, LABs and TABs of the milestone been pretested? – Have the materials LABs and TABs of the milestone been revised? – Were all changes inserted into the milestone plan? – Have the materials, LABs and TABs of the milestone been tested a second time? – Have the materials, LABs and TABs of the milestone been finalized? – Is there a final milestone plan? – Is the LAB of the milestone printed? – Is the TAB of the milestone printed? – Are all materials, LABs and TABs of the milestone been laminated and bound? – Are all materials, LABs and TABs of the milestone been stored properly? – Which information is necessary for the large-scale production of the milestone (quality checklist)? – Is there a quality checklist of the milestone? – Are there five sets of all materials, LABs and TABs of the milestone?

Fig. 11.6: Checklist of questions which support the development process of each milestone (Source: own illustration).

Personal Notes of the Authors

Since our first encounter and interviews with the Daasanach in Northern Kenya, we hear repeated expressions of grievances of them being the most marginalized language group in Kenya. Daasanach have a strong claim for the right of land, education, healthcare and peace. We often hear stories about the struggles of Daasanach women who feel deceived or tricked by shop owners for not understanding the value of banknotes or ATM relief food credit cards. We encountered unreasonable livestock bargaining and that Daasanach children face regular periods of hunger and rely on relief food even though their parents have large herds of animals. This shows the need for monetary and market economy knowledge because competition tightens especially in times of crisis after droughts when prices for livestock sink and other foodstuffs are more expensive.

During our interviews with Daasanach pastoralists there was a clear wish that the mobile schools teach their children Mathematical skills. More research has to be done in order to analyse the reasons why Daasanach pastoralists want their children to be skilled in Mathematics. Yet we can assume that there is a wish to understand market economy and to have the infrastructure to access livestock markets.

In the very beginning we tried to develop the Daasanach and the Mathematics ladder of learning in parallel because both subjects are equally important. Due to the tremendous workload and little resources of the INES project, however, the Daasanach ladder of learning was developed first. In connection with the conclusion of the Daasanach ladder of learning in 2018 we were able to refocus on Mathematics with experiences gained in other projects.[114]

Experiences with the Daasanach ladder of learning in the mobile schools and the basically trained teachers shows that the learning materials have to be easy as possible and as closely adapted to the activities of Daasanach in order not to over demand the teachers and their time spent in training. As already mentioned in this chapter, we face similar, as well as, completely new challenges in comparison with the Daasanach ladder of learning which all too often prolong the process and truly tests the patience of all team members. Nonetheless, because many conceptual ideas were already set through the previous ladders of learning, the decision making processes were easier. Also, whereas the production tools and teacher education materials for the other two subject ladders of learning were developed in a later step, all tools and materials for the Mathematics ladder of learning can be planned and worked on parallel and in less time.

---

114 The *Freie Christliche Schule* Gera, Germany is working with the *Mathemeer* (lit. Mathematics sea), a Mathematics ladder of learning for class 1 to 3. The teacher team in Gera was supported by professors and students from the University of Regensburg (Bauer, Böcker, Höldrich, Kirr, Lichtinger, Schaller, Schmutzer & Zeh). Based on these experiences in Germany and the field research in Illeret, the INES development team revised the ten milestones for the introduction of numbers. However, all other Mathematics milestones were developed independently without references to the German learning materials.

I want to become an INES teacher. I want to teach the children in Illkimere fora.

Francis Tabiye, teacher trainee

12. How Does INES Empower Mobile Teachers?

Since the Daasanach pastoralists need an educational system that is designed for mobile communities, INES does not send sedentary (governmentally trained) teachers into the *fora* (stock camps of the Daasanach) but seeks to equip pastoralists themselves to be teachers to the children of their own communities. Community affiliation of the teacher is essential to promote ownership and to avoid alienating children from their pastoralist culture – which is a fear of many Daasanach parents as depicted in chapter 4. For their *Satellite Schools*, the Indian RIVER team also chooses locals who may have a minimum of educational qualification but have strong community ties. The RIVER teacher education programme enables them to handle multigrade classrooms with the help of educational materials which were specially developed by RIVER (Rishi Valley Education Centre 1999).

INES has developed a sequential teacher education programme which empowers Daasanach pastoralists to run the mobile schools. The programme is a process and can be compared to a Daasanach *'dimi* celebration which takes months and sometimes even years to prepare. The modules of the teacher education programme are based on the mobile school concept of INES with the system Ladders of Learning. The teacher trainees learn what kind of pedagogical materials are needed to support a decentralised learning arrangement. They are shown how to handle multiple ability levels, to establish school routines, to read and write in their mother tongue Daasanach and how to work with the ladders of learning for different subjects. The education programme is designed for hands-on which implies that theory courses in Illeret and practice in the school field alternate. The aim is that teacher trainees can implement the newly learned knowledge of the workshops immediately and one to one in their mobile schools.

Even though the development and material production of the ladders of learning for various subjects are still taking place, the INES teacher education programme has already commenced with two different groups of trainees who have started with the process of becoming mobile teachers. INES has decided to run material development and teacher education parallel for several reasons: Firstly, it is possible to open a mobile school with the starter kit of the Introduction ladder of learning. Secondly, the mobile teachers need time to grow into an entirely new role as teachers which is easier when accountability and tasks increase in the course of the programme and with their experience in the field. Thirdly, INES encourages teachers to live lifelong learning which means they can be teachers and learners at the same time. Teachers are great role models if they openly show that they continue to be learners (Hattie 2009).

The community hall on the campus of the Benedictine Fathers in Illeret, where the INES head office is situated, also serves as meeting venue for the local teacher trainees and trainers, as well as, members of the material production team and the pedagogical manager. While the learning materials are produced in the INES office and the first mobile schools run out in the field, the future teachers meet here regularly for workshops and revision sessions. These meetings allow the exchange of information and experiences.

12.1 Community Participation

All these activities of INES would be useless without the genuine involvement of the community in the teacher education process. With the community's wish to have a mobile school comes the responsibility and the necessity of active participation. INES understands that the Daasanach' wish for education and their deep attachment to the nomadic lifestyle are strong forces that, with the support of INES, can be channelled into active participation in the establishment of mobile schools. Chapter 7 already talks about the importance of community participation in generating materials and activities for the ladders of learning. Furthermore, without the involvement of the community at various stages and levels of planning, implementing and running the mobile schools there is no chance of sustainability for the mobile schools.

The community's responsibility begins choosing an apprentice candidate for the INES teacher programme. INES advises the mobile communities to select a member of their own mobile community who is acquainted with the nomadic pastoralist way of life and has a basic knowledge of reading, writing and calculating. Thus, the teachers do not join the INES teacher education programme at their own request and cannot decide for themselves to start a mobile school. It is the responsibility of the community to appoint an interested candidate and to assign them to the INES teacher education programme. The community members are the ones who know their candidate best, as well as, his/her degree of attachment to the nomadic background community. Of course, the INES founder Father Florian OSB and the pedagogical manager Edwin Changamu support the process and offer consultations.

Community involvement does not stop at this point. Elders and parents of the (future) learners in the *forich* have to support the teacher in various ways. It starts with assigning donkeys which will carry the learning materials while shifting to the next stock camp and deciding which tree(s) are reserved for the learning area. The school tree decision is not without importance since shaded places are scarce and especially young animals must avoid the sun of the midday heat without occupying or demanding the school tree. In a big *forich* with many children, the community and the teacher also have to decide upon the number and age-range of learners enrolled. INES advises the teachers to start with approximately 15 learners between the age of 6 and 12 years in the beginning to ensure that the teachers can meet all requirements and demands of their learners. With time and experience, they may increase the number or start a second learning group.

Since each community structures their daily routine in the stock camp differently, each mobile community must establish a certain period during the day in which the children are not involved in fetching water, collecting firewood and taking care of livestock, but free for learning. This assigned time for schooling may vary between the mobile schools but also depending on the weather season and the present location of the stock camp whether it is near or from a waterhole and the grazing grounds. For this reason, Jeremiah Teete's community decided to start the school during the dry season at around 8 o'clock, before the learners go for their daily chores, while Joshua Esho's school begins at around 11 o'clock after the first chores have been fulfilled. These examples clearly show that only the local community can determine the decision concerning school time.

Fig. 12.1: During the school start of Joshua Esho, Father Florian OSB, Edwin Changamu and members of the INES team officially hand over the learning materials to the community and their teacher (Source: Ruth Würzle).

Additionally, the local community members take over a major part in monitoring the teacher. Of course, INES has installed monitoring tools such as registers, assessment forms and regular school visits but it is up to the community to observe the teacher's presence and the educational progress of the learners. It is an indicator of active participation and sustainability when elders and parents keep watch over the learning area and when they help to keep away any distractions. If the community finds a teacher being frequently absent they can cut the salary. INES advises the communities to pay one goat or sheep per month to their teacher. The teacher can then decide whether to keep the animal and to increase their personal flock or to sell it. INES supports the local community where necessary while making sure to transfer as much responsibility back to them as possible.

12.2 Becoming a Mobile Teacher

INES started the teacher education programme for mobile teachers in 2017. Since then two consecutive teacher trainee groups have run through the first modules. The teacher education programme is structured in a way that allows pastoralists to attend on a part-time basis and be able to start their own school as early as possible (Module 3). Before the trainees start, INES explains that becoming an INES teacher is a process with different (fixed) modules. Compulsory attendance to workshops and obligatory observations are often compared to the fixed steps which Daasanach men have to undergo to become an elder. Experience shows there is a notion that the INES teacher education programme is a single workshop with the starting of a school being immediate. The future teachers quickly recognise, however, that running a mobile school with the system Ladders of Learning involves a radically new way of teaching and learning which takes time to internalize (Rishi Valley Education Centre 2003). According to Hattie, high quality student-centred settings, as in the mobile schools with the system Ladders of Learning, require even better educated forces than teacher-centred settings (Hattie 2009).

Fig. 12.2: Elders observing the mobile school of Jakob Lon'gada (Source: Ruth Würzle).

When the two pedagogical consultants, Theresa Schaller and Ruth Würzle, or the pedagogical INES manager Edwin Changamu facilitate workshops or revision days a translator supports them.[115] When a local team member conducts the sessions they are held in Daasanach only. Long term INES hopes to employ local teacher trainers who have gone through the INES teacher education programme themselves and are familiar with leading a mobile school.[116]

---

[115] The two consultants facilitated the first round of the INES teacher education programme. From the first round, attempts were made to train local teacher trainers. Local team members, therefore, took over parts of the workshops and facilitated the teacher revision days.

[116] Schaller and Würzle have developed a series of workshops for the INES teacher education programme and a manual which introduces the INES teacher trainer to important approaches, skills and tools. Moreover, the manual provides a detailed overview of the INES teacher education programme with all its modules including background theory and the elaborated workshop plans.

Module	Components
Preparation Module 0	– Appointment of the prospective teachers – Participation and observation in an existing mobile school
Module 1	– Workshop 1 – Basics – First experience in the field (conducting assemblies, reading stories, singing songs) – Observation in a mobile school – Teacher revision days
Module 2	– Workshop 2 – Introduction ladder of learning – Experiences in the field (conducting assemblies, activities with the – 'bil 'Daasanach (initial sound chart) – Teacher revision days
Module 3	– Workshop 3 – Preparation of the school start – Start of the mobile school with the Introduction ladder of learning – Teacher revision days
Module 4	– Workshop 4 – Daasanach ladder of learning – Addition of learning materials in the mobile school with the – Daasanach ladder of learning – Peer observation – Teacher revision days
Module 5	– Workshop 5 – Mathematics ladder of learning – Addition of learning materials in the mobile school with the – Mathematics ladder of learning – Peer observation – Teacher revision days
Module 6	– Workshop 6 – Life Studies ladder of learning – Addition of learning materials in the mobile school with the – Life Studies ladder of learning – Peer observation – Teacher revision days

Fig. 12.3: Modules of the INES teacher education programme and their components (Source: own illustration).

Care is taken that the workshops are catered to fit the requirements of the participants (e.g. pace) and the various sessions are organised interactively to keep up the concentration and motivation. Even if the content outline, learning objectives and didactical materials of each training module are defined and prepared beforehand, the actual workshops are never the same due to the group of future teachers. INES workshops are facilitated in group form. Everyone is in a circle sitting on a mat around an aesthetically designed centre where either a traditional piece of cloth or stones are arranged. Often, the centre displays the current learning objective on a piece of paper to keep the session's focus. In a circle everyone, trainees and facilitators, are at eye level reducing the fear of speaking and community sharing, promoting listening to and learning from each other.

Sitting on a mat and in a circle is chosen on cultural grounds since the two domains of Daasanach men and women merge when they meet in their round huts. Everyone sits on the floor on a mat and in a circular arrangement. To visualize abstract learning contents and relationships of components within the system Ladders of Learning, the facilitators use three-dimensional materials, as well as, labelled, colourful and laminated cards which they arrange on the ground. These groundwork pictures develop within the course of the workshops and are kept on the ground to function as mind maps throughout the sessions. They also visualize and secure what was has been learned. Experience has shown that these groundwork pictures fascinate many workshop participants, lead to the intended self-reflections, discussions and also allows the perception to be prompted in an aesthetic and holistic way.

I really like these pictures. It shows everything I have learned and how it is in my head
Jeremiah Teete, teacher trainee

The daily sessions of the workshops are structured similar to the daily schedule in the mobile schools to establish and repeat daily routines as early as the first day of the teacher's education programme. In addition to the similar structure, the trainees also work according to the four social forms which are an important part of the flexible system Ladders of Learning. Most importantly, learning contents and activity types are taught in the same way as INES advises the teacher trainees to apply with their future learners.

In order to give a more vivid impression of the teacher training, each module and its components, as well as, excerpts of the didactical principles more details are in the following chapters.

12.3 Preparation Module

The preparation module of the INES teacher education programme comprises of the appointment of one or more prospective teachers, as well as, participation and observation in an existing mobile school.

Appointment of Prospective Teachers. The experience of recent years has shown that prospective teachers have to fulfil some basic requirements to successfully participate in the education programme and to start a mobile school in a nomadic community. The candidates have to be pastoralists themselves and be appointed by their mobile community. INES is reluctant to train sedentary living Daasanach because it is unlikely that they will give up their lifestyle to be a teacher for a nomadic community. So far all sedentary living Daasanach who joined the INES teacher education programme dropped out before the start of their own mobile school in a *fora* or shortly after. INES, therefore, advises the communities to choose a candidate who is a fixed member of their community, who is married and has children because a stable home attaches the teacher to the respective community.

For this reason, Edwin Changamu and Father Florian OSB gather information about the candidates' family status, pastoral management, community assignments, as well as, their allegiance to an extended nomadic family before they are admitted to the education programme.

Participation and Observation in an Existing Mobile School. From their long-term and large-scale experience in teacher education, Padmanabha and Rama Rao, continue saying *seeing is believing*. They strongly advise to set up a model school that new teachers can observe during their training. At the same time, this model school serves as a resource centre (RIVER 2003). It is crucial for the teacher trainees to observe, if not participate, in an existing mobile school at an early stage of the programme. The system Ladders of Learning strongly differs from the candidates' educational experience in conventional primary schools, so they need to see a mobile school set up in real life.

Fig. 12.4: Joshua Esho (mobile teacher) and a member of the INES production team participating in the campus school as learners in February 2017 (Source: Ruth Würzle).

During the first round of the INES teacher education programme in 2017, a semi-mobile campus school was established in Illeret to offer basic education to all illiterate INES workers. An important reason was to provide them with education and to create an opportunity for the workers to experience the learning materials which they had produced in the office beforehand. Another reason was to offer the first INES teacher trainee group, among them Joshua Esho and Jeremiah Teete, the opportunity to participate as learners and observers in a running school which is based on the system Ladders of Learning. Even though Joshua Esho and Jeremiah Teete are literate they too had the chance to experience the daily school routine, learn activities and practise reading and writing in their mother tongue.

Since the start of the semi-mobile campus school in Illeret young Daasanach girls visit as learners and the school is open to observers. Nowadays INES allows teacher trainees only to observe in this campus or a mobile school because, in the Daasanach cultural context, adult learners would always receive more attention than young learners. However, with time and increased resources, INES desires to have more involvement of trainees in the campus school.

12.4 Module 1 - Basics

Module 1 of the INES teacher education programme comprises of a workshop in Illeret (Workshop 1 – Basics), first experience in the field consisting of conducting assemblies, reading stories and singing songs, observation in a mobile school, as well as, teacher revision days.

Workshop 1 – Basics. The module 1 workshop takes place on the INES campus in Illeret and focuses on the basics of the system Ladders of Learning. Teaching ethics and personal motivation to the teaching profession are also essential parts. The workshop begins with the participants' self-introduction (personal and community details), articulation of their teaching motivation (Why do I want to be a teacher?) and the prospective schooling plans of their individual mobile communities.

I want to be a teacher because I like the children to know how to read and write. I want to advise the children in a good way. As a father, I can teach my children at home. I also want my own children to learn.
Hilary Nyakeru Nashere, teacher trainee

Once this has been established the facilitators introduce the vision, working fields and cooperation offers of INES. INES has a short explanatory film and groundwork picture cards to display the concept behind the mobile school system and the cooperation ideas between INES and the mobile communities. The groundwork pictures support a structured and viewable presentation and allow the listeners to pose concrete questions on various levels like learning materials, community participation, staffing and financing, time schedules, etc.. The next session focuses on teaching ethics, culturally appropriate handling of children and basic pedagogical principles. Care is taken that the opening and closing assemblies during the workshop days are identical to those in the mobile schools and follow the same procedure. The trainees are introduced to the schedule of the assemblies and after they have witnessed several of them, they are asked to take over these meetings at the beginning and the end of the workshops to gain first-hand experience and to receive feedback on their trials.

INES planned and set the structure of the assemblies during the initial Workshop 1 of the teacher education programme training with the members of the first group in 2017. The aim was to find a ceremonial assembly routine that has a group-strengthening effect, opens and closes the learning process and gives the learners the possibility to reflect on their learning process. It was also important to provide a framework in which success can be celebrated and special individual contributions can be recognised (Deal & Peterson 2009).

The opening assembly for the mobile schools takes place in a group circle where the event of the day consisting of the current events within the stock camp are shared. Special value was placed on the fact that the assemblies contain culturally familiar rituals and ritual elements and that the schedule follows a fixed structure. Special Daasanach' ceremonies, for example, a 'dimi celebration also follow a defined sequence of distinguished rituals.

Opening Assembly
1) Sit down in a circle around a designed centre
2) Welcome the learners
3) Take the register
4) Sing a song
5) Talk about the event of the day. Possible events of the day may be:
– Talking about the weather and season
– Talking about cultural events (e.g. 'dimi, 'gúol)
– Talking about migration and animal status
– Talking about family events (e.g. birth, marriage, death)
6) Pray together

Fig. 12.5: Procedure of an opening assembly at a workshop for teachers and mobile schools (Source: own illustration).

Fig. 12.6: An opening assembly during a workshop under a tree next to the INES office (Source: Ruth Würzle).

Rituals are important elements for both children and adults because they highlight important events, mark fixed breakpoints in life, foster community living and initiate holistic learning processes. Rituals promote community and communication; they provide orientation and strength and constitute social order (Groeben 2006). When designing the INES teacher training it was important to find ritual elements which allow sufficient scope for the individual teachers to express themselves. The teacher trainees should feel as part of the collective group but also be able to express their personality and identity within a defined framework and procedure which is always open for discussion for all trainees. Individual elements can be rearranged, altered and presented differently. Ladders of learning are learning paths and part of the learner's life path, so when a day's, a week's or a year's work is completed this is caused to celebrate the achievement. In the closing assembly, the focus is on the learner to reflect on the learning process, as well as, on feedback.

I am happy that I understood the colour-coding today. I did not understand the different colours when observing in the campus school but now I understand.
Joshua Esho, teacher trainee

Closing Assembly
1) Sit down in a circle around an designed centre
2) Ask one of the questions of the thumb-method. Possible questions for the thumb-method
– Did you enjoy learning today?
– Were you in a good mood today?
– Have you learned something new today?
– Were you a fast learner today?
– Did you support someone today?
– Were you supported by a peer today?
3) Ask 5 learners to explain their answer on the thumb-method
4) Give feedback on today's learning
5) Celebrate achievements by clapping and a song
6) Make announcements
7) Say good bye
8) Conduct a minute of silence

Fig. 12.7: Procedure of a closing assembly at a workshop for teachers and mobile schools.

Since feedback is one of the essential ingredients of learning, learners must receive feedback to successfully master the given challenges (Hattie 2012). During the feedback session of the closing assembly, the INES teacher trainees experience that constructive feedback, whether positive or negative, aims at improving performance and is thus an effective tool for continuous learning. In the INES closing assemblies, the learners not only receive feedback on whether a learning task is correct or incorrect but also informs the learners where they are in their learning process. The goal is to also suggest other directions which the learners could pursue and lead to alternative strategies of working with and understanding the learning material (Hattie & Clarke 2019).[117]

To meet these demands of promoting learning, INES teacher trainees learn how to formulate constructive feedback. However, also receiving feedback is an important component that should not be underestimated. The theoretical approach in the training session and recurring practice during the closing assemblies eventually initiate a motivating feedback culture in which giving and receiving feedback is a fixed component and possible for all, teacher trainees and trainers, as well as, learners.[118]

---

117 According to John Hattie and Helen Timperley (2007) constructive feedback has to define the goal (Where am I going?), describe what the learner is currently doing (How am I going?) and guide the learner to the next step towards attaining their goal (Where to next?). Ideally, these questions are woven together to emphasise what needs to be done for the learner.

118 Hattie discovered that the most powerful feedback is provided from learners to teachers. Teachers are advised to be open to feedback from learners. The feedback that learners give about their own learning process, what

Besides the plenary sessions, Workshop 1 also focuses on introducing the trainees to the learning ladder time, the main part of a school day. Gradually, the trainees become acquainted with the major components of the learning system: ladders of learning, milestones, activities, material bags, learner activity booklets (LAB), social forms, learning zones, assessment form and register. The facilitators use groundwork pictures to visualize the various components of the system Ladders of Learning and how they are linked to each other. At the end of this first workshop, all applied learning contents are visualized and in a large groundwork picture.

Seeing the floor of the community hall layered with all the materials, graphics and technical terms of the workshop is an impressive experience for the trainees and helps them to recall everything which was learned during the first workshop of the teacher education programme and supports the creation of an own mind map.

After this first workshop in Illeret, the trainees return to their mobile communities and report what they have learned. INES hands out richly illustrated didactical materials on the contents of Workshop 1 to the trainees, which makes the presentation to and the involvement of their Daasanach community easier.

Fig. 12.8: A groundwork picture developed in Workshop 1 – Basics (Source: Ruth Würzle).

First Teaching Experience in the Trainees' Local Community. Back home, the teacher trainees start conducting assemblies with the local children, read stories to them and sing learning songs together. They have laminated booklets compiled with stories and songs. All of them are part of the upcoming ladders of learning. Even if these teaching contents may seem few it is a necessary experience that children gather at a fixed time during the day, in

---

they know, understand, where they make errors or need help, is just as important as the feedback teachers give to learners (Hattie 2009).

order to conduct the mentioned group activities and to understand what it means to be a teacher. Also for the community and learners, it takes time to adjust to the idea of a daily school routine.

I have talked with my community about a signal for the school start. The first idea was to observe the sun, the second to start school after the animals left for grazing. Now they know, once the children see me, it is time to go to school.
Jeremiah Teete, teacher trainee

Observation in a Mobile School. In Module 1, the trainees are obliged to observe in the campus school in Illeret or a running mobile school for at least two weeks. As mentioned above in chapter 11.3, the real school life experience with a teacher colleague, who already works with ladders of learning and offers school on a daily basis, is essential to believe in the system. It also allows them to share with other mobile teachers and to compare different variations of the mobile schools working with INES learning materials. At the same time, the more opportunities teachers have in receiving feedback from a visitor the more objective their view becomes. These observations are organised by INES to make sure that not more than two trainees visit a mobile school at the same time. The trainees were introduced to observation rules during the first workshop to assure that the teacher and learners are not distracted. For the first teacher trainee group, a model school was established on the INES campus for two weeks in 2016 to offer them a place for observation.

Fig. 12.9: Joshua Esho and other teacher trainees observing in a model school with Ruth Würzle and Joseph Naliye in 2016 during the first Workshop 1 of the INES teacher education programme (Source: Theresa Schaller).

Teacher Revision Days. After some weeks of this module of the teacher education programme, the experiences in the field and observations in a running mobile school, so-called teacher revision days are facilitated in Illeret. Here, all new teacher trainees meet again and reflect on their experiences in the field. During these peer-learning reflections, the trainees also revise the contents of Workshop 1 and talk about their observations. INES poses questions to the trainees on how to adapt the learning system in their future schools and they discuss the answers as a group.

12.5 Module 2 - Introduction Ladder of Learning

Module 2 of the INES teacher training consists of the Module 2 workshop, which focuses on the learning activities of the Introduction ladder of learning, further experiences in the field (activities with the *'bil 'Daasanach* – the initial sound chart) and also teacher revision days.

Fig. 12.10: All trainees of the first INES education programme (Source: Theresa Schaller).

Workshop 2 – Introduction Ladder of Learning. Module 2 introduces the teacher trainees to all activities of the Introduction ladder of learning with subsequent practice of these learning activities on different levels. First, the trainees discover the various learning materials of the respective activity by the help of the learner activity booklet (LAB). Using a cohesive colour, symbol, number and outline system, the activity cards refer to the required learning materials, social form and the task of a specific learning activity. Each activity type implemented within a ladder of learning has an activity card and is later on used by the learners as an explanatory support tool. After the analysis of the activity card, the teacher trainees have to single out the required learning materials from a box which contains the complete set of learning materials of the Introduction ladder of learning. This task trains logo and picture identification, as well as, handling the various card and three-dimensional learning materials. Then, the activity is acted out by the facilitators (or a video is shown) where the trainees have to watch closely before trying out the activity themselves together with their peers. The trainees take turns playing the role of a teacher, individual learner or peer learner. Only if the teachers fully understand each activity type, they will be able to show them correctly to the learners and assist them with challenges.

After they have performed an activity type with the learning materials, they place the cards and three-dimensional materials into the correct bag. Each trainee gets a personal set of bags of the Introduction ladder of learning. Filling the material bags emphasises the logo system on the ladder of learning, bags and materials and reinforces the importance of a clear order and correct storage. It is important to include all trainees in this process and not to hand out a complete set of bags because the process of packing their own learning material bags creates ownership for the materials and the bag sets. The teachers can only prepare the start of their mobile school when the material bags are fully packed and they master all activities of the Introduction ladder of learning. If learning materials are missing or broken, the trainees report it immediately to the INES pedagogical manager, Edwin Changamu, who is also in charge of the material production and storage. He hands out the missing materials and ensures an immediate replacement either during the training or later in the mobile schools.

The training follows the activity sequence given on the Introduction ladder of learning. Just as their future learners, the trainees follow the procedure of attaching their name tag on the ladder of learning to indicate which learning activity they are about to discover. The training of each activity always closes by reading through the Teacher Activity Booklet (TAB), a flipbook which explains each activity step by step, what the teachers have to take care of and how to react when the learners face problems. The TABs are two-sided and provide the explanation in English and Daasanach.

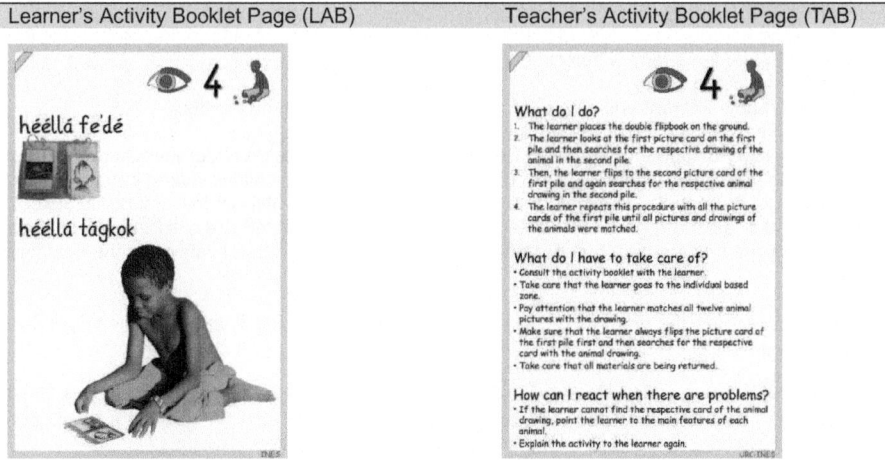

Fig. 12.11: Learner activity booklet (LAB) and the English side of the teacher activity booklet (TAB) of the Activity Eye 4 of the Introduction ladder of learning (Source: own illustration).

During this workshop, INES also invites the teacher trainees into the material production office. Edwin Changamu shows them around and asks them to help with the production of learning materials for some time. This way the trainees experience the close link between the material production workers, as well as, the teachers and the various important roles within the Illeret Nomadic Education System. To develop further team spirit, there are joint assemblies of teacher trainees and material workers during the workshop. Here, the INES team and the teacher trainees get the chance to report on their daily work and to appreciate achievements of the day e.g. that the tailor Veronicah was able to attach missing buttons to some material bags while the trainees were practising activities.

Experiences in the Field. Back in their community, the trainees continue meeting with their learners. Now the focus lies on introducing first small learning activities to children. The trainees use the initial sound chart and they teach their learners the initial sounds and pictures, as well as, the corresponding song.

The Introduction ladder of learning and the complete set of material bags are not yet given out for two reasons: the activity training often requires further practice and the start of a mobile school is planned and prepared in the following module.

Teacher Revision Days. Again teacher revision days are held in Illeret where the participants revise the activities of the first ladder of learning by means of small activity videos and their material bags.

12.6 Module 3 - Start of the Mobile School

Module 3 of the INES teacher training prepares the teachers for the start of their own mobile school (Workshop 3) and includes the official school start.

Steps of Introduction	
Step 1:	Place the Introduction ladder of learning into the centre with the ladder of learning facing the students (students form a half circle).
Step 2:	Ask: What do you see?
Step 3:	Collect many different answers from the learners. Encourage the learners to look very closely. Show appreciation for all given answers.
Step 4:	Tell the story of ladder of learning: There is a child which goes on a journey. On the journey the child visits different fora (ɗabano). In each forich (ɗab) the child is invited into the homes (lokool) of the people. The child hears, sees and learns new things. In each home (lokool) the child is asked to do a task. After visiting each home (lokool) the child is able to show what he/she has learned, before they say good bye and the child travels on to the next fora (ɗab).
...	
Step 24:	Together with all the learners get the activity booklet of Learning Together and sit down in the circle.
...	
Step 50:	Now, the learners start on their own with the Introduction ladder of learning. This time let all learners go at their own pace. To avoid crowding, let them start one after the other. The learners waiting for their start support in partner and group based activities. Stay in the teacher based zone and support the learners.

Fig. 12.12: An excerpt of the Steps of Introduction of the Introduction ladder of learning (Source: own illustration).

Workshop 3 – Preparation of the School Start. During the Module 3 workshop, each participant finishes sorting the learning materials into the personal material bag.

The main issue of the Module 3 workshop lies on how to introduce the learners to the learning system with the help of the pre-school materials of the Introduction ladder of learning. INES also supports the teachers in how to organise the start of the mobile schools in the teachers' communities. INES has developed a manual for the school start: Steps of Introduction of the Introduction ladder of learning. The very first group of learners in a mobile school require a lot of time and support to understand the learning system, the individual learning procedures and the schedule. In time, new learners who are enrolled in the mobile school will not need as much instruction by the teacher because they adapt quickly by observing their advanced peers, as experienced in the first mobile school showed with Joshua Esho and in the campus school with Bonaya Yierar. The pedagogical colleagues from Rishi Valley, India also support this experience. The Steps of Introduction of the Introduction ladder of learning were developed using pedagogic didactical basics, they were extended to include ideas of the first group of teacher trainees and revised after the experiences and observations in the model school on the INES campus in 2016 and the school start of Joshua Esho in 2017.[119] The procedure of introduction to the learning system is also used in Workshop 1 – Basics of the INES teacher education programme. Therefore, after the completion of Workshop 3 the teachers have already experienced the Introduction procedure as learners, observed it in the model school (Module 2) and are now prepared to conduct the steps as teachers themselves. For the first group of teacher trainees, INES carefully planned the school starts for these various teachers, to provide each teacher with a colleague at hand who would support as an assistant teacher during the first two weeks of the mobile school.

Start of the Mobile School with the Introduction Ladder of Learning. As soon as, all organisational issues are addressed the teachers start their own mobile school and begin teaching with the Introduction ladder of learning. The whole INES team accompanies the official school start, as soon as, the trainee has accomplished the Modules 1, 2 and 3 of the teacher education programme.

Before the INES team comes for the official function, the teachers have to inform their community, they have to identify the first group of learners, a school tree has to be chosen (if not already done) and sticks and ropes have to be prepared in order to be able to fix the hanging bags below the school tree. Providing an appropriate fixation system for the learning material bags and the ladder of learning is in the teacher's responsibility and may be solved differently in each community. Jeremiah Teete and Bonaya Yierar attach the bags directly to the branches of a big shady tree while Joshua Esho fixes sticks into the ground below a cluster of short trees to provide sufficient stability against the wind. INES advises the new teachers not to enrol more than 15 learners between the age of 6 and 12 years at the beginning of the mobile school. Often, the communally living and shifting community may not even exceed this number of school-age children, however, larger communities will impede a too high responsibility on their teacher if they allow all children to attend the school. This is a complex decision process in which the whole community must participate in order to avoid dispute. INES advises the teachers to start with a fixed group of learners to get the learning system across to as many learners as possible and to install a school routine as fast as possible. Both,

---

119 After the school start of the first group of teacher trainees, the Steps of Introduction of the Introduction ladder of learning was revised and adapted. This manual is intended to be a guidance and support for the teachers, not a rigid system of obligatory rules.

Joshua Esho and Jeremiah Teete chose a group with more girls than boys between the age of 6 and 12. For the official school start, to which all community members of the stock camp are invited, Father Florian OSB (founder of INES) and Edwin Changamu (pedagogical manager of INES) visit the teacher's community together with a translator, the assistant teacher and other interested INES members. The opening speeches address the cooperation between INES and the community and talk about who carries which part of the responsibility of the learners' education. The teachers are honoured for their efforts during the training process and then the learners and the learning materials of the Introduction ladder of learning are officially given to the new teacher. The teachers then have the chance to explain the basic idea of the learning system to their community and allow plenty of time for questions. The meetings usually end with a prayer and sometimes the community slaughters a goat and prepares a meal for the visitors.

The next day after the ceremony the mobile school starts. The teacher and the assistant teacher use the Steps of Introduction of the Introduction ladder of learning to guide the learners into the individual learning procedure. Experience has shown that during the first days and weeks various community members join the daily learning sessions and observe from a distance in order to get an impression of how the mobile school works. Especially during the beginning phase, Edwin Changamu and the two consultants Theresa Schaller and Ruth Würzle, visit on a regular basis to accompany the teachers on their first steps of leading their own mobile school. After class, any observations are shared and together answers and solutions are gathered.

Fig. 12.13: Joshua Esho and his learners hanging up the ladder of learning and the material bags in their mobile school (Source: Ruth Würzle).

Teacher Revision Days. After some time of teaching with the Introduction ladder of learning the teachers meet in Illeret to share their experiences. At this point, the teachers get the opportunity to report on their everyday schooling, ask questions and discuss problems. They share how many learners have attended school since the official school start, the average number of daily attendances, they reflect on the learner's answers in the closing assemblies concerning the daily school offer and how they like it. The mobile teachers are also encouraged to give feedback on the learning materials (e.g. if they noticed some activities which are not manageable by the learners or which ones are constantly done incorrectly) and the procedure (e.g. if they would like to suggest some changes in the Steps of Introduction of the Introduction ladder of learning). Of course, focus also lies on how the teachers themselves enjoy their roles and tasks and how the INES team can provide further support if needed.

12.7 Further Modules – Additional Subject Ladders of Learning

After the mobile school has used the Introduction ladder of learning for some time and, as soon as, the first learners have passed the compulsory two rounds of the ladder, the teachers get introduced to the structure and content of the Daasanach ladder of learning (Workshop 4). Workshop 4 introduces the teachers sequentially to the activities of the Daasanach ladder of learning by the help of video clips and teacher activity booklets (TABs). Since many of the activity types are already known to the teachers from former activity trainings, a shorter period of time is scheduled for the introduction to the Daasanach activities.[120] Additionally, the teachers go through the handbook Steps of Introduction of the Daasanach ladder of learning which gives a step-by-step instruction on how to introduce the new ladder of learning in the mobile school. After the introduction of each of the four phases of the Daasanach ladder of learning the teachers pack all necessary learning materials into their personal red Daasanach material bags.

This procedure is repeated in Module 5 (Mathematics ladder of learning and addition of learning materials in the mobile school with the Mathematics ladder of learning) and Module 6 (Life Studies ladder of learning and addition of learning materials in the mobile school with the Life Studies ladder of learning). After each workshop of the subject ladders of learning in Illeret, the teachers receive the learning materials for their mobile schools.

In Module 4, 5 and 6 of the INES teacher education programme, there is continuous peer observation. This ensures that the teachers can observe their colleagues, see alternating ways of teaching, how to address learning-related challenges and receive direct feedback and discuss problems.[121] The INES team visit the individual mobile schools on a regular basis for evaluation, monitoring, for consultation and to supply the teachers with missing learning materials.

---

120 The Daasanach ladder of learning is divided into 4 phases visualized by a growing herd of goats. For more information on the phases of the Daasanach ladder of learning see chapter 10.4.
121 The teachers of the Indian schools teaching with the MGML-Methodology also meet periodically. In a question-answer session discussing the MultiGradeMultiLevel-Methodology, Padmanabha Rao from RIVER highlights the importance of the teachers themselves meeting on a regular basis to share experiences and to confer about suitable activities. "It is important that the teacher does not begin to feel isolated and unsupported in the newly set up schools." (RIVER 2003: 153).

Conclusion

This book has shown that education participation of mobile pastoralists remains a controversial issue worldwide. History shows that attempts have often failed due to the unsuitable linking of educational offers and the existing life situation of mobile pastoralists (Krätli & Dyer, 2009). Differences between education providers and education recipients are a general problem around the globe. If schools handle learners all equally, in administrative, as well as methodological terms, with no or little regard to their context, a significant number of learners will be under- or over-challenged. When learners drop out or are left behind, schools do not reduce educational disadvantage but rather contribute to increasing it. (Schröder, 2012).

The conceptual difficulty behind this is that formal school systems usually take the general conditions in which children and adolescents grow up to define the learning objectives and tasks. The formal school system in Kenya takes the general conditions of communities who live in cities or from agriculture to determine the educational objectives in the national curriculum, the form of teaching through direct instruction and the place of learning in fixed school buildings. The life situation of mobile pastoralists is not considered even though large parts of the country are homeland to communities like the Daasanach who secure their livelihood through mobile pastoralism. Schools that focus on the context and life situations of children and adolescents, however, refer more strongly to the biographical requirements, which include the learners' social and cultural background, their physical, mental and emotional conditions, their previous knowledge and aspects of livelihood. Around the globe, educational concepts are required, in which the heterogeneous contexts, learning objectives, teaching forms and methods are interlinked (Schröder, 2012).

The educational concept presented in this book has been developed in close relation to the precarious life situation of Daasanach pastoralist children while taking into account the educational objectives that are required by the Kenyan national curriculum. The local INES team and its consultants started with a precise analysis of the everyday life of the Daasanach pastoralists and clarified which decisions and demands Daasanach parents and children have in terms of livelihood and formal education. Through intensive talks with pastoralist children, parents and elders, the international INES team identified the legal, organisational and normative barriers for Daasanach to access formal education. Only after the controversial issues of the Kenyan formal school system and the existing life situation of Daasanach pastoralists were clarified and Daasanach children, parents and elders had formulated their wishes regarding schooling and education, could a suitable educational concept and learning arrangement be developed.

The INES team adapted the Indian MultiGradeMultiLevel-Methodology and its ladders of learning to the specific context of the Daasanach pastoralists and established a suitable organisational variation through mobile schools. For this, the national curriculum, the traditional textbook contents and methodological designs of what is taught and learned in Kenya were analysed and reconstructed, adapted to the needs of the Daasanach pastoralists and designed into learning plans for the lower primary level. The system Ladders of Learning allows learners to work individually, at their own pace, yet in heterogeneous learning groups.

Further, the INES team developed a teacher education programme, trained local men and women as mobile teachers and started the piloting phase with first mobile schools. The system Ladders of Learning allows teachers to offer a well-equipped learning environment in which they have sufficient time to support individual learners instead of constantly directing the whole learning group. Numerous Daasanach communities have identified young men and women and have applied for the INES teacher education programme.

Because also life situation oriented educational concepts bear risks and can lead to further disadvantage and other forms of discrimination, educational research must observe them critically (Schröder, 2012). Concerning the mobile INES schools, the learners are evaluated regularly to assess whether they meet the national standards of lower primary level. The learners have to be able to transfer to national schools at any time. If the mobile schools with the system Ladders of Learning do not increase literacy and numeracy in Northern Kenya, they could easily be labelled as schools for disadvantaged Daasanach pastoralists, which offer some form of basic education but do not meet the national standards. This would strengthen rather than weaken the existing social discrimination of Daasanach pastoralists.

Likewise, Daasanach pastoralist themselves have to experience how basic education improves their lives and future perspectives. If this is not the case, the mobile schools with the system Ladders of Learning will not be sustainable. Long-term educational research is necessary, to assess the learning standards and the local ownership and perspective of this adapted educational concept.

Given the current situation of the Daasanach in Northern Kenya, the INES team has mainly trained mobile pastoralists in the teacher education centre in Illeret because these men and women are able to live and teach in this harsh and remote environment. Only with their own livestock and embedded in their pastoral production team can they provide a school offer for the children in the temporary stock camps. This, however, confronts the trainees and teachers with a double task. They have to maintain a mobile lifestyle to take care of their own livestock and run their mobile school at the same time. The INES team has to supervise and support them closely to assess how much time the mobile teachers can dedicate to their school. With time and more trained teachers, team teaching could be a solution for this double task, just as pastoral production maintains itself only through teamwork.

This book has given a practical insight that the cooperative development of a mobile school system that is oriented towards the context and everyday life of pastoralists is a time-consuming process. Of course, not all school development contexts pose the challenges of the INES project such as lack of infrastructure, existing educational material and financial resources. Nevertheless, the time required analysing the life situation, transforming the national lesson plans into learning plans, adapting learning tasks and materials for several subjects to the specific context, empowering a local team of material workers, establishing a suitable teacher education programme and supporting the mobile teachers in their school starts must not be underestimated. In the context of international cooperation and external fundraising, ambitious school development projects have to possess immense power of perseverance and a tenacious commitment to overcoming opposition and setbacks.

In our global society, the question remains how formal education can be designed to foster maturity in different life situations. Children and adolescents need to be equipped so that they can handle the tasks and responsibilities as individuals in an increasingly complex and controversial global society. Educational questions are universal, for rural children in South India, urban children in German and pastoralist children in Northern Kenya. The system Ladders of Learning provides and improve context-oriented educational opportunities for them all.

Afterword – What Do We See Now?

The journey to one of the mobile schools begins early, well before the sun rises because we often only have a rough idea where the stock camp is at the moment. The first kilometres the jeep follows a track that hints at a road then, however, our driver goes off-road. Skilfully he navigates through the thorny bushes, crosses dry riverbeds and never-ending stone fields. Finally, after a-three-hour drive, a large herd of cattle appears on the gentle hills in the glimmer of the rising sun. As we get closer we recognise the round huts covered with goatskins, iron sheets and black plastic foils. The recently built stock camp blends in perfectly with the colours of the earth with its barren landscape and the brittle ground. We arrive at the forich just as the men drive out the herds from the thorn hedges which have guarded man and cattle during the night.

We join some children and elders below a tree in the nearby riverbed and observe as the teacher and some learners fasten the different school bags with ropes and sticks below an Acacia bush. After a few hand movements, everything is firmly tucked away to resist the wind and the colourful ladder of learning stretches like a sail. Then the teacher settles down with the children who eagerly await for him in their circle. The teacher opens the morning assembly with a song. Sixteen children sing and clap joyfully. The strong wind carries their melodic singing to the round huts where the mothers are preparing tea. Now the individual learning time starts. Learners approach the ladder of learning and set their personal nametag one step further. We observe a girl who cannot close the safety pin of her nametag by herself but with the help of a classmate, she finally manages. With such self-confidence, the learners move to the bags, search for the logo of their current milestone and then carefully go through the different materials of the bag until they have found their required card. In the meantime, we observe the teacher together with a boy, both speak quietly with each other. Another girl sits down next to them and observes the short instruction of the activity with interest. Just outside the shade of a tree, three children dance, sing and giggle as they perform their activity. This elicits a smile from the respectable elders at the tree to our left. We are moved as we realise in this most remote savannah plain below an acacia, active, individual, flexible and cooperative learning is happening.

Appendix – Photographs and Graphics

Page 15: Paul Gosh Kwanjang (Source: Philipp Laurer)
Page 37: Joshua Esho (Source: Ruth Würzle)
Page 51: Father Florian OSB (Source: Philipp Laurer)
Page 59: Felicitas Muer (Source: Ruth Würzle)
Page 73: Eveline Momanyi & Daasanach group (Source: Ruth Würzle)
Page 81: Padmanabha & Rama Rao (Source: Ashoka, Innovators for the Public)
Page 89: Edwin Changamu (Source: Ruth Würzle)
Page 125: Kamate Longaye (Source: Ruth Würzle)
Page 139: Jacob Long'ada (Source: Ruth Würzle)
Page 155: Bonaya Yierar (Source: Philipp Laurer)
Page 171: Francis Tabiye (Source : Ruth Würzle)

Fig. 1.1 Joshua Esho with his family in traditional dress at the '*dimi* celebration (Source: Ruth Würzle).

Fig. 1.4: Eastern shore of Lake Turkana with view on Northern Island (Source: Ruth Würzle).

Fig. 1.5: A Daasanach boy tending goats and sheep (Source: Ruth Würzle).

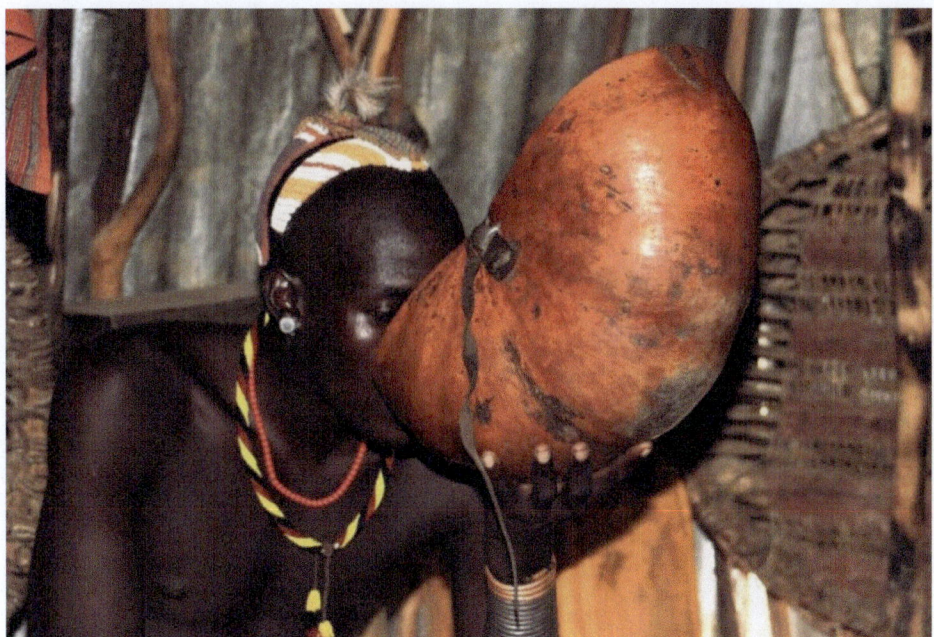

Fig. 1.6: A Daasanach man with traditional hair drinking *bie kulláá* from a *'daate* (Source: Ruth Würzle).

Fig. 1.8: Two Daasanach girls of the generation-sets *nabus* and *kobier* (Source: Ruth Würzle).

Fig. 1.9: A Daasanach man tending his goats (Source: Ruth Würzle).

Fig. 1.10: A Daasanach woman carrying a grass mat, two calabash and her grandchild (Source: Ruth Würzle).

Fig. 1.11: A Daasanach girl milking a goat (Source: Philipp Laurer).

Fig. 1.12: A small *forich* with a few round huts, covered with black tarps (Source: Ruth Würzle).

Fig. 1.13: A hut with an iron sheet roof in a *manyatta* (Source: Ruth Würzle).

Fig. 1.14: Daasanach men celebaring *'gúol* (Source: Philipp Laurer).

Fig. 1.15: A Daasanach man celebrating *'dimi* in Nang'oleiy in 2016 (Source: Ruth Würzle).

Fig. 4.1: Theresa Schaller conducting surveys in Illgele (Source: Theresa Schaller).

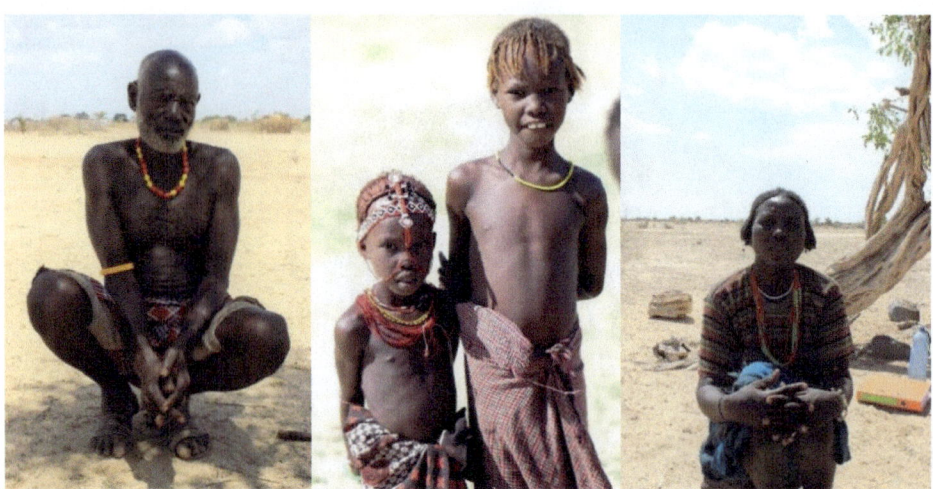

Fig. 4.3: Interviewee Lokoringole Hakualata, two Daasanach girl interviewees with traditional hairdress and interviewee Laboro (Source: Theresa Schaller).

Fig. 5.0 Eveline Momanyi (INES team) speaking with Daasanach mothers and children (Source: Ruth Würzle).

Fig. 8.1: Classroom of the MGML-school Sundravanam, Andhra Pradesh, India (Source: Ruth Würzle).

Fig. 8.2: MGML-school Sundravanam, Andhra Pradesh, India (Source: Ruth Würzle).

Fig. 8.3: Daasanach girls are attaching their nametags on the Introduction ladder of learning (Source: Ruth Würzle).

Fig. 8.4: (On the left) Indian systemic ladder of learning for EVS (RIVER) (Source: Ruth Würzle); (On the right) linear ladder of learning for preschool in Northern Kenya (INES) (Source: own illustration).

Fig. 8.5: Linear arrangement of the milestones in the INES Daasanach ladder of learning (Source: own illustration).

Fig. 8.10: Joshua Esho conducting an opening assembly in his mobile school (Source: Ruth Würzle).

Fig. 8.11: Jeremiah Teete fixing the material bags in the school tree by means of ropes (on the left) material bags on a complex carrier system made from sticks (on the right) (Source: Ruth Würzle).

Fig. 8.12: Jeremiah Teete supporting a learner (on the left), Bonaya Yierar watching learners (on the right) (Source: Ruth Würzle).

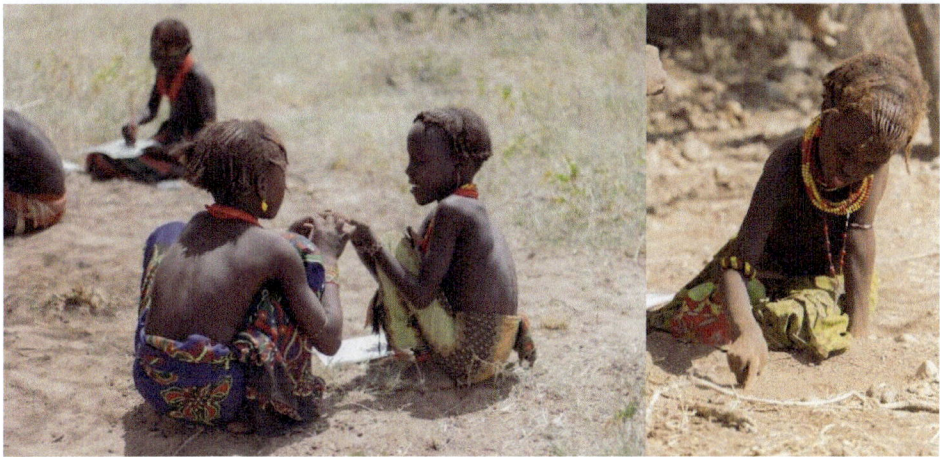

Fig. 8.14: Two girls working together on a learning activity in the partner based zone (on the left); a girl working individually (on the right) (Source: Ruth Würzle).

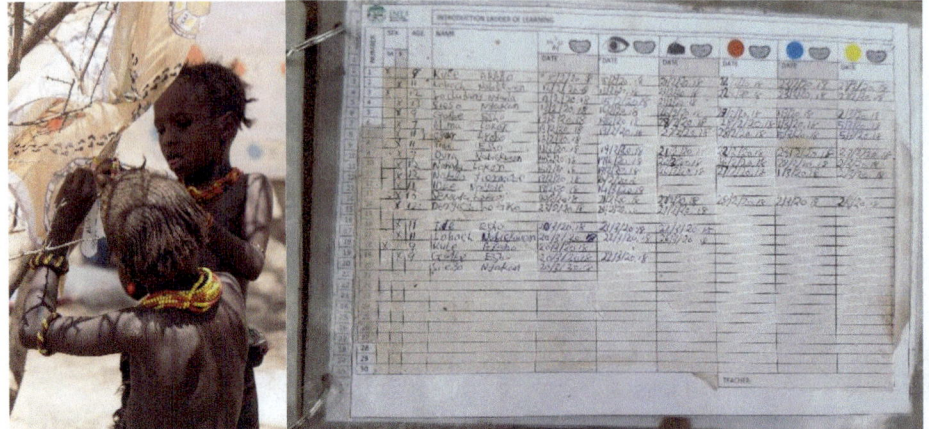

Fig. 8.15: Two girls attaching their name tag on the Introduction ladder of learning (on the left); the assessment form of one of the mobile teachers (on the right) (Source: Ruth Würzle).

Fig. 9.1: Daasanach children building play huts (Source: Theresa Schaller).

Fig. 9.2: Introduction ladder of learning of INES (Source: own illustration).

Fig. 9.3: The Introduction ladder of learning with the nametags of all learners (Source: Ruth Würzle).

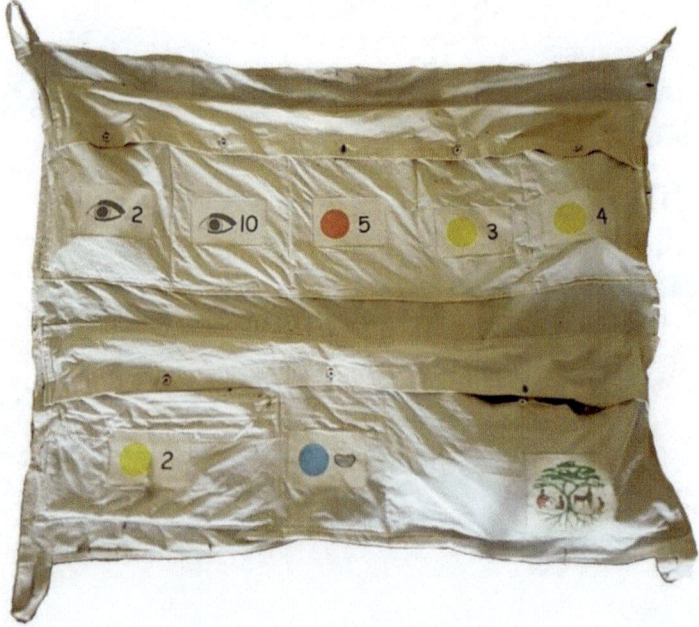

Fig. 9.10: One of the four material bags of the Introduction ladder of learning (Source: Ruth Würzle).

Fig. 10.6: Learning materials for the milestone mM of the Daasanach ladder of learning (Source: Ruth Würzle).

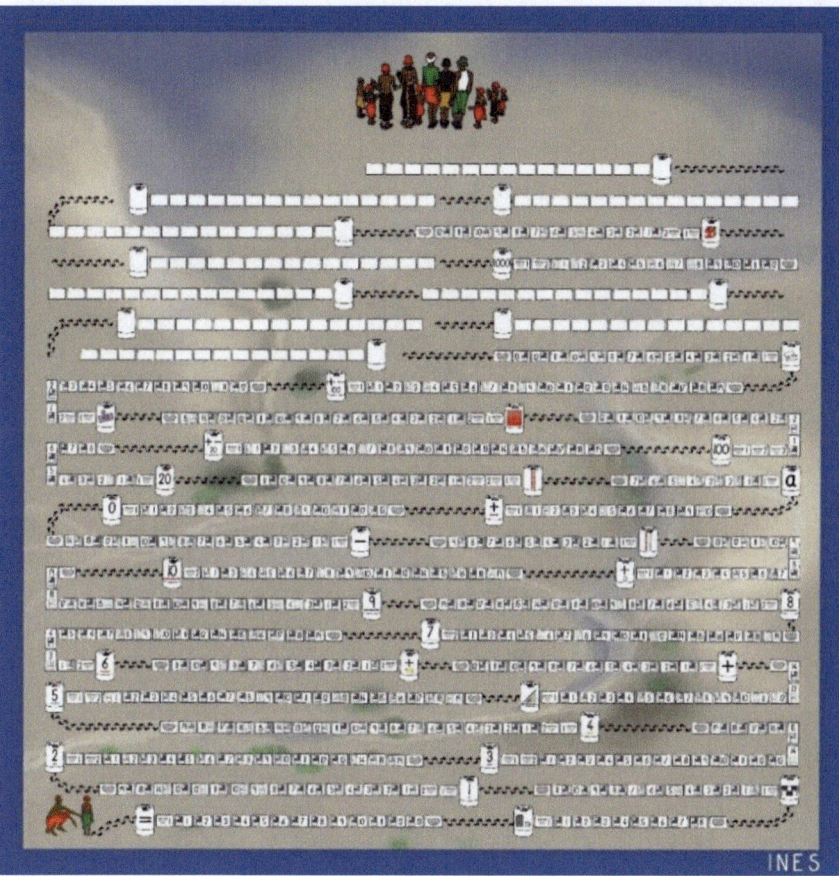

Fig. 11.5: First sketch of the Mathematics ladder of learning (Source: own illustration).

Fig. 12.1: During the school start of Joshua Esho (Source: Ruth Würzle).

Fig. 12.2: Elders observing the mobile school of Jakob Lon'gada (Source: Ruth Würzle).

Fig. 12.4: Joshua Esho participating in the campus school as learners in February 2017 (Source: Ruth Würzle).

Fig. 12.6: An opening assembly during a workshop under a tree (Source: Ruth Würzle).

Fig. 12.8: A groundwork picture developed in the course of Workshop 1 (Source: Ruth Würzle).

Fig. 12.9: Teacher trainees observing Ruth Würzle and Joseph Naliye in 2016 (Source: Theresa Schaller).

Fig. 12.13: Joshua Esho and his learners hanging up the ladder of learning and material bags (Source: Ruth Würzle).

Fig. 13.1: Joshua Esho and learners in their mobile school (Source: Ruth Würzle).

Fig. 13.2: Learners in Jacob Long'ada's mobile school (Source: Ruth Würzle).

Fig. 13.3: Learners in Jacob Long'ada's mobile school making their own name tag (Source: Ruth Würzle).

Fig. 13.4: Two girls in Bonaya Yierar's mobile school (Source: Ruth Würzle).

Fig. 13.5: Learners walking to their school tree (Source: Ruth Würzle).

Fig. 13.6: Joshua Esho with his goats early in the morning before he opens school (Source: Ruth Würzle).

Fig. 13.7: Two learners in Joshua Esho's mobile school (Source: Ruth Würzle).

Fig. 13.8: Girl holding a kid (on the left); four boys tending the community's goats together (on the right) (Source: Ruth Würzle).

Fig. 13.9: Laminated learning material cards in the mobile schools (Source: Ruth Würzle).

Fig. 13.10: Learners working with rubber letters and the *'Bil 'Daasanach* in a mobile school (Source: Ruth Würzle).

Fig. 13.11: Livestock leaving the *forich* early in the morning (Source: Ruth Würzle).

Fig. 13.12: Opening ceremony of Jacob Long'ada's mobile school (Source: Ruth Würzle).

Fig. 13.13: Learner with the Daasanach material bag (on the left); two learners with the Introduction material bag (on the right) (Source: Ruth Würzle).

Fig. 13.14: Edwin Changamu during a visit at Jacob Long'ada's mobile school (Source: Theresa Schaller).

Fig. 13.15: Theresa Schaller and Felicitas Muer during field research (Source: Ruth Würzle).

Fig. 13.16: Ruth Würzle visiting Jeremiah Tete's mobile school (Source: Theresa Schaller).

Fig. 13.17: Eveline Momanyi and Edwin Changamu checking learning materials (Source: Ruth Würzle).

Fig. 13.18: Women crafting learning materials in the INES office in Illeret (Source: Ruth Würzle).

Fig. 13.19: Elisabeth tailoring the Daasanach material bags in Illeret (Source: Ruth Würzle).

Fig. 13.20: First material development workshop of INES in Illeret in 2015 (Source: Ruth Würzle).

Fig. 13.21: Edwin Changamu and three trainees in the Daasanach teacher training workshop (Source: Ruth Würzle).

Fig. 13.22: Joshua Esho and explaining a task to the whole learning group (Source: Ruth Würzle).

Fig. 13.23: Joshua Esho and explaining a task to an individual learner (Source: Ruth Würzle).

Works Cited

Agostini, Evi/Risse, Erika/Schratz, Michael (2018): Lernseits denken – erfolgreich unterrichten. Personalisiertes Lehren und Lernen in der Schule. Hamburg: AOL-Verlag.

Almagor, Uri (1978): Pastoral Partners. Affinity and Bond Partnership among the Dassanetch of South-West Ethiopia. Manchester University Press.

Anderson, John (1970): The Struggle for the School. The Interaction of Missionary, Colonial Government and Nationalist Enterprise in the Development of Formal Education in Kenya. Longman Group Ltd.

Anini, Nyingole Felix (29 March 2017): Personal Interview.

Anyder, Neete (19 June 2017): Personal Interview.

Barnard, Alan/Spencer, Jonathan (2002): Cattle Complex. In: Barnard, Alan/Spencer, Jonathan (Ed.): The Routledge Encyclopedia of Social and Cultural Anthropology. Routledge, p. 91-92.

Bewa, Nyatemura (21 March 2017): Personal Interview.

Birch, Izzy/Cavanna, Sue/Abkula, Dauod/Hujale, Diyad (2010): Towards Education for Nomads. Community Perspectives in Kenya. International Institute for Environment and Development.

Bohl, Thorsten (2010): Offener Unterricht heute. Konzeptionelle und didaktische Weiterentwicklung. Beltz.

Borke, Jörn/Keller, Heidi (2014): Kultursensitive Frühpädagogik. W. Kohlhammer GmbH.

Brügelmann, Hans (1989): Die Schrift entdecken. Beobachtungshilfen und methodische Ideen für einen offenen Anfangsunterricht im Lesen und Schreiben. Libelle Verlag.

Brügelmann, Hans/Brinkmann, Erika (1994): Stufen des Schriftspracherwerbs und Ansätze zu seiner Förderung. In: Brügelmann, Hans/Richter, Sigrun (Ed.): Wie wir recht schreiben lernen. Libelle Verlag, p. 44-52.

Brügelmann, Hans/Brinkmann, Erika (1994): Stufen des Schriftspracherwerbs und Ansätze zu seiner Förderung. In: Brügelmann, Hans/Richter, Sigrun (Ed.): Wie wir recht schreiben lernen. Libelle Verlag, p. 44-52.

Buke, Catherine (2012): Abuses of Girls by Cultural Practices. Pastoral Office Marsabit Diocese.

Bundesministerium für wirtschaftliche Zusammenarbeit und Entwicklung BMZ (2020): Vereinte Nationen einigen sich auf 17 Nachhaltige Entwicklungsziele bis 2030. http://www.bmz.de/de/presse/aktuelleMeldungen/2015/august/20150803_Vereinte-Nationen-einigen-sich-auf-17-nachhaltige-Entwicklungsziele-bis-2030/index.html. [Accessed: 8 Oct 2018].

Bundesministerium für wirtschaftliche Zusammenarbeit und Entwicklung BMZ (2020): Entwicklungszusammenarbeit. http://www.bmz.de/de/service/glossar/E/entwicklungszusammenarbeit.html. [Accessed: 22 Jan 2020].

Bundesministerium für wirtschaftliche Zusammenarbeit und Entwicklung BMZ (2020): Ownership. http://www.bmz.de/de/service/glossar/O/ownership.html. [Accessed: 22 Jan 2020].

Carr, Claudia J. (1977): Pastoralism in Crisis: The Dasanetch and Their Ethiopian Lands (University of Chicago Geography Research Papers). Committee on Geographical Studies.

Carr, Claudia J. (2017): River Basin Development and Human Rights in Eastern Africa – A Policy Crossroads. Springer.

Carr-Hill, Roy/Peart, Edwina (2005): The Education of Nomadic Peoples in East Africa: Djibouti, Eritrea, Ethiopia, Kenya, Tanzania and Uganda. Review of Relevant Literature. ADB/UNESCO-IIEP.

Changamu, Edwin K. (28 September 2019): Personal Interview.

Chen, Hongyan (2016): Dynamics in Circle Rituals. Daily Life at a German Reform Pedagogic School. European Studies in Education 33. Waxmann.

Chilisa, Bagele (2012): Indigenous Research Methodologies. SAGE Publications.

Clark, Nick (2015): Education in Kenya. https://wenr.wes.org/2015/06/education-kenya. [Accessed: 16 Aug 2020].

Cowan, Gray (1970): The Cost of Learning. The Politics of Primary Education in Kenya. Columbia University Teachers College Press.

Daseking, Monika/Petermann, Franz (2009): KET-KID. Kognitiver Entwicklungstest für das Kindergartenalter. Manual. Hogrefe.

Deal, Terrence E./Peterson, Kent D. (2009): Shaping School Culture. Pitfalls, Paradoxes, and Promises. John Wiley & Sons, Inc.

Dei, George Jerry Sefa (1994): Afrocentricity: A Cornerstone of Pedagogy. In: Anthropology and Education Quarterly 25, 1, p. 3–28.

Demuth, Carolin/Keller, Heidi/Relindis, D. Yovsi (2012): Cultural Models in Communication with Infants: Lessons from Kikaikelaki, Cameroon and Muenster, Germany. In: Journal of Early Childhood Research 10, 1, p. 70-87.

Dinucci, Alessandro/Fre, Zeremariam (2003): Understanding Indigenous Knowledge and Information Systems of Pastoralists in Eritrea. Food and Agriculture Organization of the United Nations.

Dyer, Caroline (2006): The Education of Nomadic Peoples. Current Issues, Future Perspectives. Berghan Books.

Dyer, Caroline (2015): Background paper prepared for the Education for All Global Monitoring Report 2015. Education for All 2000-2015: Achievements and Challenges. Evolution in Approaches to Educating Children from Mobile and Nomadic Communities. https://unesdoc.unesco.org/ark:/48223/pf0000232422. [Accessed: 23 Aug 2020].

Dyer, Caroline (2016): Does Mobility Have to Mean Being Hard to Reach? Mobile Pastoralists and Education's Terms of Inclusion. In: Arnot, Madeleine/Schneider, Claudia/Welply, Oakleigh (Ed.): Education, Mobilities and Migration. People, Ideas and Resources. Routledge.

Earl, Sarah/Carden, Fred/Smutylo, Terry (2001): Outcome Mapping. Building Learning and Reflection into Development Programmes. International Development Research Centre.

Eisemon, Thomas Owen (1988): Benefiting from Basic Education, School Quality and Functional Literacy in Kenya. Pergamon Press.

Elfmann, Peggy (2005): Women's Worlds in Daasanetch, Southern Ethiopia. Working Papers. Mainz: Johannes Gutenberg-Universität Mainz/ Institut für Ethnologie und Afrikastudien.

Würzle, Ruth (2014): Individualisierter Englischunterricht mit Lernleitern. Eine Untersuchung der Lernleiter als Lernmethode für die Inhalte von Unit 7 aus Go Ahead 6 Realschule 2000 für die 6. Jahrgangsstufe. Student Paper (unpublished).

Esho, Joshua (17 March 2017): Personal Interview.

Esho, Joshua (14 June 2017): Personal Interview.
Ezeomah, Chimah (1997): The Education of Nomadic Populations in Africa. UNESCO.
Farrant, J. S. (1980): Principles and Practice of Education. Longman.
Feez, Susan (2010): Montessori and Early Childhood. A Guide for Students. SAGE Publications.
Frith, Uta (1986): Psychologische Aspekte des orthographischen Wissens. Entwicklung und Entwicklungsstörung. In: August, Gerhard (Ed.): New Trends in Graphemic and Orthography. Augst. De Gruyter, p. 2018-233.
Fuson, Karen C. (1988): Children's Counting and Concepts of Number. Springer.
Galaty, John G. (2005): Time, Terror, and Pastoral Inertia: Sedentarization and Conflict in Northern Kenya. In: Fratkin, Elliot/Roth, Eric Abella (Ed.): As Pastoralists Settle: Social, Health and Economic Consequences of Pastoral Sedentarization in Marsabit District, Kenya. Kluwer Academic Publisher, p. 53-68.
Gaskins, Suzanne (1999): Children's Daily Lives in a Mayan Village. A Case Study of Culturally Constructed Roles and Activities. In: Göncü, Artin (Ed.): Children's Engagement in the World. Socio-cultural Perspectives. Cambridge University Press, p. 25-60.
Gaskins, Suzanne (2006): Cultural Perspectives on Infant-Caregiver Interaction. In: Levinson, Stephen C./Enfield, Nicholas J. (Ed.): Roots of Human Sociality. Culture, Cognition and Interaction. Berg, p. 279-298.
Gerlach, Maria/Ricken, Gabriele/Fritz, Annemarie (2007): Kalkulie, Diagnose und Trainingsprogramm für rechenschwache Kinder. Cornelsen.
Gillies, Robyn M. (2016): Cooperative Learning: Review of Research and Practice. In: Australian Journal of Teacher Education 41, 3, p. 39–51 [online]. https://files.eric.ed.gov/fulltext/EJ1096789.pdf [Accessed: 16 Aug 2020].
Girg, Ralf/Lichtinger, Ulrike/Müller, Thomas (2012): Lernen mit Lernleitern. Unterrichten mit der MultiGradeMultiLevel-Methodology (MGML). Prolog-Verlag.
Habara, Nyakaro (22 March 2017): Personal Interview.
Hall, Nathan C./Goetz, Thomas (2013): Emotion, Motivation, and Self-regulation. A Handbook for Teachers. Emerald Group Publishing Limited.
Hartig, Johannes/Klieme, Eckhard/Leutner, Detlev (2008): Assessment of Competencies in Educational Contexts. Hogrefe Publishing.
Hattie, John/Timperley, Helen (2007): The Power of Feedback. In: Review of Educational Research 77, 1, p. 81-112.
Hattie, John (2009): Visible Learning: A Synthesis of Over 800 Meta-Analyses Relating to Achievement. Routledge.
Hattie, John (2012): Visible Learning for Teachers. Maximizing Impact on Learning. Routledge.
Hattie, John/Clarke, Shirley (2019): Visible Learning. Feedback. Routledge.
Helekua, Nyabatang' (21 March 2017): Personal Interview.
Jacobs, Claus/Petermann, Franz (2008): Rechenstörung. In: Petermann, Franz (Ed.): Lehrbuch für klinische Kinderpsychologie. Hogrefe.
Johnson, David (2009): An Educational Psychology Success Story: Social Interdependence Theory and Cooperative Learning. In: Educational Researcher. 38, 5, p. 365–379.
Johnson, David/Johnson, Roger (1975): Learning Together and Alone. Cooperation, Competition, and Individualization. Prentice Hall.

Johnson, David/Johnson, Roger (1999): Learning Together and Alone: Cooperative, Competitive, and Individualistic Learning. University of California.

Johnson, David/Johnson, Roger/Holubec, Edythe (1994): Cooperative Learning in the Classroom. Association for Supervision and Curriculum Development.

Johnson, David/Johnson, Roger/Smith, Karl (2013): Cooperative Learning: Improving University Instruction By Basing Practice On Validated Theory. University of Minnesota [online]. http://personal.cege.umn.edu/~smith/docs/Johnson-Johnson-Smith-Cooperative_Learning-JECT-Small_Group_Learning-draft.pdf [Accessed: 16 Aug 2020].

Keller, Heidi (2003): Socialization for Competence: Cultural Models of Infancy. In: Human Development 46, 5, p. 288-311.

Keller, Heidi (2007): Cultures of Infancy. Lawrence Erlbaum Associates.

Keller, Heidi (2011): Kinderalltag. Kulturen der Kindheit und ihre Bedeutung für Bindung, Bildung und Erziehung. Springer.

Kenya Institute of Curriculum Development (2017): Pre Primary PP1. Kenya Institute of Curriculum Development.

Kenya Institute of Curriculum Development (2017): Pre Primary PP2. Kenya Institute of Curriculum Development.

Kenya Institute of Curriculum Development (2017): Lower Primary Level Curriculum Designs. Volume 1. Subjects: Kiswahili, Literacy and Indigenous Languages and English Activities. Kenya Institute of Curriculum Development.

Kenya Institute of Curriculum Development (2017): Lower Primary Level Curriculum Design. Volume 2. Subjects: Mathematics, Environmental, Hygiene and Nutrition Activities. Kenya Institute of Curriculum Development.

Kenya National Bureau of Statistics (2014): Demographic and Health Survey 2014. https://dhsprogram.com/pubs/pdf/fr308/fr308.pdf. [Accessed: 20 Dec 2015].

Kibera, Mercy Wangu/Gakunga, Daniel/Imonje, Rosemary (2013): Provision of Education for Pastoralist Children. The Case of Mobile Schools in Kenya. LAP LAMBERT Academic Publishing.

Komarek, Kurt (2006): ‚Bildung für alle' durch muttersprachlichen Unterricht. In: eins Entwicklungspolitik 18, 19, p. 30 - 33.

Krätli, Saverio (2000): Education Provision to Nomadic Pastoralists. A Literature Review. IDS Working Paper. https://www.ids.ac.uk/download.php?file=files/Wp126.pdf. [Accessed: 16 Aug 2020].

Krätli, Saverio/Dyer, Caroline (2009): Mobile Pastoralists and Education: Strategic Options. IIED/SOS Sahel.

Krajewski, Kristin (2005): Vorschulische Mengenbewusstheit von Zahlen und ihre Bedeutung für die Früherkennung von Rechenschwäche. In: Hasselhorn, Marcus/Marx, Harald/Schneider, Wolfgang (Ed.): Diagnostik von Mathematikleistungen. Hogrefe, p. 49 – 70.

Krajewski, Kristin/Schneider, Wolfgang (2006): Mathematische Vorläuferfertigkeiten im Vorschulalter und ihrer Vorhersagekraft für die Mathematikleistungen bis zum Ende der Grundschulzeit. In: Psychologie in Erziehung und Unterricht 53, 4, p. 246 – 262.

Kucharz, Diemut/Wagener, Matthea (2007): Jahrgangsübergreifendes Lernen. Eine empirische Studie zu Lernen, Leistung und Interaktion von Kindern in der Schuleingangsphase. Schneider Verlag Hohengehren.

Kude, Kerstin (2019): Personalentwicklung für Fachkräfte. Lernen im Dialog und durch Personelle Zusammenarbeit (PEZ) In: AGIAMONDO e.V. (Ed.): Vom Entwicklungsdienst zum Weltdienst. MVG Medienproduktion und Vertriebsgesellschaft mbH, p. 62 – 67.
Kuijstermans, Christian (2019): Managing Outcomes. A Practitioner's Manual For Analysis, Planning, Monitoring and Self-Evaluation Based on Outcome Mapping. Arbeitsgemeinschaft für Entwicklungshilfe (AGEH) e.V..
Kwanjang', Paul Gosh (26 June 2018): Personal Interview.
Lawton, Denis (1975): Class, Culture and the Curriculum. Routledge & Kegan Paul Ltd.
Lewis, M. Paul (2009): Ethnologues. Languages of the World. SIL International.
Lichtinger, Ulrike/Höldrich, Antonie (2016): Buchstabenberge. Lernmaterial zum flexiblen Lernen mit Lernleitern und Unterrichten mit der MultiGradMultiLevel-Methodology (MGML). (Buchstabenlernen, 1. Lernjahr). Roderer Verlag.
Little, Angela/Hoppers, Wim/Garder, Roy (1994): Beyond Jomtien. Implementing Primary Education for All. Macmillan Press.
Lokono, Paul (17 March 2017): Personal Interview.
Lokoringole, Hakualata (29 March 2017): Personal Interview.
Long'ada, Jakob (22 March 2017): Personal Interview.
Long'ada, Lokolom (22 March 2017): Personal Interview.
Longaye, Kamate (11 October 2018): Personal Interview.
Lübben-Chambí, Regine/Jackson, Hannelore (2001): Kinder spielen für ihr Leben gern. Oncken Verlag.
Lücking-Michel, Claudia (2019): Nomen est Omen. In: AGIAMONDO e.V. (Ed.): Vom Entwicklungsdienst zum Weltdienst. MVG Medienproduktion und Vertriebsgesellschaft mbH, p. 12-17.
Ma, Vaunne/Schoeneman J. Thomas (1997): Individualism Versus Collectivism: A Comparison of Kenyan and American Self-Concepts. In: Basic and Applied Social Psychology 19, 2, p. 261-273.
Matsumoto, David (1997): Culture and Modern Life. Cengage Learning.
Meck, Margarete (1971): Problems and Prospects of Social Services in Kenya. A Study with Special Regard to Education and Health in the Light of Regional Needs and Demographic Trends. Weltforum Verlag.
Milimo, Britta (2004): "Richtige" und "falsche" Umweltwahrnehmungen: Sichtweisen und Handlungsfelder mobile Tierhalter und externer Hilfsorganisationen zur nachhaltigen Nutzung von Weidepotenzialen in einem ereignisgesteuerten Ökosystem in Nordkenia. Diss. Bayreuth: Universität Bayreuth/Fakultät für Biologie, Chemie und Geowissenschaften.
Ministry of State for Development of Northern Kenya and Other Arid Lands (2010): Getting the Hardest-to-Reach: A Strategy to Provide Education to Nomadic Communities in Kenya Through Distance Learning. https://pubs.iied.org/pdfs/G02742.pdf. [Accessed: 16 Aug 2020].
Molteno, Marion/Ogadhoh, Kimberly/Cain, Emma/Crumpton, Bridget (2000): Towards Responsive Schools: Supporting Better Schooling for Disadvantaged Children - Education Research Paper No. 38. Department for International Development.
Montessori, Maria (2007): Education for a New World. Montessori-Pierson Publishing Company.

Müller, Thomas et al. (2017): The MultiGradeMulitLevel-Methodology and Early Childhood Education. Ladders of Learning for children from 3 to 4 years and children from 4 to 5 years. Teacher's Manual. RIVER, Universität Würzburg.

Müller, Thomas/Lichtinger, Ulrike/Girg, Ralf (2015): The MultiGradeMultiLevel-Methodology and its Global Significance. Ladders of Learning. Scientific Horizons. Teacher Education. Prolog-Verlag.

Muer, Felicitas (26 June 2017): Personal Interview.

Nabul, Mary (20 March 2017): Personal Interview.

Närman, Anders (1995): Education and Nation Building in Kenya. Perspectives on Modernization, Global Dependency and Local Development Alternatives. Diss. Göteborg: University Göteborg/ Department of Human and Economic Geography.

Naliye, Joseph (25 June 2017): Personal Interview.

Nashere, Hilary Nyakeru (19 June 2019): Personal Interview.

Ngome, Charles (2006): Mobile Schools Programme for Nomadic Pastoralists in Kenya; Pilot Project in Wajir, Ijara and Turkana Districts. A Report Prepared for ALRMP. Institute for Research and Development, Kenyatta University.

Nohlen, Dieter (1991): Entwicklung. In: Nohlen, Dieter (Ed.): Lexikon Dritte Welt. Länder, Organisationen, Theorien, Begriffe, Personen. Rowohlt, p. 196.

Nyingole, Benedict Lokono/ Kwanyang', Paul Gosh (2013a): Af 'Daasanach Onisinyle. Mé Gáá Koon. BTL.

Nyingole, Benedict Lokono/ Kwanyang', Paul Gosh (2013b): War'gát Hátlé Ke Túóy Muogká 'Déé Um Ke Oonootká. BTL.

Nylim, Artukatch (29 March 2017): Personal Interview.

Organisation for Economic Co-operation and Development OECD (2012): Better Aid. Aid Effectiveness 2011. Progress in Implementing the Paris Declaration. OECD Publishing.

Osamor, Pauline Ejemen/Owumi, Bernard Ejuromu/Dipeolu, Isaac Oluwafemi (2015): Socio-Cultural Context of Developmental Milestones in Infancy in South West Nigeria: A Qualitative Study. European Scientific Institute.

Pauli, Sabine/Kirsch, Andrea (2016): RAVEK Handbuch zum Ravensburger Erhebungsbogen fein- und grafmotorischer Kompetenzen – Befunderhebung von 4-10 Jahren. Verlag modernes lernen.

Petersen, Susanne (2001): Rituale für kooperatives Lernen in der Grundschule. Cornelsen.

Piaget, Jean (1950): The Psychology of Intelligence. Routledge.

Reich, Kerstin (2012): Konstruktivistische Didaktik: Das Lehr- und Studienbuch mit Online-Methodenpool. Beltz.

Ricken, Gabriele/Fritz, Annemarie/Balzer, Lars (2011): Mathematik und Rechnen – Test zur Erfassung von Kompetenzen im Vorschulalter (MARKO-D) – ein Bespiel für einen niveauorientierten Ansatz. In: Empirische Sonderpädagogik 3, 3, p. 256 -271.

Rishi Valley Education Centre RIVER (1999): Redesigning the Elementary School: Multilevel Perspectives from Rishi Valley. Rishi Valley Education Centre.

Rishi Valley Institute for Education Resources RIVER (1999): Redesigning the Elementary School. Multilevel Perspectives from Rishi Valley. KFI Rishi Valley Education Centre.

Rishi Valley Institute for Education Resources RIVER (2001): A Multigrade Trainer's Resource Pack. A Trainer's Module 1. KFI Rishi Valley Education Centre.

Rishi Valley Institute for Education Resources RIVER (2003). A Multigrade Trainer's Resource Pack. Background Document 1. KFI Rishi Valley Education Centre.

Rolff, Hans-Günter/Buhren, Claus G./Lindau-Bank, Detlev/Müller, Sabine (2000): Manual Schulentwicklung. Handlungskonzept zur pädagogischen Schulentwicklungsberatung (SchuB). Beltz Verlag.
Rubin, Kenneth H./Menzer, Melissa (2010): Culture and Social Development. In: Boivin M./Peters, RDeV./Tremblay, RE (Ed.): Encyclopedia on Early Childhood Development [online]. Centre of Excellence for Early Childhood Development, p. 1-9. http://www.child-encyclopedia.com/documents/Rubin-MenzerANGxp.pdf. [Accessed: 27 May 2019].
Sangmeister, Hartmut (2009): Entwicklung und internationale Zusammenarbeit: Eine Einführung. Nomos.
Sasse, Hans-Jürgen (1975): The Extension of Macro-Somali. Research Report (unpublished).
Sassenroth, Martin (1991): Schriftspracherwerb, Entwicklungsverlauf, Diagnostik und Förderung. Haupt Verlag.
Sattgast, Linda J./ Kwanyang', Paul Gosh/ Komoi, Job Yergalech (1995): Hibano War'gat Waa'giet. Harvest House Publishers.
Schmalenbach, Christine (2018): Learning Cooperatively under Challenging Circumstances. Springer.
Schröder, Joachim (2012): Schulen für schwierige Lebenslagen.: Studien zu einem Sozialatlas der Bildung. Waxmann Verlag.
Shizha, Edward (2005): Reclaiming Our Memories. The Education Dilemma in Postcolonial African School Curricula. In: Abdi, Ali A./Cleghorn, Ailie (Ed.): Issues in African Education: Sociological Perspectives. Palgrave Macmillan, p. 65-84.
Sousa, David A. (2005): How the Brain Learns to Read. Corwin Press.
Steeb, Michael (2019): Vom Entwicklungsdienst zum Weltdienst. Mehr als 60 Jahre Geschichte. In: AGIAMONDO e.V. (Ed.): Vom Entwicklungsdienst zum Weltdienst. MVG Medienproduktion und Vertriebsgesellschaft mbH, p. 48 – 53.
Tabiye, Francis (19 June 2018): Personal Interview.
Teete, Jeremiah Loki (27 June 2017): Personal Interview.
Teete, Jeremiah Loki (1 July 2017): Personal Interview.
Teete, Jeremiah Loki (16 November 2016): Personal Interview.
Tetzlaff, Rainer/Jakobeit, Cord (2005): Das nachkoloniale Afrika: Politik, Wirtschaft, Gesellschaft. VS Verlag für Sozialwissenschaften.
Thaman, Konai Helu (1993): Culture and the Curriculum in South Pacific. In: Comparative Education 29, 3, p. 249–260.
Tosco, Mauro (2001): The Dhaasanac Language. Grammar, Texts and Vocabulary of a Cushitic Language of Ethiopia. Köppe.
Tröster, Heinrich/ Flender, Judith/ Reineke, Dirk/ Wolf, Sylvia Mira (2016): DESK 3-6 R. Dortmunder Entwicklungsscreening für den Kindergarten – Revision. Hogrefe.
UN General Assembly (2018): Universal Declaration of Human Rights. United Nations, 217 (III) A, 1948, Paris, art. 26. http://www.un.org/en/udhrbook/pdf/udhr_booklet_en_web.pdf/. [Accessed: 10 Aug 2018].
United Nations Development Programme/United Nations Children's Fund/World Bank (1990): World Conference on Education for All – Meeting Basic Learning Needs, Jomtien, Thailand, 1990. Inter-Agency Commission (UNDO, UNESCO, UNICEF, World Bank).

Von der Groeben, Annemarie (2006): Was sind und wozu brauchen Schulen gute Rituale? In: von der Groeben, Annemarie (Ed.): Rituale in Schule und Unterricht. Hamburg: Bergmann und Helbig Verlag, p. 11-18.

Weber, Erich (1974): Zur moralischen Erziehung in Unterricht und Schule: pädagogische und psychologische Überlegungen. Auer Verlag.

Willemsen, Michael/Gottschalk, Wiebke (2015): Erziehung und Entwicklung. Ernst Klett.

World Population Review (2020): Kenya Population 2020. https://worldpopulationreview.com/countries/kenya-population. [Accessed: 16 Aug 2020].

Würzle, Ruth (2014): Individualisierter Englischunterricht mit Lernleitern. Eine Untersuchung der Lernleiter als Lernmethode für die Inhalte von Unit 7 aus Go Ahead 6 Realschule 2000 für die 6. Jahrgangsstufe. Student Paper (unpublished).

Yierar, Bonaya (21 March 2017): Personal Interview.

Yierite, Ar'gudo (29 March 2017): Personal Interview.

Zurbriggen, Eveline (2011): Prüfungswissen Schulpädagogik – Grundlagen. UTB.

Petra Strehmel | Johanna Heikka
Eeva Hujala | Jillian Rodd
Manjula Waniganayake (eds.)

**Leadership in
Early Education in
Times of Change**

Research from five Continents

*2019 • 308 pp. • Pb. • 36,00 € (D) • US$50.00 • GBP 32.00
ISBN 978-3-8474-2199-3 • eISBN 978-3-8474-1224-3*

The collection brings together the latest work of researchers from Australia, Africa, Asia, and Europe focusing on early childhood leadership matters. It covers different aspects of leadership in early education: professional education and development, identity and leadership strategies as well as governance and leadership under different frame conditions.

The book is an **Open Access** title, which is free to download or can be bought as paperback.

www.barbara-budrich.net

Marta Kowalczuk-Walędziak
Alicja Korzeniecka-Bondar
Wioleta Danilewicz
Gracienne Lauwers (eds.)

**Rethinking
Teacher Education for
the 21st Century**

*2019 • 402 pp. • Pb. • 76,00 € (D) • US$105.00 • GBP 67.00
ISBN 978-3-8474-2241-9 • eISBN 978-3-8474-1257-1*

This book focuses on current trends, potential challenges and further developments of teacher education and professional development from a theoretical, empirical and practical point of view. It intends to provide valuable and fresh insights from research studies and examples of best practices from Europe and all over the world. The authors deal with the strengths and limitations of different models, strategies, approaches and policies related to teacher education and professional development in and for changing times(digitization, multiculturalism, pressure to perform).

The book is an **Open Access** title (DOI: 10.3224/84742241) , which is free to download or can be bought as paperback.

www.barbara-budrich.net